Bunco Artists in Richmond, 1870–1920

ALSO BY HARRY M. WARD
AND FROM MCFARLAND

Children of the Streets of Richmond, 1865–1920 (2015)

*Public Executions in Richmond,
Virginia: A History, 1782–1907* (2012)

*For Virginia and for Independence: Twenty-Eight
Revolutionary War Soldiers from the Old Dominion* (2011)

Bunco Artists in Richmond, 1870–1920

*Sharpers, Snatchers,
Swindlers, Flimflammers
and Other Con Men*

HARRY M. WARD

McFarland & Company, Inc., Publishers
Jefferson, North Carolina

Publisher's note: The author died on October 4, 2016, after completing the manuscript for this book but before seeing proofs.

ISBN (print) 978-1-4766-6692-1
ISBN (ebook) 978-1-4766-2617-8

LIBRARY OF CONGRESS CATALOGUING DATA ARE AVAILABLE

BRITISH LIBRARY CATALOGUING DATA ARE AVAILABLE

© 2017 The Estate of Harry M. Ward. All rights reserved

No part of this book may be reproduced or transmitted in any form or by any means, electronic or mechanical, including photocopying or recording, or by any information storage and retrieval system, without permission in writing from the publisher.

Front cover: financial trickery image © 2017 whitemay/iStock

Printed in the United States of America

McFarland & Company, Inc., Publishers
Box 611, Jefferson, North Carolina 28640
www.mcfarlandpub.com

Table of Contents

Preface   1

1. River City   5
2. Resurrectionists   10
3. Clairvoyants   19
4. Plungers   35
5. Confidence Men   47
6. Money Sharks   53
7. Fakir Paradise   59
8. "Shoving the Queer"   77
9. Larceners   83
10. Footpads   93
11. Cracksmen   99
12. Dips   103
13. Suspicious Characters   109
14. "American Nobility"   118
15. Narcoticists   127
16. Kidnappers   133
17. Fugitive Felons   142
18. Forgers   148
19. Embezzlers   156
20. Impostors   164

21.	Drummers	174
22.	Postal Robbers	184
23.	Railway Disrupters	190
24.	On Board Troublemakers	195
25.	The "Big Train Robbery"	199
26.	Gold Brick Caper	204

Glossary 213
Chapter Notes 217
Bibliography 230
Index 233

Preface

Every locality—urban or rural—had its tricksters, swindlers, flimflammers, and the like. In addition, there were those who stole from under the very eyes of their victims. Combining the two, we might refer to a dreaded sub-society called bunco-land. Though hold-ups properly belong to another category, we will include some of the criminals in this vein, simply because of the excitement they caused. Richmond was a sharply divided community between those with at least a modicum of wealth and the large mass of citizens comprised of poorly paid industrial workers and domestics, with a number of unemployed and homeless. As the poor were victimized by society at large, so were they the easy dupes of criminals on the prowl. This is not to say that bunco men did not target men of means when they could.

Bunco artists, with a little patience and resourcefulness, could reap ample gain from the unsuspecting, and then hightail it out of sight to avoid detection.

"Bunco," for a long time, did not appear in the American lexicon. Today it may simply be defined as a swindle, in which a person is cheated at gambling, persuaded to buy a nonexistent, unsalable, or worthless object, or is otherwise vitictimized.[1] "Bunco" first appeared in the *Century Dictionary* in the late 19th century. The word, it was pointed out, was of Italian origin, meaning a bank money changer.

> The *Century* defines "bunco" as being a swindle practiced by two or more confederates upon a stranger (generally by gaining his confidence on the grounds of alleged previous acquaintance with himself or some of his friends). He is lured to a house, and there the victim at some game, is openly robbed or otherwise victimized. This definition is probably correct, except in one particular; there was certainly no effort on the part of the original professionals in this line to use violence or openly rob their victim.[2]

Whereas the city could be considered one of the least desirable places to live in the United States because of its smells of open sewage, slaughterhouses, horse manure, and overcrowding, it at least had a rather effective law enforcement. The Black Hand, or Mafia, never took root in Richmond as it did in some other Southern cities. By always clamping down on vagrants, tramps, and suspicious persons, misbehavior was often nipped in the bud. Still, there was enough swindling and snatching in the community as to reflect unfavorably on the quality of society. The middle and upper classes seemed to exhibit an exclusiveness apart from the poor and the many transients who drifted in and out of the city. By looking at the lower sort of crime involving gain mainly by deception, one can glimpse the fringe of society.

We are indebted to the indefatigable crime reporters of Richmond's newspapers of long ago for glimpses into the wide variety of misbehavior. Most of the revelations came from the Police Court. This was not a court

"Woodman Don't Spare that Tree," read the caption for this political cartoon from the *Richmond News Leader*, July 17, 1906.

of record, but, nevertheless, extensive newspaper coverage with great detail of the goings-on in the court was offered to the public. Since most of those brought to the bench for judgment were drunks, vagrants, hot-headed individuals, and even wayward children, there was always opportunity for humor. None other than the long-serving justice of thirty-two years on the bench, Justice John J. Crutchfield, was better fitted for the role of the discerning, humor-spouting judge. Although he worked in the city, Crutchfield was the epitome of the country judge, delivering words of wisdom that could match that of Solomon. Defendants did not always prevail. Malefactors wound up in jail, the penitentiary, on a chain gang, being run out of town, and/or paying a fine. Judge Crutchfield was sort of a gamester himself, his showmanship attracting spectators to his court from far away.

A portrait of the renowned Justice John Jeter Crutchfield (1844–1920), who presided over the Police Court for 32 years, with showmanship and the wisdom of Solomon (courtesy the Valentine).

The period that embraces our narrative forms a definite segment of Richmond's history. It is a time of transition whereby the city recovered from the disaster of war and achieved a rebuilding of its industrial base. Population quintupled from the end of the Civil War to 1920. The era coincided with what authors Elaine Hatfield and Richard Rapson have called the "Golden Age of the Con," when hordes of gamblers, thieves, grifters, and con artists plied their trade across the country.[3]

Richmond was a fairly accommodating place for the enterprising petty criminal. One, however, had to keep a watchful eye for approaching policemen who seemed to come out of nowhere. Of their imminent presence, it was said, only the small boys and the squirrels had that kind of knowledge.[4]

I wish to thank, especially, the Richmond Public Library and the Virginia Historical Society for the use of their collections (primarily microfilm) of Richmond newspapers. More so than the periodicals of our own time, these newspapers relished the printing of human stories and records, even if at times they dwelled gratuitously on gore and misery. Martha Beitner provided final copy and skillful editing. My thanks also to Lissa Searfoss for the illustration and photo restorations.

1

River City

The social milieu of Richmond abetted easy victimization by swindlers and thieves. The large number of poor people crowded together in slums aided that prospect. In 1904 the city, within its corporate bounds of five-and-a-half square miles, had the greatest density of people in the United States, with the exception of Hoboken, New Jersey.[1] The number of inhabitants measured 65,000 in 1880, 85,000 in 1900, and with a large expansion of boundaries 127,628 in 1910 and 171,667 in 1920.[2]

Many Richmonders were first- and second-generation Americans. At the time of the Civil War, Irish and German immigrants made up one-half of the population. At the turn of the century came Syrians, Italians, Chinese, Russians, Greeks, and a scattering of individuals who had drifted down from northern cities or had disembarked at Richmond's port. The Chinese, despite their immigration prohibited by Congress in 1882, came in under special work visas known as "chuck-cee"; they resided in Richmond's little Chinatown, at the intersection of Belvidere and Broad streets. The Irish occupied principally Oregon Hill and areas bordering the penitentiary; the Italians were mostly found in and around Jackson Ward; the Germans were dispersed, some of them being prosperous businessmen.[3] Other than in Jackson Ward, blacks could be found in nooks and niches throughout the city and principally at Fulton Bottom. The most notorious slums were at Butchertown (on the slopes east of the Capitol) and among the dwellings in the shacks and shanties in downtown's forty or so alleys.

"What Five Points used to be to New York, Penitentiary Bottom is to Richmond," declared a reporter in 1999. Many ex-criminals took up residence in Penitentiary Bottom.

> Lying at the foot of the State Penitentiary, and embracing within its confines scores of unsightly abodes and tenements, it gives to the criminal a place of shelter secluded and safe from the eyes of the average citizen.
>
> From this locality has arisen a peculiar society, and the perpetrators of crime are often traced to this section by the shrewd police.[4]

Poverty was extensive in Richmond. Nearly one in twelve persons sought relief or shelter from the public funds of the city in 1911.[5] In 1905, 1,440 were listed as homeless (half white, half black).[6] Among Richmond's "unseen poor" at a house on Exchange Alley, twenty-seven persons slept on the first floor, and the stairway "swarmed" with lodgers; "the stench was terrible."[7] Abandoned and starving children were discovered on the streets, along with castaway dead infants.[8] A boy died of starvation in November 1901.[9] Rations of any kind were severely limited for the poor. A reporter and a Salvation Army volunteer, in their visits to people in need at Christmastime, found many individuals suffering from lack of food. Arriving at one particular abode, they found a poor woman and her family were sitting down to supper:

> The children divided the gravy from a minute piece of bacon, which they spread over a very small piece of bread, while the mother and the brother divided the bacon and had slightly larger pieces of bread. There was nothing more. Not even coffee or tea.[10]

The best a poor family could expect from the city's Department of Outdoor Poor was some free wood or cordage in wintertime, and, if they were lucky, assistance of a few cents a week.[11] The Children's Home Society of Virginia cared for children for short periods,[12] and there were several orphanages serving the city.

Not the least of the problems facing all residents was the horrible sanitation conditions. Streets were used to drive "hogs, sheep, and beeves to the slaughter-pens."[13] Until the advent of the automobile, horse manure polluted the roads, along with virtually every kind of refuse. In 1900, 12,143 animals, 7,800 fowl, 5,200 barrels of fruits and vegetables, 8,700 barrels of offal, and 4,100 loads of garbage were carted off.[14] Garbage dumps within the city sometimes rose higher than buildings; they contained about everything, including tin cans, paper, garbage, rags, dead animals, and fecal matter. When it rained, water flowed down from the dumps, carrying "the dirt and filth into the neighboring yards and under the houses."[15]

Polluted water afforded a major propellant of disease. Smallpox and cholera, epidemics of an earlier time, had somewhat been conquered, but there were still to be hurdled tuberculosis, diphtheria, scarlet fever, and typhoid fever. Shockoe Creek, which ran through the center of the city, was an open sewer.[16] Richmond depended on the James River for its drinking water. The river cleaned itself over a 350-mile stretch; unfortunately, the city of Lynchburg, 146 miles from Richmond, dumped its entire sewage into the James.[17] Streets without sewers abounded in the city.[18] At one time the city had 400 surface wells, considered a major source for typhoid fever; not until the early 1900s did the city begin ordering the closing of the wells.[19] Richmond did not have a complete purification system until the 1920s.

Much mischief could be expected at nighttime. When the sun went down and most all stores were locked (except for the 220 saloons, some of which remained open all night), it was as if it were a different city. Children stayed out in the streets. It was estimated that as many as a hundred boys never went home at night.[20] Rowdies, gangs, brothel denizens, street fighters, drunks, and simply the curious were out and about. One might find a crowd of "negro children and youths who congregate around a plug on street corners."[21] After dark, crowds were attracted to night-auctions, where "every variety of article, from a paper of pins to an overcoat, is disposed of cheap 'for cash.'" Revelry prevailed.

> Around "Cash Corner," Seventeenth and Grace streets, Tenth and Byrd streets, Pink alley, and in some other outlawed localities, at times the most deprived specimens of humanity congregate, dance to mean music, and drink meaner whiskey until daylight doth appear, unless—as is frequently the case—a first-class row is raised and the police of the First district disperse the revellers.[22]

Richmond's hundred-man police force was hard pressed to keep abreast the multitude of criminals. Arrests generally averaged around 12,000 persons a year. Of the 12,728 detentions in 1915, 875 were for those between the ages of ten and seventeen; 1,734 were anywhere from seventeen to twenty-one, and 5,157 were between twenty-one and twenty-seven.[23] In 1919, of the 12,463 arrests, 1,520 were of those under the age of eighteen; 1,831 between eighteen and twenty-one, and 4,191 between twenty-one and thirty.[24]

Most miscreants who found themselves in Police Court were charged with misdemeanors. At one time, felons were taken to the same court, although the venue for trying more serious crimes later became Hustings Court. Bunco artists and other swindlers could expect little sympathy from the "Great Dispenser," as Justice John J. Crutchfield (1849-1920) was often called. His first inclination was to run such pests out of town.

The major source for petty crime in Richmond, as one reporter noted in January 1909, was the large number of "loafers" on the streets. Hence the city's periodic crackdown on vagrants, persons who suddenly appeared in the community without any visible means of support. In the opinion of one Richmonder, "If more vagrants arrested were sent out to work on the roads, there would probably be an appreciable decrease in crime."[25]

Incarceration came under the most dismal of prospects. The Richmond jail, at Marshall Street and Jail Alley, usually held about 160 prisoners. In 1895, the facility housed twenty-nine white prisoners in nineteen cells; 132 blacks in thirty-eight cells; and, in an upstairs tier, about a dozen women in seven cells. Worst of all, the jail had a dungeon, measuring nine by nine feet, adjoining a solid front wall; whatever light and air came into this dark hole was admitted through eight slots bored in the door.[26] The dungeon, with "its hideous solitude and scanty food" only exacerbated a prisoner's mental imbalance. Inadequate sanitation and contagious diseases were also major problems.[27]

Until about 1910 a punishment that returned dividends to the city was the Chain Gang. For a long time, Squire "Sugar Bottom" Frank Jones had charge of this group, consisting mainly of thirty to forty vagrants, tramps, and those charged with the lightest of offenses. Time served amounted to fifteen to sixty days. Persons deemed disorderly in the streets or those not meeting security bonds were also likely candidates. The "tough toilers" performed the whole gamut of city-maintenance chores.[28]

The state penitentiary in Richmond incarcerated felons from all over Virginia. As many as seven persons were held in each of the prison's 198 cells. In 1897, there were 998 black men, 255 white men, and seventy-nine females (of whom seventy-five were black, and four, white).[29] As with the Richmond Jail, the penitentiary, before reformatories took root at the turn of the century, accommodated child prisoners. In 1883, the penitentiary housed some 140 prisoners, aged eleven to twenty-one. The State Farm, established in 1895, in adjacent Goochland County, attended largely to "idiots, imbeciles and juveniles not yet having reached their teens."[30]

The whipping of children by order of the Police Court and by even its successor, the Juvenile and Domestic Relations Court, continued until about 1920. Men and women of color were also subject to flogging during this time.[31]

For swindlers, time spent in a jail cell or beneath the lash could be avoided by simply hightailing it out of town, ahead of the law. But, if the miscreant was caught, he was taken to Justice John's Police Court, where, in the least objectionable scenario, he might be expected to pay a small fine or be sentenced to a brief stay at the local lockup. A bunco man, like any other minor criminal, faced the irony of being hauled before a court not too unlike the world of finagling to which he had become accustomed. Two commentaries of the 1890s suggest the typical showcasing that ensued in the Police Court:

The White Chamber swarmed with the colored population yesterday, they looked as grave as a Filipino commission while Justice John was cracking his richest jokes, the guffaw of an old time negro breaking the sullen silence as the Great Dispenser commented on their misdoings in his characteristic way.[32]

There was a queer-looking variety of bystanders around the railing at the Temple yesterday morning. It was a regular Dickens' tea party, the bald-headed man towering above the others, while the sportive flies played prisoner's base with a decided relish on the smooth cranium.

Among the audience was the shaggy-browed man, the man with the Van Dyke beard, the peg-legged hero of Appomattox, the colored dude with the high, laundered collar, the brawny sons of Italy and Ireland and the blue-black representatives of Africa. If "variety is the spice of life," life at the Sanctum is well seasoned.[33]

2

Resurrectionists

Not long after the Civil War, a spate of body-snatching from graveyards appeared in Richmond and vicinity. The purpose of this so-called "ghoul traffic" was to supply corpses for anatomical study at the Medical College of Virginia in Richmond and the University of Virginia Medical School in Charlottesville.

Body-snatching was, in fact, a common occurrence throughout the country. Headlined incidents included the attempt to remove the bodies of President Abraham Lincoln from his marble sarcophagus at Springfield, Illinois; Roman Catholic Archbishop R. V. Whelan in Wheeling, West Virginia; and President William McKinley in Canton, Ohio.[1] In 1894, ghouls dynamited a stone tomb, thirty-five-feet high and twenty-feet deep, to steal jewelry from Colonel E. E. Norton's family vault near Stroudsburg, Pennsylvannia.[2] A gang of seven black men was taken into custody in Indianapolis for having robbed an estimated one hundred graves.[3]

The main period for body-snatching in the Richmond area occurred before 1884, when the state legislature enacted an anatomy bill that provided for legal means for medical schools to obtain corpses.

The "Resurrection Men" preferred corpses of African descent to those of the Caucasian variety. The reason for this is simple: White decedents were packed in ice and salt and placed in hermetically sealed caskets; when lowered into the earth, their bodies thawed and rapidly decayed. Black decedents, on the other hand, were merely buried in pine caskets; as the untreated bodies took longer to decompose, they were therefore better suited for the medical dissecting table.[4]

Indeed, most body-snatching involved black cadavers, simply because they were more available. Even living black men and women were not immune to the so-called "sack-'em-up men" who prowled the streets after dark, searching for victims to send on to an anatomy class held in the Medical School of Virginia's Egyptian Building. The perpetrators were said to throw cloth bags over their victims' heads, suffocating them. It was rumored that two of the most notorious practitioners of these abduction-murders were janitors at the school—Chris Baker and a man who went by the nickname "Old Billy."[5]

One frightful experience involved the death of Mollie Vaughan, a black lady, and the whereabouts of the body. Her husband, Charles, it turned out, was too poor to afford a proper burial for his wife; instead, he had the "Black Jane"—the dead-cart of the city—come by and pick up the corpse. Charles was paid fifteen dollars in cash. Normally, the body would have then been taken to the almshouse and subsequently buried in Potter's Field. After much confusion and a formal investigation by newspaper reporters, it was finally determined that the missing corpse wound up at the medical college. A physician there was asked, "Where do you suppose the body is just at this moment?" His reply was incredibly insensitive: "Chopped to pieces by the students."[6]

While virtually all cemeteries in and around Richmond fell victim to grave robbing, the body-snatchers relied chiefly on the black section of Oakwood Cemetery (on Nine Mile Road in Church Hill); the all-black Evergreen Cemetery (three-quarters-of-a-mile distance); and Potter's Field, adjacent to the Almshouse at 5th and Hospital streets. The convict burial ground next to the penitentiary was also a source. Riverview and Shockoe Hill cemeteries supplied a few bodies.[7]

During 1879–80 the resurrectionists were particularly busy mining graves at Oakwood Cemetery. In one particular month, forty bodies disappeared. Although the corpses were those of African descent, whites soon became alarmed that the predators might begin desecrating their burial grounds. While authorities initially overlooked the problem, a guard placed in a cemetery served to discourage disinterment.[8]

> Grave robbing in Richmond entailed three steps. First, one had to have intelligence of any impending burial. Next came reconnoitering the interment site, often going about pretending to be a hunter. The final step involved arriving at the grave, using a shaded lantern, observing the arrangement of stones and flowers so as to replace them exactly as they were, placing a tarpaulin on the ground next to the grave to receive the excavated soil, and making a three-foot-square hole at the head of the grave, through which the head of the coffin was reached about four feet down through the loose dirt. Bodies were easy to remove, because graves were shallow, no more than three feet deep. After removing the lid of the coffin, the body-snatchers, to prevent any disfiguration, put a harness strapping the arms and containing a ring through which a rope was inserted for pulling up the cadaver. The exhumed body was placed on a second tarpaulin and wrapped in it. Quickly the ghoulish booty was hauled to a waiting wagon.[9]

Bodies shipped out of Richmond to Charlottesville were usually preserved in kerosene oil barrels.[10] At times they may have been packed in bran. Outside of Richmond, grave robbers resorted to hay and even apples to encase corpses for shipment. One Midwestern physician recalled using apples. "The fruit absorbs all the bad odor," he noted. The doctor said that one time he and some cohorts

> brought a subject into Toledo in a barrel, all so nicely packed in apples that if a head had been taken out spectators would swear there was nothing in it but Baldwins, or Ramboes, or whatever they were. We got it up to the college all right and after dark the stiff was lifted up the elevator into a dissecting room, leaving the barrel and the apples in the alley. Next morning some Polish women came along, found the apples, and carried away every blamed one of 'em.[11]

Sometimes the body-snatchers visited burial plots outside of Richmond. Near Manchester (across the river and, later, part of the city), John Walke, a well-known African American blacksmith, was interred in a cemetery. On the evening following the burial, Joseph Williams, who lived in the neighborhood, passed by the cemetery and spotted a hack parked on the road. Upon inquiry, Williams was informed by the driver of the hack that he was returning from a wedding, and having traveled a long distance, was resting the horses. Moving on toward Manchester, Williams looked back and saw two men carrying what appeared to be a wrapped body to the hack. Williams hurried into town, and while stopping at a store to report what he had seen, the hack "passed by at a rapid rate, going in the direction of Richmond, and in a moment was out of sight." Police, notified by telephone, immediately went to the Mayo Bridge, but the hack had reached Richmond. News of this event incensed black citizens. But nothing was found as to the whereabouts of the deceased. The thieves had fled the gravesite so suddenly that they neglected to refill it. Resurrectionists thereafter refrained from robbing the cemetery.[12]

Of course, there are stories of cadavers for anatomy classes suddenly appearing to be alive and frightening the janitorial help. A similar incident was reported concerning the delivery of a body to the undertaker's. At nighttime of October 3, 1904, two "negro men and a [seventeen-year-old] boy" in a wagon, carrying a dead body, stopped on a city street. A streetcar conductor passing by saw the two men leave the boy to watch over the corpse.

> The conductor looked at the body a minute and said: "What are you winking at me for? If you are dead, why don't you keep your eyes shut?" ....
> About this time the boy on the wagon turned and said: "Look heah, boss, is dat man done wunk at you?" The conductor assured the boy that the man had not only winked at him, but had "cut his eyes around" at him. The now-thoroughly

Chris Baker, known as a body snatcher, was a longtime janitor at the Medical College of Virginia, assigned to the Dissections Room (Warner and Edmonson, *Dissection: Photographs of the Rite of Passage in American Medicine*).

terrified boy jumped off the wagon and started up Hull street running as fast as he could go, after saying, "Den here I go. Dat man aint dade and he can't ketch me, cause Ise gwine to flew." When the men came out of the store, they found the wagon standing where they had left it and the body undisturbed, but the boy could not be found.[13]

At long last, the state legislature enacted, on January 28, 1884, a law "to promote medical science and to protect graves and cemeteries from desecration within the commonwealth of Virginia." An anatomical board, consisting of medical school faculty, would preside over the "distribution and delivery of dead human bodies. The Medical College of Virginia could now receive unclaimed corpses. All officials who may have charge over dead bodies were required to notify the board of the death of anyone in their custody who would be buried at public expense. The board could order the removal of all such bodies to be used within the state for the advancement of medical science." After the bodies had been used for instruction, they should be "decently interred." The board could employ a carrier for transport of dead bodies. A fine was levied for the selling or buying of cadavers and/or for sending them out of state; body-snatching was made a felony, punishable from five to ten years' imprisonment.[14]

Although the new law put an end to grave robbing, fear among members of the black community remained high over the possible continuation of this evil practice. Chris Baker, a janitor at the medical college, still had "the unenviable reputation of being a body-snatcher," a charge which led to his life being threatened. In 1884, Baker, a fellow janitor named Billy, and two students were convicted of robbing a grave at Oakwood Cemetery. Fortunately for them, they were eventually pardoned by Governor William E. Cameron. On another occasion Baker was caught stealing a body from "the dead-house at the almshouse," replacing the body in the coffin with a heavy log. In March 1887, Baker was under suspicion of having been instrumental in the disappearance of the bodies of a Mrs. Walker, a Mr. Wrenn, and a Mr. Rudolphe. Baker was so frightened that he dared not leave the college, sleeping and taking his meals there. Actually, according to one commentator: "As for Wrenn and Rudolphe, the former is no doubt in Chicago and the latter in Milwaukee, and poor Mrs. Walker either wandered off into the country or into the river."[15]

The city also had regulations concerning body-snatching. Edwin Phaup, an undertaker, was fined $25 for the misdemeanor offense of moving the body of T. L. Brannan, who had died in Sheltering Arms Hospital in the city, to Hanover County, where it was buried. A city ordinance provided that no one who had died in the city "or within its sanitary jurisdiction" could be moved without a permit from Richmond's board of health.[16]

Chris Baker continued on as the janitor, working for the dissection department until the end of his life, in 1919 at age seventy. He had lived his whole life residing at the Egyptian Building of the Medical College of Virginia, having been born in its basement, which his father had established as the family home while he held the janitor role; Chris took over the position in 1860. In 1890, a census listed Baker's occupation as "Anatomical Man." He also reportedly had a wife and a son.

Chris took charge of the bodies that found their way into the Egyptian Building, the entire top floor of which was used for anatomy. Chris put the corpses into a formaldehyde solution in vats, which looked like old metal bathtubs. The building had no windows, only skylights, the reason being supposedly to prevent an outraged public from viewing the goings-on. The bodies were brought to the large dissecting room where they were placed on tables; six to eight students were assigned to each table. As one alumnus of MCV has noted:

> It was their business to dissect out and expose all the soft parts (as they were called) of the body. In this way the muscles were demonstrated together with their origin and insertion so that their function could be shown and understood. The dissection also included the blood supply [the heart, arteries, and veins], and the viscera, that is to say the stomach and intestines, liver and kidneys, and also the brain and all the other organs that go to make up the human anatomy.

After the dissections were concluded, the bodies were taken to the basement and covered with quick lime. In this way, all soft tissue disappeared, leaving only clean, white bones. Baker then assembled the bones into a complete skeleton; the bones not joined together were placed in a box. He then sold the boxes for $5 apiece to students.[17]

An amusing anecdote about Chris Baker was told by the celebrated folklorist/musician Polk Miller. He had a friend of his, a ventriloquist, who "in league with a student," hid in the dissecting hall about the time Chris would arrive to attend to the bodies.

> Chris approached the covered form. From beneath came a voice: "Niggah, you doan want me." Never flinching, Chris passed to another table where another inert sheet-covered form greeted him verbally. Unperturbed, the old Negro went to the third body. He lifted the shroud and was greeted by a sepulchral voice and in a similar vein of protest. Chris looked down with supreme indifference and replied, "Dam you Niggah, I gwine take you anyways."[18]

Problems other than body-snatching plagued the burial grounds. Poor blacks who could not afford to have a loved one buried in a cemetery, and were too proud to resort to Potter's Field, would creep into a cemetery at night and bury a body themselves on unassigned ground or simply put a corpse into an already occupied grave. In March 1897 a reporter visited the Evergreen Cemetery, where there had been a regular appearance of mysterious graves. The suspicious graves were at the lower end of the cemetery alongside a "narrow, shallow brook." A body could be planted in this locality "at high noon without interference or detection" and just as well at night because the cemetery keeper seemed to have important business elsewhere. The reporter spent an entire afternoon in the cemetery waiting for someone to appear. At about six p.m. the silhouetted figures of a boy and a dog were seen at the edge of the cemetery.

> A series of whoops and yells attracted the attention of the boy and brought him into the cemetery. He sat down on a tombstone and kicked the dead turf off a mound while answering the reporter's questions. He was a dwarfed, oldish looking boy with a shock of yellow hair and a wart on his ear.
>
> "Where does the keeper live?" asked the reporter.
> "Dunno," said the boy.
> "Where are the two graves that were made without permit?"
> "Dunno," said the boy.
> "When was the last funeral here?" …
>
> He said "Dunno" to [this and] half a dozen other queries and then the reporter, to test him, inquired: "Do you know the name of this cemetery?"
>
> "What cemetery?" said the boy sullenly.
> "Where we are now," said the reporter. "Do you know where you are?"
> "Naw," said the boy.
> "Where do you live?"
> "Up yonder in that house on the hill, 'cross the field."
> "Don't you know what use they make of this field?" groaned the reporter.
> "Yes," said the boy, and relapsed into his favorite occupation of kicking the stuffing out of the turf.
> "Well, do they grow beans in it?"
> "H-ll, naw," said the boy, "it's nigger berryin' ground."
> "Of course it is," exclaimed the reporter, greatly encouraged. "Now we're getting to the point. Somebody, you know, has charge of the place—to keep it in order, and all that. You ought to know who it is. Don't you see somebody fixing up the graves—turfing them and shaping the mounds sometimes?"
> "Naw," said the boy doggedly.
> "Never see anybody come in here or go, or stop at the gate?" pleaded the newspaper man. The boy brightened up.
> "Say, I know now. You mean him.... I reckon he's the keeper. He comes down here on Thursdays and spending his time in the house."[19]

Small private cemeteries had some of the same troubles affecting larger burial grounds. An interview with a grave digger for Mechanics and Ebenezer cemeteries by an attorney representing neighbors of the cemeteries revealed a longtime practice of multiple bodies occupying single graves. Robert Dickerson, a black man of "Herculean proportions," who had been a grave digger for four years, revealed that at the two cemeteries "there was hardly a foot of ground that had not been buried over once, and a great portion of the cemeteries had been gone over twice and three times." The superintendents of these cemeteries had instructed Dickerson to remove the bones in a grave into a hole at the bottom, with new remains filling the space vacated. Dickerson asserted that he often had to mutilate bodies to make room for the added corpses. One time while digging a grave, which lapped over another, he "had been forced to cut the head of a white man off, as it protruded in the newly-opened grave." Dickerson buried the head "in a hole beneath the box for the new corpse, and covered up the protruding neck in the next grave with the end of the box."[20] There were reports at the various cemeteries of the occasional find of as many as three bodies in one grave.[21]

Flower thieves and vandals persistently caused trouble at the cemeteries in and around Richmond. Girls as young as age ten, collected flowers in full bloom. More determined robbers, at nighttime, raided cemeteries to get flowers to resell, preferring plants pulled up by the roots.[22] Wade McGruder, in 1891, was jailed for six months for pilfering flowers from graves in Richmond's Hollywood Cemetery.[23] A year later William Harris, a black man, went before the Police Court for stealing flowers, also at Hollywood Cemetery. As it could not be proven from which graves the flowers had been taken, Harris was ordered to put up security for future good behavior, which he could not meet, and, hence, wound up with sixty days in jail.[24] One Sunday in November 1896, three young women, rambling "about in Oakwood Cemetery, enjoying the beauties of that well-kept place," showed "their appreciation" by "pulling sundry souvenirs from the blooming plants." After being apprehended, the "fair pilferers" were let go by order of the cemetery's superintendent, on grounds that there was no willful violation of the law; but the ladies were informed that next time the law would be strictly enforced.[25]

From time to time, police were called in to investigate cemetery vandalism. "Bands of young toughs" frequented Riverview Cemetery during 1908–9. A "novel depredation" committed by a gang of small boys in a pasture adjoining the cemetery was the regular milking of the superintendent's cow. Boys, believed to be of the same band, set fire near the keeper's house and stole prized chickens. At other city cemeteries, vandals, believed to be between ages of twelve and sixteen, committed such deeds as breaking glass in a greenhouse and stealing flowers. Eventually, at Riverview and other cemeteries, keepers were awarded police power to pursue the boys to their homes and arrest them.[26] At least, with medical institutions now legally able to appropriate dead bodies that had come under public custody, body-snatching from cemeteries was a thing of the past.

Unrelated to body-snatching, but having the same sordid appeal to Richmonders, was the knowledge that in their midst was a "real, live cannibal," who happened to be in the state penitentiary. In June 1895, Eso Aso, the cannibal, who now went by the name of Antonio Frederick, a cognomen he had acquired as a sailor, was the subject in a report in the Richmond *Times*. He claimed to be fifty-eight years old, but appeared to be in his early thirties.

> He is six feet two inches high, weighs 174 pounds, and has a magnificent physique. Of a ginger-bread complexion, bright intelligent eyes, low forehead, straight nose, and lips unusually thin for an African, he is by no means a bad-looking negro. He reads and writes well, talks intelligently, with a foreign accent leaning towards the Oriental brogue, and has a nervous, jerky way of noticing things generally.... He is a remarkable athlete, muscular, active, and fleet of foot. He has been known to climb around on balconies and verandas at the prison where none of the other prisoners would dare venture. During his thirty-two years' residence in America and Europe he has picked up a great deal of information and grown accustomed to civilization, yet cherishes many of the legends and customs of his native land. He claims to be proselytized to the Catholic faith, and wears his beads and cross. He prays three times a day and reads his Bible regularly.
>
> Despite all this, Eso Aso still has a keen appetite for human flesh....

Eso Aso told about his life back in Africa, and of battles he fought.

> "We killed the prisoners and cooked them by putting them on a cross bar, back down and roasting them over a fire made in a square pit underneath. The hams and shoulders are the best to eat, and the muscles of the arm were eaten to make us strong and brave. With the meat was served a sauce made by boiling certain herbs. There is no better eating in the world than that. It is tender and juicy, and very wholesome. When once you eat it and get used to it nothing will take its place.
>
> "After the meat was all taken off the bones and skull were then given to the boys to play with. The skull was then dried in the sun, and the children found much amusement in filling it up with sand and letting it run through the eye sockets. That was nearly all the means of amusement we had."[27]

3

Clairvoyants

Clairvoyants were tricksters of the mind and spirit world just as various hucksters were of the material world. The mediums (spiritualists), fortune tellers, palmists, hoodoo-conjurers, mind readers, divine healers, and mesmerists (hypnotists) all claimed preternatural insight and ability to impact the lives of others. To all of this one might add the appearance of ghosts.

The Spiritualist Movement reached its high point in America at mid–19th century, owing largely to the influence of the Fox sisters, Margaret and Kate. Even in the 1880s, when the duo exposed the trickery of their frauds, Spiritualism retained much of its appeal. Through mediums, clients were induced step by step into "entering the silence," while a medium went into a trance. The ensuing séance brought forth a host of supposed manifestations of the spirit world, most notably communication with a deceased loved one. In a trance, the medium, tapping his or her subconscious, remained awake and was able to read the minds of others "even to give names, to see the absent, to visit strange places, to even leave this earth and visit other spheres."[1]

One of the most popular mediums in the country, seventy-year-old Dr. Louis Scheisinger of California, put on a demonstration at the Murphy Hotel on September 30, 1899. Everything he did proved to be accurate. He gave information on persons in the spirit world as well as those living in distant towns. The doctor claimed to have the power to cure disease, as well as break addicts of their need for morphine, tobacco, opium, and liquor "in a single sitting."[2]

In January 1894, Miss Anna Eva Fay, of Richmond, was labeled as "an indescribable phenomenon" in the performance of "unexplainable" feats while performing séances. During one such session, Justice Crutchfield of the Police Court and the sergeant of the city jail were allowed to attempt to expose trickery, but failed to do so. These two officials "kept the audience in one continual stream of laughter during the entire evening" and "Justice Crutchfield's hair was seen to stand on end several times."[3]

One particular séance, held one night in June 1901, attracted press coverage. The medium, a fifty-year-old who was said to have sixteen children, held forth on the second floor above a vacant store at 503 Pine Street. Some fifty persons were seated in the darkened room. The medium announced that she did not have power to summon the spirits; they would appear on their own. The session began with everyone singing the hymns "Nearer My God to Thee" and "Rock of Ages." Soon there was a sound resembling that of a tapping pencil. A muffled voice asked for "John, John Hooper." Then came from the beyond an utterance identifying the speaker as John Hooper's sister-in-law, Rebecca. When asked to prove this statement, the voice simply said "mail bag." Hooper's brother, it turned out, had been a mail carrier.

John R. Hooper, superintendent of Hollywood Cemetery, had come to the meeting along with police officer John Sales. Hooper addressed the voice from beyond. "How about grandmother? Is she with you?"

"Yes, and happy."

"Grandfather?"

"Yes, he is here, too."

Then the voice went quiet. The medium said that "the bright star who kept her in touch with the spirit world" had departed. Once again, however, she was able to recall the spirit. Bob McClintlock, Hooper, and Sales then posed questions to the spirit, some of which dealt with mythical persons, and, of course, they received unsatisfactory replies. That was enough to bring an end to the séance.[4]

"The question is not whether spiritualism is a fraud, but whether it is of God or Satan," declared a Richmond clergyman. Indeed, the issue for Richmonders came down simply to the conflict in a spiritualist's claim of being able to communicate with the dead and that of Christian doctrine that held that the dead are asleep and that only resurrection can restore life.[5]

Exposers of the methods of the spiritualists performed to capacity audiences in Richmond. Most proficient of such demonstrators was Professor H. Cooke. At his final appearance in the city at the opera house, he debunked the cabinet tests, rope-tying tests, and the "materializing test" (a mainstay of the Fox sisters) as the "Spirit Bride" appears on the stage. The "magical changing of water into wine and *vice versa* was not exposed," but at the "conclusion of the entertainment the secret was imparted to all who were willing to pay three dollars for it."[6]

3. Clairvoyants

Hoodooism (also known as voodooism) had it claimants in Richmond. Conjurers of this kind could cast spells, maleficent or beneficent, on other persons. In the African American communities from time to time there were alleged cases of conjuration causing physical harm. Instances of alleged death by conjuration were reported.[7]

In the fall of 1897 "intense excitement" prevailed "among the negroes in the district east of 23rd street and north of Main, over the 'hoodooing' of a colored woman" who cooked for a white family. It was reported that a "religious mania broke out among the colored people of Church Hill and everybody who was anybody became converted and professed religion." Eliza, however, was too busy with her kitchen duties to pay any attention. Several "old[er] sisters who had been converted," her relatives, and church deacons all came by her house to beg her to join the church, but she paid them no mind. Finally, she became very disturbed, and decided to go along with the entreaties. Deacons and several "sisters" came by her house and picked up Eliza in a wagon and took her to the location of the revival being held in King William County. Eliza, however, still had her doubts. At the end of a sermon the preacher gave a long exhortation, demanding that Eliza make a confession of faith. Again, she demurred. All the members of the congregation joined in the appeal, but with no success. The preacher again entered the pulpit, repeating his exhortation and adding a personal request that she come forward and be saved. But there was no compliance.

> Finally, the preacher lost his temper. Provoked by the obstinacy of the unrepentant Eliza he flew into a fit of rage. Again ascending the pulpit, he hurled volley after volley of curses on her head. The woman listened, aghast, to the maledictions coming from the preacher's mouth. She heard herself consigned to the most terrible places in punishment for her obstinacy, and ran out of the place in horror. She found her way back to the city and the next day became possessed of the belief that she had been "hoodooed."

Some church members told her that the preacher's curses had caused snakes and toads to enter her body. Eliza became delirious, believing that dozens of vipers and toads had crawled into her stomach. A half dozen "hoodoo" doctors treated her, without success. Her suffering was said to be extreme.[8]

On a lighter note, Richmonders were attracted to conjuring simply as a means of showmanship. In March 1900 at the Bijou Theater, Ching Ling Foo, the "marvelous Chinese conjuror and his company of high caste Orientals" gave an exhibition of "magic balancing legerdemain, and illusions from the Far East."[9]

Fortune tellers enjoyed immense popularity in Richmond. These prognosticators gleaned their special knowledge in a variety of ways, chiefly through astrology, card-reading, or palmistry. They especially seemed capable of conducting scams. Two such "get-rich-quick" clairvoyants were a "Professor Lee" and a "Professor Jackson," who practiced out of several rooms in different parts of the city, doing a "land office business," attracting as many as two thousand clients in a month's time. They advertised extensively by passing out cards and placing notices in newspapers. Although the two fortune tellers conned a number of citizens out of money and valuables, one episode in particular led them to hightail it out of town. This was when a young lady left her $150 diamond ring with Lee, who promised that within a few days, with a "proper treatment," he could make the ring, which was similar to rings worn by "the great Seers of India," into "a magic talisman." As he explained to the gullible woman, "Just leave the ring with me until Wednesday morning. I will, by a certain experiment, infuse a lot of magnetism into the diamond, and then it will become a talisman of good luck to you as long as you wear it."

When she called to retrieve her ring, not surprisingly, Lee was nowhere to be found. The "Professor" had left the ring at a pawnshop for $60.[10]

In December 1897 Mary Reid, a "colored" licensed fortune teller, was arrested for eliciting large sums of money from one Charles Priddy by promising to cure him of dyspepsia. Mary received ninety days in jail for petty larceny.[11]

Authorities clamped a "young clairvoyant," George Howard, alias Parker, in jail in May 1912, on the charge of being "a suspicious person." Given that the police lacked any solid evidence, the prisoner was released. Subsequently, a prominent local woman came forward to accuse Howard of swindling her out of two diamond rings, valued at $200, and $50 in cash. She swore out a warrant against the fortune teller. The woman, who remained unnamed, said she had consulted Howard "as a medium of the spirit world," and was told that "she was under a spell of evil influence and that if she wished to have it cast off" she must present Howard with something valuable, which would later be returned. The woman went home and came back with the two diamond rings. Howard examined them and said that they carried an "ill omen" for her and, to free herself, the woman should throw them away. The clairvoyant then directed the owner of the rings to accompany him to the James River, and there, standing on the Free Bridge, he threw them into the water. The woman was then required to come up with a fee of $50 for the medium's services. That was the last the woman heard of him until she learned he had been arrested as a suspicious character. This arrest had occurred when a girl, named Mary Blackmore, tried to pawn the rings. She had been arrested along with Howard as a suspicious person. The two swindlers, however, were released before they could be prosecuted, and disappeared from the city.[12]

"Professor Blair, alias for A. J. Morris, a fortune teller who worked 'the ancient envelope trick'" on W. E. Kahn, was arrested in Baltimore in August 1914 for the crime committed in Richmond six years before. Kahn had given the "professor" a thousand dollars as a deposit for the purpose of Kahn finding a person who had robbed him. When Kahn returned to the "professor" to collect his deposit, he was given an envelope to be opened later, which contained only "scraps of paper." The "professor" (Morris) was extradited to Richmond, and was sentenced to twelve months in the city jail. After serving six months of his sentence, the seriously ill con man was pardoned by Governor Henry C. Stuart.[13]

Gypsies' specialty was fortune telling. Once, it was said, they performed a whole evening before Queen Victoria and the royal household. In October 1900, a gypsy band stopping in Richmond charged between a nickel and two dollars per sitting—or whatever a customer could bargain for. Of this group, Princess Viola, daughter of Queen Cynthia, was asked how old one must be before discovering she had the ability to tell fortunes. Viola replied that "the power came to all gypsy girls who were descendants of gypsy parents on both sides for five generations," on their thirteenth birthday at 6 a.m.[14]

In September 1895, a group of several dozen gypsies pitched seven small tents at the edge of the fairgrounds, west of the city's border with Henrico County. The tents were without "the sheet of canvas which is thrown over the front at night," leaving the interior "exposed to the gaze of the crowd that flocks about the camp all day."

> "Tell fortune. Tell fortune. Two dollars." This was the greeting of the reporter from several of the women. "Five shent! five shent!" yelled half a score of children tugging at his clothing. The young beggars ranged in age probably from two to six years. One of them was dressed in a blue bead necklace and one sock. With their bronzed skins, coarse matted hair, piercing black eyes and dirt-covered faces they resembled young savages. They swore like pirates. "Five shent!" they screeched, "five shent!" and when the coin was not speedily forthcoming they heaped maledictions upon the reporter, themselves and the world in general.

A "countryman" entered the tent and asked that his fortune be told. "How much?" he asked. "Two dollar" was the answer. After much haggling, he agreed to pay one dollar. Then a black girl, named Sarah James, stepped forward, and again the soothsayer demanded two dollars; the fortune, however, was told for the price of five cents. But after Sarah and the gypsy woman had been "closeted together" several minutes

> angry voices emanating from within came to the ears of those outside the tent. Then Sarah appeared dragging the fortune teller through the entrance. "I give you a quarter and you ain't gimme no change," Sarah shouted for the benefit of the crowd. "Gimme twenty cents fo' I tears yo heart in pieces." Several of the Gypsies ran to the assistance of their companion and Sarah was driven off. She returned to the attack, however, and by threats of the police she contrived to get her change out of the gypsy's pocket five cents at a time.[15]

Sometimes, gypsies were admitted into private homes to give fortune readings. Thus, a gypsy woman, weighing two hundred pounds, who was "swarthy complexioned and wearing the many-colored garments of her kind, entered the home of Mrs. M. E. Wharton, 2008 Floyd Avenue. Once inside, the woman became angry when told her services as a fortune teller were not needed. The gypsy woman threw a handful of sand in Mrs. Wharton's face and then knocked Mrs. Wharton down, stealing her purse, containing $11. The gypsy woman escaped without anyone in the neighborhood having noticed her."[16]

Palmistry became a staple in Richmond's clairvoyant scene. Reading palms involved a combination of two methods: chirognomy, which deals with the shape of the hands; and chiromancy, which deals with the lines and marks on the palms. Among various possibilities, it may be noted that persons with big thumbs had "awful will power"; those with fat forefingers had a love of justice; and those with club-like forefingers were incapable of tempering justice with mercy.

So anxious were Richmonders about palmistry that the *Richmond News* in early 1900 ran a feature whereby readers could send in their palm prints and obtain a reading from the noted zaneigs (palmists). All one had to do to enter the testing was to take smoke-blackened paper and place a hand over it, draw an outline of the hand with a pencil, and submerge the blackened paper with the image into alcohol slowly with the smoked side up. A palmist could then use the dried paper to foretell the individual's future. The following are some examples of applicants' letters and the analysis they received:

> To the Zaneigs, Palmists:
> Enclosed find imprint of my left hand. Please answer through the *Richmond News*.
> M. B. S.
> This is the hand of a highly sensitive and somewhat nervous woman. The health line shows some enemy at work in the constitution, and a change would be advis-

3. *Clairvoyants*

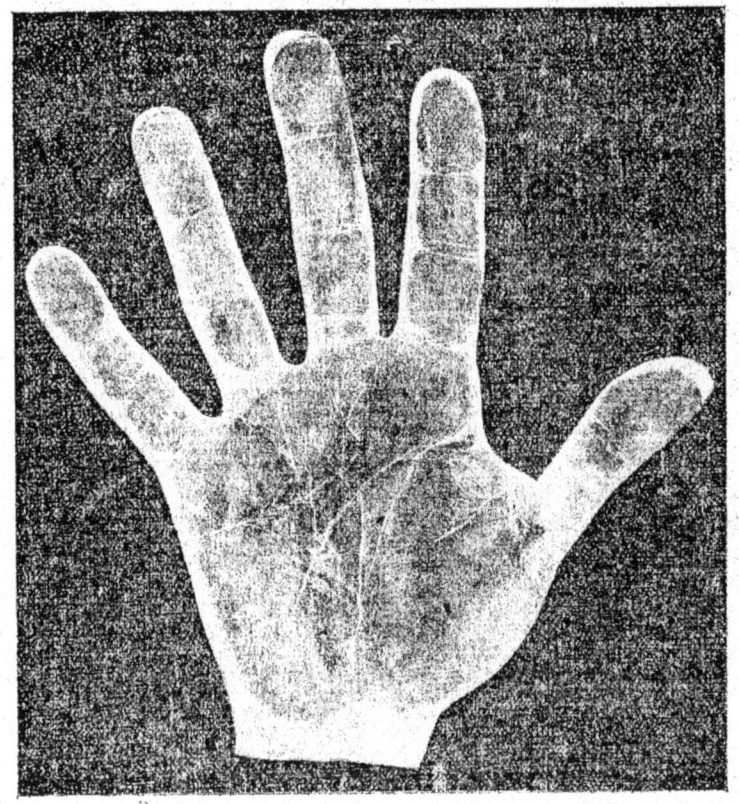

MAYOR TAYLOR'S HAND.

This hand represents the square spatulate type, showing the power to command with a great love of justice and fair play. The nature is resourceful and there is much generosity with independence in thought and action and great self-control. The first impressions should be followed. The head line indicates caution and bright imagination. The heart line shows sensitiveness where the affections are concerned with a high ideal. The hand shows love of home and family. There is inventive genius and much originality. The life line promises long life with a good constitution to enjoy it. There is some danger from the heart, that organ showing weakness towards sixty. The death will be from natural causes, though rather suddenly. From fifty on the career shows a gradual rise and the gratification of the main desire. From thirty-five to fifty much opposition and some prejudice which is entirely overcome. In reference to health some rheumatism or tendency to gout and danger to the digestive organs. In the main the future will be bright and bring much satisfaction with it.

"Mayor Taylor's Hand," as seen in the *Richmond News,* February 21, 1900.

able. There is great generosity and the affections are strong. There is a love of excitement and fresh air, but more rest should be indulged in. The heart shows three strong affections, with a possibility to two marriages. One threatens to end in separation, caused by some domestic trouble, jealousy, or interference by relatives. It will take a great deal of will power to overcome the influence of Fate in the life. The money affairs will prosper, and there is a somewhat pleasant change in the life at or near thirty-two. Some unpleasantness in the near future, but the middle and latter part of the year shows traveling and much pleasure. The life will always be eventful and the love of romance and sentiment will be fully gratified. Will not have a large family. Will always have admiration and be considerably spoiled by others. The life may be long if care is taken of the constitution.

To the Zaneigs, Palmists:
Please read my hand.
H. E.
This hand shows love of detail, good reason and much originality and independence of character. The nature is affectionate, and the long little finger shows diplomatic talent. The life line shows many changes and there will be a change on account of the health within a few years. The respiratory organs are very weak, and great care should be taken to avoid colds. The executive ability is good, and much money will be made. There is some sorrow close to thirty, before or after, and later a change of places. Much traveling, and, altogether, an eventful life. There will be two strong attachments and maybe two marriages. The life will end through an inherited weakness, but with care it may last until old age.

To the Zaneigs, Palmists:
What does my hand foretell?
H. R. K.
This hand shows the power to lead, manage and execute; great resourcefulness and adaptability; much versatility and wit. The health needs looking after at the present time; there is a tendency to rheumatism. The respiratory organs are delicate, but there will be nothing serious in that direction if caution is taken in regards to exposure. There is much traveling, and the life is made up of changes. No great success is a shown until thirty, but quite a successful career is promised. The life is protected all through from hardships.

To the Zaneigs, Palmists:
What do the lines in my hand indicate?
A. R. K.
There will be two marriages and four children. The life will end far from place of birth, at an old age.[17]

A famous palmist from England appeared in Richmond during May 1903. She offered consultations at 703 West Clay Street, daily from 10 a.m. to 9 p.m. for a fee of one dollar. Mrs. Masson, as she was known in a newspaper notice, asked that she not be confused with the "so-called 'Gypsy Queens,' humbug clairvoyants, trance mediums, slate writers and others who have done so much to bring discredit upon the science of Palmistry."

This eminent palmist did not give personal descriptions nor did she sell "spirit pictures" or "lucky charms." But she could confidently provide a reading of a person's entire life: ailments (both past and to come); the length of one's life; the work best suited to the individual; the mistakes one has made and how to avoid their repetition in the future; and that individual's potential success, be it financial, social, or artistic. Mrs. Masson asserted that she did not appeal to "ignorant superstition, but to the highest intelligence."[18]

In 1914, a city ordinance was passed requiring all "fortune prophets" to take out licenses.[19] Other than arresting those palmists and other fortune tellers who did not apply for such a license, it was very difficult to pin any malfeasance on them. For being caught in playing the "envelope game," of switching good into bad money, the punishment usually did not exceed being run out of town.[20]

One palmist turned out to be a sort of a Dickensian Fagin who was in cahoots with a gang of boy thieves. "Professor" Wilbur Lonzo, fifty-four years old, was arrested in his rooms at 510 East Marshall Street for receiving stolen goods, mostly jewelry designed for men. Three of the hoodlums, ages fifteen through sixteen, went to the reformatory. Lonzo, arrested on felony charges, was remanded for a trial in the Hustings Court. He ultimately received a six-year sentence.[21]

There were also practitioners of mind reading. A most prominent visitor of this stripe entertained at the Richmond Theater in March 1876. J. Randall Brown, a "fair-faced young man, with long silky black hair thrown back in piously poetic style, and eyes noticeable for their brilliancy," performed on a stage illuminated by an "unusual number of gas jets." With the participation by a "committee of well-known gentlemen" seated onstage, Brown showed such feats of dexterity as, upon being blindfolded, locating hidden objects and naming words written down secretly by audience members.[22] Fourteen years later (1890), Brown was back in Richmond, this time at the Mozart Academy, giving a much more sophisticated performance than previously, with such demonstrations as a "mock tragedy," "wire test," and "a charming little lady" undergoing a "materialization séance." Brown, over the years, had performed throughout the world, from the Far East to a command appearance before Queen Victoria and her royal household at Balmoral Castle.[23]

Another crowd-pleasing mind reader was Mrs. Kittie Baldwin. A feature of her show at the Academy of Music, in February 1896, had her husband distribute paper and pencils to the audience, who were then requested to jot down questions, fold up the paper, and place it into a pocket. Mr. Baldwin then hypnotized his wife. Audience members were asked to take out the paper and hold it in their hands. Individual persons stood up, and Mrs. Baldwin answered their concealed questions. In the process of responding to a question, Mrs. Baldwin's face expressed the nature of a question, ranging from sorrow to smiles. One time she told of a murder and "sent cold chills through many of her auditors by a frightful yell." Another time she said, responding to a question, "The lady was killed for $700. Her name was Mrs. Pollard. She lived in Londonburg, Lowenburg, Lunenburg." A Sergeant Brooks was told who had shot him at the railroad depot some years previously, and that his assailant now resided in Buffalo.[24]

Not all mind readers enjoyed the goodwill of the community. In May 1916, two gypsy mind readers, Marie and Anna Keslo, were each fined $100 and given thirty-day jail sentences, for stealing $5 from a client. The two women cut up the bill into pieces, which they then proceeded to swallow. But enough evidence was found to convict them. Also pertaining to the case, the two gypsies claimed that they had permission from the "big chief" of the city to practice mind reading, but the record revealed that neither woman had been granted a license.[25]

In the 1890s, Richmonders eagerly welcomed lecture/demonstrations by hypnotists (mesmerists). The hypnotists had free rein as the state had no laws affecting this practice. Hypnosis was now more or less regarded as a science.[26] The city even had its own noted authorities on hypnotism. In January 1896, Dr. John Henry delivered a series of well-attended lecture/demonstrations at the Richmond Theater, the University College of Medicine, and the Virginia General Assembly convening in the Senate Chamber of the Capitol. Dr. Henry asserted that Moses was "a great fakir," had worked miracles among "an assemblage of subjective persons," and that "under the same conditions he could do exactly what Moses did." The esteemed hypnotist conducted a class at the Capitol on how to hypnotize persons, emphasizing the necessity of concentration during the procedure.[27]

Dr. G. Stanley Hall, another Richmond physician, also became a locally recognized expert on hypnotism. Huge crowds attended his presentations. For his Thomas Memorial Lecture at Richmond College on the evening of April 1, 1897, attendees began arriving an hour early, continuing to come "on foot, in carriage, on every street car, until every accessible place in the chapel was taken." Hall's lecture on this occasion, "The Border Land," dealt with the "strange revival of so many kinds of mysticism represented by theosophy, mind cure, faith-cure, spiritualism, telepathy,

3. Clairvoyants

hypnotism, symbolism, and many others." Dr. Hall noted that the belief in "disembodied spirits" was almost universal. He went on to expose some of the trickery used by exponents of conjuring. Hypnotism, however, which Hall considered scientific as well as "a really fine art," could be beneficial, in spite of it conveying a "dangerous power." Hypnotism, said Hall, "sharpens the senses and strengthens the muscles," and could be defined as "normal sleep with great intensification of dreams."[28]

Another Richmond physician, Dr. W. H. Parker, Sr., experimented with hypnotism by telephone. Two participants in one of Dr. Parker's phone sessions, within five seconds, fell into "a complete hypnotic sleep." Among the results was the "complete rigidity" of one of the subjects, suspended between two chairs, while two men weighing in the "aggregate" of three hundred pounds, sat on him without causing the slightest bending. During this ordeal, the subject repeated, word for word, a newspaper notice that had been read to him.[29]

In January 1910, the public was informed that Sylvain A. Leopold, better known as Sylvain A. Lee, the oldest practicing and most widely known hypnotist in America, was in the city jail "awaiting examination by a commission in lunacy." The fifty-two-year-old Lee and his wife were residing at a local boarding house when he became incoherent and allegedly attacked and threatened to murder his wife. Lee had abandoned his public demonstrations two years before and had, in the meantime, failed in opening a "school of hypnotism" for treating "by mental suggestion all diseases flesh is heir to." Lee's last professional tour had been through the South, billed as "Lee, Wizard of the Mind." While making this circuit of theaters, Lee frequently exhibited erratic behavior; he especially took offense at something said or done in the audience, and proceeded to scold the wrongdoers from the stage.

During his lunacy hearing, Lee discoursed at length on his talent for hypnotism, noting that he employed the principles of the leaders of the Emanuel Movement in Boston. He, however, faulted the teachings of Mary Baker Eddy (Christian Science) because she referred too frequently to Jesus Christ, attaching little reverence to His name. The commission of lunacy decided that Lee was suffering from temporary insanity and he was removed from the city jail to the state mental hospital in Williamsburg.[30]

In the psychotherapeutics arena, faith-healing ranked, along with spiritualism, as the extreme end in conjuring. Disabled Richmonders eagerly sought cures through supposedly eminent healers whenever they came to town. One of the most popular of these "miracle workers" was

James Deane, who hailed from Kansas. In January 1896, he set up headquarters at the Henry Walker house at the corner of Clay and Thirty-Sixth Streets. "Consumptives, cripples, and people suffering with almost every known disease flocked to the house from every section of the city" and adjoining counties. Deane was "a very ordinary looking man with a full black beard covering a rather serious face"; he wore "semi-clerical garb." When he first arrived, he announced: "I am sent here by Jesus, and whatever cures I effect are through His divine power." Because of the enormous turnout, Deane was able to accommodate only a portion of all persons seeking his help. Several of those treated observed that a clasp from the faith healer's hand showed that "the man's system was evidently heavily charged with natural electricity."[31]

About a year later, August Schrader, another renowned divine healer who had caused excitement "all over the United States," arrived in Richmond. Accompanied by his private secretary, George R. Berriman, he took up rooms at a house at 912 East Marshall Street. Schrader, age twenty-six, had a "high, smooth forehead, a large nose, somewhat flattened, and small bluish-gray eyes." His thick hair fell to his shoulders. He wore a black robe and a white collar, similar to that worn by Catholic priests. On his breast pocket, attached to a small chain, were "two silver crosses and a crucifix." All persons who called on Schrader carried handkerchiefs which were blessed by the healer. Schrader also received many letters each day containing handkerchiefs to be blessed and returned to the sender. Approximately two out of every ten senders thought to include return postage. Schrader never asked for donations but accepted offerings placed on a table. He spent one morning receiving members of the African American community exclusively. Upon request, he made house calls for which he did require fees. Much of Schrader's miracle working involved the restoration of hearing.[32]

In December 1898, the Rev. Charles McLean, also known as Schlatter, delivered a series of lectures at the Mozart Hall, after which he gave a demonstration of the power of healing. Afflicted persons walked onto the stage, where the Reverend McLean prayed over them. Remarkable recoveries ensued.[33]

Not all divine healers visiting Richmond could claim success, however. Henry C. Blanchard, the "long-haired faith-cure apostle," after spending two weeks performing in rented rooms at Murphy's Hotel, found it expedient to make a sudden exit after most of his miracles did not last.[34] In his rooms on Marshall Street, thirty-two-year-old Dr. Wynne Hayden, another self-professed divine healer, became "a great favorite among a small circle of acquaintances." When it was discovered that he was involved in a plot to acquire money illegally, he committed suicide.[35]

Every year, one or several magicians drew large audiences in Richmond. Children and adults alike greeted Wyman the Wizard, who, for a decade, performed annually at the state fair and also at the Richmond Theater and the Virginia Opera House. Audiences were drawn to his "fascinating tricks," such as his ventriloquism and the "wonderful egg-bag," and the giving-away of presents.[36]

Zera Semon, a native Richmonder, a popular magician and ventriloquist, performed at Richmond Theater in 1881 and 1883. Included in the show was Billy Diamond, "the delineator of Ethiopian characters."[37] Keller, the Illusionist, and Bosco, the Magician, also gave performances at the Richmond Theater.[38]

Two performers experimented "beyond the domain of the ordinary magician." At the Academy of Music in October 1893, Powell, as he was

Howard Thurston in His Great Levitation Act, as depicted by the *Richmond News Leader*, April 5, 1913.

simply known, promised to penetrate "the most hidden secrets of his art," expounding upon the "wonderful feats of the Orientals and the theory of the Theosophists of Mahatmas."[39] A magician by the name of Bancroft brought to Richmond more scenery than any other performer. Much of the "apparatus and paraphernalia" had been purchased in India. Appearing at the Academy, he presented a "startling series of acts," titled, "The Midnight Mysteries of the Yogi of India." His extravagant backdrops included "The Palace of the Magician of Fable," "The Princely Abode of the Japanese Juggler," "Midnight in the Hindoo Temple of Magic," and "Bancroft's Home of Mystery." Bancroft expounded on "mystical subjects," ranging from "the lore of the Hindoos" to the "dark diablerie of Egypt, Japan, Turkey, and Persia." In all, Bancroft's show blended "fascinating fun and fantasy."[40]

The young Harry Houdini, just starting out at the turn of the century on his fabled career in "the lowest venues of show business [including the dime museums which featured freaks of nature]," performed in Richmond. Seeking to duplicate Houdini's tricks, particularly those of the handcuffs and being locked in a trunk, were Ching Ling and Young Lee (Moses May and Mr. Lee Reinheimer). These two "conjurers" specialized in appearing before small and select gatherings.[41]

While conjurers sought to contact the other world, apparitions from the supernatural world intruded into the lives of humans. Richmond, as elsewhere, had its share of ghost sightings.

In the summer of 1887, an eighteen-year-old black man, out at midnight on Buckingham Road (across the river a short distance west of the city), saw the figure of a woman dressed in black, and further down the road spotted the image of a headless man, who had on his shoulder a bag, much as one that might be "filled with chickens"; subsequently, the phantom followed the young man closely as he ran away. A commentator said that the behavior of this apparition was much like most of the ghosts known to history, behaving in "such a meaningless and senseless way as to lead one to suppose that their mental faculties had been interred with their bones."[42]

From a four-story brick house at 115 South Third Street appeared a "specimen of the genus ghost as ever cavorted through the brain" of Edgar Allan Poe. Many residents of the street saw the spook. This "ghost of Marshall Flats" carried a pail. His "programme," lasting an hour, included mystic dances, "contortion acts," and disappearances. Some persons connected this ghostly display with two suicides that had occurred in the house. One rational explanation for the ghost was that it was from a gas jet reflected upon window panes.[43] At another site, a brick house at the corner of Fourteenth Street and Exchange Alley, a woman dressed in black glided through the rooms; the apparition was said to have a sweet face, rendering her unthreatening.[44]

In the Brookland district (now part of northern Richmond) in Henrico County, women and children feared to venture out after dark toward the bridge between Hermitage and Broad Streets. A "wild man" haunted the structure. Usually appearing naked, the intruder had a long beard and shaggy hair, which covered most of his head and chest. One man claimed that this creature had pursued his little daughter. He never came forth in daylight, and it was assumed that he resided in the woods, near the bridge. All efforts to apprehend this mysterious person failed, including using a policeman's son outfitted in feminine attire as a decoy.[45]

There were other ghostly occurrences. An old, deserted house, built in antebellum times, had the reputation of being haunted; even a poor black family that moved into it rent free were soon scared away.[46] Similarly, a dilapidated house on Hague Street was reportedly inhabited by ghosts, including a woman in white. Yet another black family, allowed to live in the house, however, had no complaints. Others insisted they saw ghosts there. "A delegation from one of the colored churches" visited the house, and offered to hold a prayer service there. The family refused, saying that "they did not wish to have the Lord and the devil in the house at the same time."[47]

Ghostlike goings-on sometimes happened in unusual places. In the "upper end of East Main Street," door bells continually—and inexplicably—rang some nights, between midnight and 4 a.m.[48] On West Main Street one afternoon, a gentleman heading home claimed to have met a ghost. It was, he said, a woman, dressed in black, who walked up to him "and just as he was about to raise his hat she disappeared."[49] At the Henrico County jail in downtown Richmond, what was described as the ghost of James Austin, who had been hanged in the jail yard in 1905, so terrified three black prisoners that they slept only in the daytime and stayed awake at night "in order to protect themselves."[50]

One night, at approximately 11:30 p.m., W. Allen Dickinson, superintendent of Oakwood Cemetery on Richmond's East Side, while coming down the driveway of his house, saw the "figure of a tall man, dressed in a linen-duster down to his heels, and on his head was a helmet of light color, shaped something like a police-man's hat." Dickinson stopped his horse and ran towards the stranger; just as he did, the man vanished. Dickinson was convinced he had seen "a real spook."[51]

In the late 1890s, Richmond's new city hall was said to have spirits roaming its corridors at night. One particular specter made its nocturnal presence felt "until the crowing of the cocks force[d] it to take flight into the vast unknown." Nick McGiffin, the night-watchman, gave the most telling testimony of the haunting: "Gaunt figures, draped as though in the gruesome winding sheets, in the folds of which they were committed to the tomb, have started up from gloomy recesses and glided noiselessly." The ghosts, he added, were thoroughly illuminated. As they ambled along in front of McGiffin, they were "quiet and peaceable tenants as one would wish to have, never spitting on the floors nor disturbing any of the valuable documents in the various departments."[52]

Some of the supernatural phenomena, with a little careful investigation, could be explained. In May 1897, at a big four-story building that had once been a theater, all sorts of "spooky happenings" occurred. "Strange, unearthly noises" penetrated through the inside walls of the building. The "colored porter" refused to go upstairs. "With the whites of his eyes almost popping out of his head," he declared the premises "haunted." Soon, all the occupants declared they also had heard the weird sounds. Their faces "began to show the pallor that results from loss of sleep, and lines of care and mental labor corrugated the brow of all." Eventually, a woman, who proclaimed herself a spiritualist, investigated, and asserted that "the spirit of John Brown, the guerilla chieftain, had taken up temporary lodgment in the walls, and that it was crying out against the Turkish victories." The building's (living) occupants decided to take action. They sent for a carpenter who bored a hole about six inches in diameter into a wall, from which the "strange cries" emitted. Then came the startling scene, rolling out of the boarding in the aperture, "with many howls," was "a small white kitten." The "crowd in the room breathed freer as they watched the little animal crawl about the floor." A mystery remained, however; how the parent cats entered into the wall and then managed to live in the dark masonry.[53]

4

Plungers

Gambling flourished in Richmond because of the public's toleration of it and police evasion of strong enforcement of anti-gambling laws. What hostility to the waywardness of plungers, as reckless bettors were called, was owing to the reaction against skin games (hustling players through cheating and trickery) rather than of the games themselves.

Gambling by the public had been in Richmond since it became an incorporated town in the late 18th century. A traveler passing through Richmond in the early 1790s commented: "Perhaps in no place of the same size in the world is there more gambling going forward than in Richmond."[1] The principal forms of gambling in Richmond, exclusive of wagering on the stock exchange, were card playing, rolling dice (chiefly craps), and betting on games of "skill and speed."[2] Some gambling required paraphernalia, such as slot machines and lottery wheels.[3]

Playing cards and rolling dice were the main indoor games of chance, although occasionally one could catch such action outdoors. Poker and faro (which flourished more in the antebellum period than later) were the exclusive card games.

Many poker games were a "freeze-out," when, in the beginning, stakes were small but progressively (and vastly) increased. Gambling at poker occurred about everywhere—in saloons, "poker clubs," hotel rooms, and private residences.[4] Sometimes, a whole second floor of a business or home would be converted into a poker parlor, with tables set up for as many as thirty or more patrons.[5] It was not uncommon to find children engaged in poker with stakes. In August 1909, a gang of white boys and "pickaninnies" held poker games in an alley near Ninth and Broad Streets.[6]

One Richmond phenomenon was the appearance of poker rooms, or "poker resorts," which catered specifically to the game of draw poker. At one time it was estimated that there were one hundred such places in the

"He's Talking to a Stranger"—from the *Richmond Times-Dispatch*, April 4, 1916.

city. Some proprietors went to the trouble to establish a "chartered club" in order to cloak what would normally be an illegal operation.[7]

Faro was played with a full deck of cards. The dealer, known as the "gaff," assisted by a "looker-out" at his right, dealt out thirteen cards of one suit from a box. The drawn cards were arranged in two parallel rows, with four connecting cards. Players were given cards on which they bet to match a card or cards on the table in twenty-one different ways.[8] This game also had its gambling rooms featuring "Italian faro"; in one instance twenty-five African American men were caught in that pursuit during a police raid.[9]

Shooting craps was the most pervasive game of chance; it required only a pair of dice, and a game could be struck on the spur of the moment at any place, from street corners to a secluded place out of town. Although somewhat complicated, winning at craps generally meant rolling a seven or eleven. The bone-breakers were on the constant lookout for police. Since the game, as often as not, had young down-and-out black participants, they were easy prey for the police, who preferred to ride herd on lowlife gambling than to disturb well-to-do bettors. Fines, levied in Police Court, were generally in the $2.50 range.

Craps seemed to provoke more violence than other games. Arguments arising from the dice-throwing all too frequently led to a knifing or a shooting.[10] Robbing a crap game meant stirring a hornet's nest. One day in August 1908, Ifrey Shelton, who still had cuts on his face from an earlier encounter for allegedly having stolen money from a crap game, was pursued by five other African Americans wielding razors. At 5 a.m. he appeared at the First Police Station and begged for help. His tormentors stood outside the station for a while before entering. Their "jabbering" left the attending sergeant with a feeling that he was "being visited by a contingent from Coxey's army." [This is in reference to a protest march in Washington, D.C., in 1894, by U.S. workers, led by Ohio businessman Jacob Coxey.] While seeking warrants against Shelton, the complainants, however, were locked up for "disorderly conduct and fighting in the street." Shelton fared much better, receiving "comfort and consolation"; after being stitched up by a physician, he was "put to bed in a cell."[11]

"There was a hot time in Pink Alley" on Saturday night October 9, 1897. An "ever-seductive bones" game, run daily by John Thomas and John Wall at a "joint" in the alley, which ran between Sixth and Seventh streets between Broad and Marshall streets, and a "ranch" called Mundy's Hall nearby at the corner of Pink Alley and Market streets, experienced police raids. Accordingly

> a cordon of blue-coated officers assembled at the mouth of the alley, and with silent tread surrounded the two houses. As they stood without the windows the click of the bones could be distinctly heard, and a mirthful peal of laughter would ever and anon break the stillness of the night as some more fortunate gambler would roll his "seven" or capture "Big Dick."

The officers rushed in, and the players

> made for the doors and the windows like rats scampering for a hole, but at every turn they were confronted by brass buttons ... three of the darkies had secreted themselves beneath the table, and had endeavored to pull it down upon them and thereby escape detection, but like the ostrich, they had hidden only their heads, and were soon pulled forth.

Taken to jail the next morning, they made their appearance in Police Court.[12]

Many times the police unsuccessfully tried to raid a recurring crap game at a place in Weatherford's Row. Finally, upon a tip from a disgruntled insider, supplied with the password, the police knocked on the door in the darkness, and a deep bass voice rang out from the other side.

"Who dat?" said the man.

"Me-one," said the police captain.

"O. K. me," replied the voice. and the door swung open with a creaking sound.

All eight "brothers in black," who were "gambling for their Sadie" at a game of craps, were arrested. At the time that the policemen burst in, thirty cents lay on the floor, and a player was calling out loudly, "Little Joe—come, Joe, two duce, three, one hit 'im a lick."[13]

In July 1909, Harrison Bundy, the "erstwhile Beau Brummell of Pink Alley, sporting man, restaurant-keeper and operator of the leading crap game in the city," was undone by the combined efforts of his pie-maker, Alberta Lacy. Alberta was angry because almost every time she baked pies and put them on the window sill, somebody jumped out, and "the athlete generally took window sash and pies with him." Bundy was arrested for "cursing, assaulting, abusing, biting and otherwise inflicting bodily harm and mental injury" on Alberta Lacy. The police ordered Bundy to move "his headquarters to some other cover because his place had become a common nuisance," a decision reinforced by the building inspector, who deemed Bundy's crap joint as uninhabitable. It is presumed that Bundy relocated. He had "run a crap game since he was old enough to tell a deuce from a six spot, and he had many friends and had a lot of money."[14]

Crap shooters regularly turned up in Police Court. Among a "bunch" of such gamesters appearing before Justice Crutchfield, on January 13, 1907, was one who had "whirling discs in his dome."

> "Watcher name?" asked the court.
>
> "It might be John."
>
> "Please God: it might for a fact; but what in h—-, but what is it?"
>
> "William Robinson?" inquired the negro politely.
>
> "It may be Johnson," suggested the court.
>
> "That's it, judge; sorry I forgot it."
>
> "Get out of here; I'm not running the bug-house. Go get christened and come back."
>
> Then his honor dismissed court.[15]

Another dice game that had a run of popularity was chuck-a-luck. It was played with three dice. Bets were made that a certain number would come up and that all three dice would total a designated number or that total would be an odd, even, high, or low number. The game required a box in which to shake the dice. Police raids were fairly successful in deterring this form of gambling.[16]

A "game of policy," also called a "jug game," involved paying off on

4. Plungers

"The Crap Game Under the Big Culvert," *Richmond Times-Dispatch*, April 4, 1916.

numbers drawn from a rotating wheel (jug). Tickets were sold from policy shops and elsewhere, and the numbers were selected from a central location. The "house" usually took a 15 percent commission. Typically, the "jug," noted one observer, is

> very much like a swinging ice-pitcher; but it has only one aperture, and that is at the bottom when the "jug" is at rest. This aperture is quite small, and is closed with a spring. Seventy-six round balls about the size of marbles, numbered from one to seventy-six, are put in the "jug." The "jug" is made to revolve once or twice, and when it comes to rest the aperture is opened and thirteen balls allowed to drop out one by one, and as they come out their numbers are taken and recorded.

GAMBLING PARAPHERNALIA CAPTURED BY OFFICER WYATT

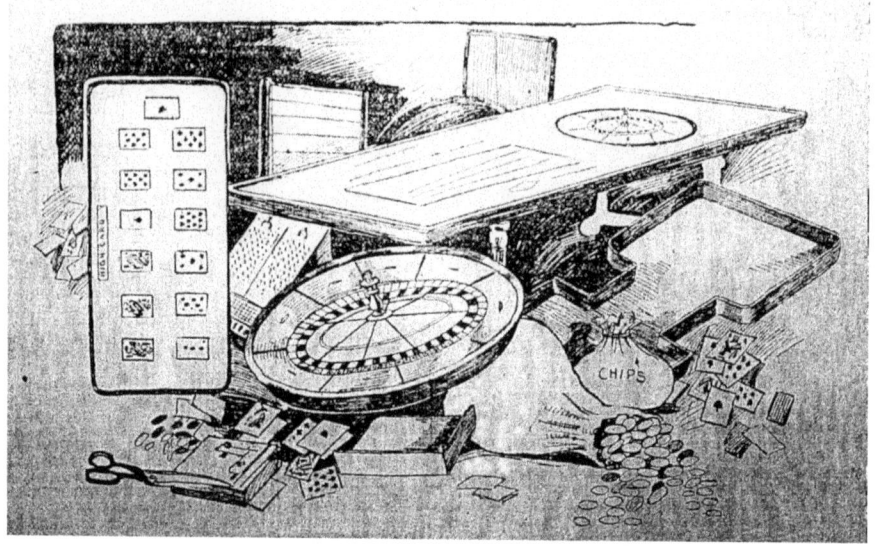

"Gambling Paraphernalia Captured by Officer Wyatt," read the caption for this photograph in the Richmond *Daily Times*, September 21, 1902.

The "writers" then settle with the ticket holders. Selecting three consecutive numbers as winners leads to the reward of 100 to 150 times the amount of money invested.[17]

A "Policy King" of Richmond was Marshall Brown (died in May 1895). Brown "opened more poker rooms, policy shops and crap joints" than any other person in Richmond. He had three "jug games" within fifty yards of the intersection of Cary and Eighteenth streets.[18]

Occasionally, those who conducted policy games were hauled into Police Court. But the perpetrators usually had an advantage of being forewarned of impending raids. The most effective enforcement against lotteries was an "anti-lottery law," which prohibited the use of the mails for anything pertaining to the conducting of a lottery, including promotional materials.[19]

Resembling lotteries, raffles were a cause for concern only if fraud was suspected. Favorite raffle prizes were turkeys and cigars. Authorities investigated whether prizes were actually delivered or if they were even worth the price of a raffle ticket.[20]

4. Plungers

Working a shell game rarely brought arrests.[21] This game involved putting a pea or pellet under something that resembled a shell (e.g., a thimble), and after moving around the shells, betting under which one was the object.

Pictured is the "Winner of the Big Pot in Kelly Pool," as seen in the *Richmond Times-Dispatch*, December 29, 1913.

Another game of chance held sway for a decade or so. "Nickel-in-the-slot" machines made their appearance in the mid-1890s. Originally, the machines dispensed candy, gum, or cigars, but were soon converted to mete out cash.[22] Some saloons boasted as many as three dozen slot machines.[23] At first, annual license fees were required for the devices.[24] A state law of 1905, however, prohibited all slot machines in which there was an element of chance. Persons caught maintaining slot machines faced a penalty of up to twelve months in jail and a five-hundred-dollar fine; normally, a conviction brought a hundred-dollar fine and court costs.[25]

The sporting life showed its most aggressive side relating to gambling on events involving skill. The outdoor variety were chiefly horseracing and cockfighting, while indoor pool (billiards), with bets to win and side wagering, was popular.

"A race track plunger, like a poet or a gambler, is born and not made," a reporter commented in 1893. Plunging on horse-races, however, should be left alone if one did not know "horses from A to Z and has not the traits of a gamester."[26]

For most of the period, Richmond and its vicinity had three race courses: Fairfield, two and a half miles southeast of the Capitol in Henrico County; Broad Rock, across the river in Chesterfield County (today's site of McGuire's Veteran Hospital); and at the fairgrounds, just west of the city, on Broad Street.[27] Bookmaking occurred throughout the city. The main off-track betting for several years could be found at the Turf Exchange at 101 Government Street; although allowed to operate, the owners had difficulty in meeting the $2,500 annual license fee required by the city.[28] Bookmaking mostly evaded the Maupin Act of 1896, which aimed at prohibiting all forms of gambling.[29]

Cockfighting, though illegal, drew enthusiastic crowds, with spectators often coming from afar, particularly from Washington, D.C., the Carolinas, and Florida.[30] Local venues for the cruel sport could be found at buildings on Main Street, between Seventh, Eighth, and Ninth streets, 615 West Main Street, corner of Ninth and Clay streets, a hall on Third Street, the Casino on Broad, near Seventh Street, and along the eastern borders of the city, with Chesterfield and Henrico counties.[31] For a while, nearly every boy in the city who raised chickens kept two "skags" for fighting.[32]

On January 14, 1891, a major cockfight took place at the Casino in downtown Richmond. To reach the scene of action, one had to produce a pass for a guard and climb two flights of stairs. Attending were ninety-nine ticket holders. At the start of the action at 10 a.m., around the pit were gathered cockfight aficionados from "all walks of life—merchants, bank clerks, traveling men, capitalists, druggists, barroom keepers, gamblers, men-about-town, and nobodies whose lives are mysteries." The fight was between cocks from Washington, D.C., and North Carolina. These birds were described as "beautiful specimens, and had the look that is unusually apparent on a well-groomed and well-fed horse. They were stylish-looking roosters, but would break up the peace of any barnyard." There were five fights during which lesser important combat between other roosters was held. A fight broke out among drunken spectators that was "more brutal than the poor birds themselves"; the men "were as bad and depraved as the devil would have them to be." A raid elicited some arrests.[33]

A similar event occurred on February 3, 1899, at "an old barn-like house just west of the Old Reservoir," with two hundred spectators in attendance.

> The tip had been given quietly, early in the week, and every sport in the city knew the various signals, countersigns and other things, together with the price of admission [50 cents] and the exact location....
> All during the night sentries had been on the lookout from various posts assigned them, and no man who did not know the countersign could pass them.[34]

Dog fighting cropped up from time to time, but law enforcement bore down harder than with cockfights. It was more difficult to cover up as more space was required. Dog events, nevertheless, were staged in a building on the corner of Ninth and Clay streets and on Brown and Vauxhall islands.[35] Dog stealers, for the purpose of providing the contestants, menaced the community. "The town's full of 'em fakirs that stand on the corners and put pink ribbons on pups that ain't worth drowning," noted one "canine burglar."[36]

Pool (pocket-billiards) rooms proved a major attraction. Too often boys and young men "acquired bad habits and evil associates by spending the evening around the green cloth covered tables." The "alluring click of the ivory balls and the excitement of the game" fascinated youths who were "bought into contact in these places with men from whom they learn nothing calculated to improve their morals." These young men went on to squander their pocket money.[37] Exhibition games by professionals drew large crowds.[38] Some pool parlors were elegantly furnished to attract upscale clientele.[39] With the passage of an ordinance of 1909, however, minors (under age eighteen) could not enter pool rooms except on business and with permission of parents, guardians, or employers.[40] In August 1918, the city's police department, in cooperation with local draft boards, in announcing a "work or fight program," required that all men between ages of twenty-one and thirty-one, who were regarded as "habitués" of poolrooms or "not having visible means of support," be drafted. If these "slackers" could not explain their situation, they would be "given tickets good for a trip to France."[41]

Over the years, Richmond had its share of well-established gambling "resorts." Among these, such places were at 704, 806, and 811 East Broad Street; 1343 and 1708 East Franklin Street; 913 Bank Street; corner of Fourteenth and Franklin streets, 1708 Franklin Street; 610 Buchanan Street; and 1313 North Thirty-fourth Street.[42] Downtown social clubs that permitted gambling included the Albemarle Club, Manhattan Club, Virginia Club, Monroe Club, Richmond Club, Gladstone Club, and the Paradise Club.[43] In Henrico County, just beyond the city limits, the Henrico County Country Club had the appearance—at least for a while—as a "gambling

THE INFLUENCE OF A GOOD FACE.
1.

2.

This, according to one cartoonist, is "The Influence of a Good Face," as seen in the Richmond *Daily Times*, May 2, 1897.

resort."[44] Gambling establishments usually retained "ropers" or "steerers," who operated outside, fishing for "suckers." They were constantly on the lookout for anyone with money. Over a pool game many a "sucker" was cultivated.[45]

Except when a police raid was imminent, the doors of the gambling places stood ajar. But to gain admission one had to pass inspection by an entrance guard.[46]

Mostly poor men patronized the "fake clubs." All of these places had bars for dispensing alcoholic beverages. If, upon arrival, an entrant seemed too reserved for gambling, he was soon loosened up under a wave of booze, and with his will power gone he became a fool, and a fool and his money were soon separated; the wife and children at home suffered, and certain policemen profited by raking off some of the profits for not conducting raids.[47] Among the fake clubs were the Richmond Home Social Club and the Jewish Club. Despite its moniker, the latter was "a gambling resort patronized by Gentiles."[48]

By the early 1900s, state law had become rather strict in exacting penalties for those attempting to entice the public to gamble. Any form

THE WOLVES OF THE CITY

"The Wolves of the City," depicted in the *Richmond News Leader,* February 5, 1906.

of running a gambling establishment entailed a jail sentence of two to twelve months and a fine of between a hundred and a thousand dollars.[49] In the rare events that raids were conducted, these occurred late at night and usually on weekends. Those who were arrested faced fines as low as $5.[50]

Gambling places designed for blacks, more than those frequented by whites, came under the arm of the law. On December 3, 1907, a typical raid on an African American social club was reported:

> Paradise Hall was aglow with many ruddy lights, beneath which the sable swells and dusky belles of the ultra-exclusive Society of the Lilies of the Valley, were tripping the light fantastic ... when the moon was high, when Henry Taylor, who is not on the visiting list of any of the Lilies, loomed upon the horizon, dark as a thundercloud and just as threatening....
>
> "Brush by niggah; brush by," said Henry to the door-tender.
>
> The door-tender drew himself up haughtily. "Show yo' c'yard of invite," he demanded, obstructing the progress of Henry.
>
> Then the battle began. When the police arrived the dusty beaux were engaged in a desperate struggle. The belles were shrieking hysterically.
>
> Out of the tangled mass of dark men which was rolling down the steps of Paradise Hall, the cops dragged Henry Taylor, Roscoe Walker and Richard Tyler.
>
> "What sort of an aggregation is this Lilies of the Valley herd?" demanded Justice Crutchfield as the prisoners were lined up before him.
>
> "Cullud 'ciety folks, sah," replied Walker.
>
> "What do you do in that joint—drink whiskey?"
>
> "Not of we knows it," retorted Tyler, which offended dignity.
>
> "Play cards?"
>
> "Not as we knows."
>
> "Eat dope?"
>
> "Great heavings, no."
>
> "Then you read the newspapers when you get together in the club-house, eh?" Walker and Tyler admitted their guilt.
>
> "Fine you $5. Call the next case, sergeant."[51]

5

Confidence Men

Persons engaging in confidence tricks were consummate bunco artists. They readily found willing victims for a wide variety of scams.

Typically, in April 1872, Joseph B. Williams, of Dinwiddie County, visited Richmond, and while out strolling met a man who gave his name as William Martin. Martin asked Williams if "he was acquainted." Upon the answer of "no," Martin said he also was a stranger in the city and had arrived to buy tobacco and needed assistance. Williams agreed to help and went with Martin to the American Hotel. There Martin ran across a friend, William G. Austin, who asked Martin to pay a bill of $28. Martin did not have the cash but offered to pay with a $500 draft. Austin said he could not provide the change. Williams then stepped in and gave Martin all the money he had, with Martin giving Williams as security the draft and a pocket book containing "a lot of gold." Austin then went into another room to make out a receipt. Meanwhile, William Kersey came up and made conversation with Williams, preventing Williams from following Martin and Austin. The latter soon disappeared. Martin and Austin were later arrested. The police believed that Martin and his cohort were part of an "organized band of confidence men operating in the city."[1]

A favorite swindle was to present false claims of injury from transportation facilities to insurance companies. There was also the "old card game." In May 1897, H. Dillard, "a bright skinned negro" and having just been released after serving eight years in the penitentiary, was charged with swindling John Collins, a Pamunkey Indian, who had come to Richmond from his reservation some thirty miles north of the city. Not familiar with Richmond, Collins, running across Dillard on a street, asked for directions to a place on Main Street where he was headed. Dillard said he worked for a local dry goods firm. The two men stepped into an alley, whereupon Dillard pulled out a pack of everyday business cards. Some of the cards had names of prizes written on them. Collins willingly drew several lucky cards. Then Dillard said, "Bet twenty to ten you can't do it again." Meanwhile, another African American man came on the scene. Collins pulled out a ten-dollar note, and, just as he did, the newcomer grabbed the money and fled. Later, Collins, along with a policeman, saw the two culprits coming down a street; the two thieves were arrested.[2] The scam was performed in other variations, simply two men being involved in enticing a victim to bet against two to one on the drawing of a winning card.[3]

"A game of bunco that rivals some of the achievements of the long-fingered and loose-moralled [sic] gentry of New York and Chicago" occurred in Richmond. The intended victim, J. H. Callaway of Georgia, came to Richmond, accompanying a herd of cattle which he hoped to dispose of. Callaway checked into the St. Claire Hotel. There he was approached by a man who introduced himself as B. F. Stanley of Nashville, Tennessee. Claiming to be a horse dealer, Stanley suggested that "we dealers ought to stick together." Callaway and Stanley ended up sharing a hotel room. In the meantime, Callaway was able to dispose of his cattle for $550 and received part of this sum up front. Stanley persuaded Callaway to step inside a saloon. Stanley proposed winning money at craps from someone who was in the bar. Callaway refused to join the game, but, being taunted that he did not have any money, pulled out a roll of bills to show that he did, whereupon Stanley (or his accomplice) grabbed the money and "bolted through the door."[4]

Buncoing continued on a regular basis. Two swindlers saw one Catherine Chambers pull out a bulky roll of banknotes in the purchase of a railway ticket for her niece at a station. One of the men asked Catherine to change a hundred-dollar bill. She drew out $215, forgetting the exact amount demanded. In return, one of the swindlers presented what was supposedly a banknote and put it into an envelope, sealing the flap. After handing Catherine the envelope with the worthless paper inside, the two bunco men skedaddled.[5] The list of those con artists securing money with false collateral had no end. One of the many examples was a woman lending $300 to a swindler who left watches with her as security, but which proved valueless.[6]

In October 1910, a newspaper reported that "a confidence man, an adept at his game, has invaded Richmond, separated some of the gullible from their coin, and hastened to greener fields." Working among state fair visitors, the swindler would offer a person in need of a job the opportunity to work at the company store at Coy, a new town being formed near Williamson, West Virginia. The salary offered was $75 a month. A young man jumped at the chance for employment and put up $55 bond and paid train fare across two states. Of course, there was no such town and certainly no reception committee or welcoming band that had been promised upon his arrival.[7]

Another lure-for-employment swindle sought to enlist washerwomen to work at the Hotel Jefferson. A man who went by the name of Smith went into the poorer sections of the city and knocked on the doors and signed up volunteers to work at the Jefferson as washerwomen for three dollars a week (and having to work only three days a week). Smith required the women each put up fifty cents as his fee for arranging the employment. Smith put a prospect's name in a little book, told her she would receive a load of wash on Saturday by 4 p.m.; if the wash should not arrive then, she was to go to the hotel to pick it up. Smith then took his leave and disappeared. In a half a day Smith had signed up over a hundred workers, netting him fifty dollars. The "fun" began about 4:20 p.m. on Saturday

"Buncoed," read the caption of this political cartoon featured in the Richmond *Daily Times*, August 17, 1902.

> when the women began to arrive at the Jefferson, and for the next two hours "Mr. Smith" was greatly in demand. The man who answered the rings at the servants' door grew weary of the name of Smith, and in his heart cursed the whole generation of that ilk.
>
> For nearly two hours, it is said, the sable stream flowed up to the doors of the Jefferson, and the name of Smith was upon every lip. The last one to arrive in quest of him was an old negro woman carrying upon her head a basket large enough for all the washing of the Jefferson. She advanced to the door with brisk and confident steps and rang the bell. The weary waiter opened the door and glared out at her.
>
> "Is Mr. Smiff here," she queries. "I wants dat washin.'"
>
> "Naw, Smiff ain't here, and derr ain't no washin,' an' here's been ninety-nine here befo' you, and youse left" and bang went the door in her face.
>
> No news has since been received from Smith and his ill-gotten halves.[8]

The following advertisement appeared in the *State* on December 5, 1895: "Wanted, stenographer and typewriter for responsible position. H. F. Gibson, advertising agency, city." A Mr. Goodman, son of William Goodman, a "well-known commercial traveler," and a young lady were among the many who answered the advertisement. They went to Gibson's office on Main Street, where he represented himself as an agent for the George. P. Rowell Advertising Company of New York. Gibson offered to employ each applicant at a salary of twelve dollars a week on condition that security to the amount of fifty dollars be given to him by both applicants. Goodman's father became suspicious of Gibson. Upon investigation, it was discovered that Gibson was not in the employ of the Rowell Company, and that the company had no branches. An arrest warrant was sworn out for Gibson; if convicted, he faced up to eighteen months in prison and a $500 fine.[9]

Soliciting donations for a fictional organization could bring jail time as well. Such was the situation of R. A. Turner, whose last name was really King. Turner faced twenty charges for illegally obtaining sums ranging from $2.50 to $10 as a contribution for the fictitious "Virginia Library for the Blind." Two other persons were involved with Turner in the scheme, but disappeared at the time of his arrest. At trial in Police Court, Turner took the stand in his own defense. He claimed that he had been made a scapegoat and that he believed that he was engaged in a legitimate enterprise. Justice Crutchfield was unsympathetic and sentenced Turner to twelve months in jail.[10]

A bunco case in fall 1877 resulted in the perpetrator receiving a five-day jail sentence and "ten lashes well laid on." Samuel Houston had hoodwinked George A. Wingfield into buying three sticks of corn medicine, throwing in two boxes, one with five dollars in it and the other with ten. The price of the purchase was five dollars. By sleight of hand, a switch was made and the result was that neither box contained any money.[11] Similar scams involved selling a boxful of stove polish at the Old Market. When the recipient brought his purchase home, he discovered that the box was filled with paper.[12]

Disposal of phony jewelry provided an easy route for bunco trickery. In March 1897, Joe Grimes, a "fakir who works the wedding ring racket," received fifteen days in jail, as did his pal Willie Johnson. Grimes, in working this racket, would meet someone on the street, and "taking the ring from his pocket" would let go "a story about a destitute family. The wedding ring must go for food and fuel. He got a couple of dollars, and the buyer a 'phoney' ring."[13]

5. Confidence Men

H. C. Reed, who operated under a variety of aliases, was lodged in the Richmond jail in December 1910 under suspicion of being a "penny-weigher," one who disposes of false diamond rings after allowing a dupe to examine and appraise them. A city policeman in civilian clothes was in a Broad Street cigar store one afternoon when Reed entered and engaged the owner in conversation. The talk turned to diamonds, and Reed pulled out what he claimed was an unset diamond valued at four hundred dollars, which he would sell for one hundred. The policeman had his doubts, and Reed was taken into custody. Upon examination at the station, it was determined that the "diamond" was worth only four dollars. Although a real stone was often used in a diamond ruse, none was found on Reed's person. Upon further investigation, it was discovered that the prisoner had been arrested a number of times in similar swindles along the East Coast.[14]

"The first case of what is known as 'bunco-steering' or confidence-gaming ever officially reported in this city came to light this week," reported the *Daily Dispatch* of February 10, 1888. Two men rented an unfurnished front basement room for one day, paying the charge of seventy-five cents. The men said they were literary agents and wanted space to store books. The next day the room again was rented at the same rate. Meanwhile a young, well-dressed man approached Dr. A. G. Wollard, who was walking down Main Street. The stranger passed himself off as a nephew of a friend of Dr. Wollard. The young man's companion interjected: "I've got something for you, Doctor." He then said that his aunt had died, and before she passed away she left two books, one with Dr. Wollard's name in it. "She asked me to give it to you," said the companion, "and if you'll come with me I'll get it."

Dr. Wollard consented to go in pursuit of the book. When they arrived at the rented room, there was another person seated at a table on which were money, writing materials, and some books. The man who had first approached Dr. Wollard said,

> "I understand that my ticket has drawn two books, and I want to get them and make my friend a present of one of them."
>
> "What is the number of your ticket?" inquired the office-keeper, as he reached for a book.
>
> The young man named a number, and after his confederate had looked over the book, he asserted: "Yes, you have drawn two books and $50 with it," and turning to the Doctor: "Your friend is very lucky, but there is a larger prize here now," and he endeavored to get him to take a chance, but the Doctor began by this time to catch a whiff of the rodent, and as soon as possible he got outside into pure, honest air.

Dr. Wollard immediately went to a police station, and an officer was sent to the house in question, but the bunco artists had fled, leaving behind only a few blank envelopes and note paper. A "wanted" notice went out for the two would-be swindlers, one of whom was young and had a clean-shaven face, and the other a taller man with a black mustache and wearing spectacles—"probably as a disguise." Although it was thought that the two confidence men did not leave the city, they remained at large.[15]

6

Money Sharks

Usurers reaped profits from the misfortunes of the poor, legally and illegally. Pawnbrokers legally provided loans on merchandise for persons in dire need, giving out tickets for which the items could be redeemed. Loan sharks simply advanced money, as a last resort for the borrower, on the promise to pay; because of the allegedly high risks, interest fees were exorbitant. Then there were the second-hand clothing dealers who functioned much like the pawnbrokers. Junk dealers also gave financial aid on items received, but were more likely to operate as fences for stolen goods than the pawnbrokers.

Pawnshops in Richmond generally loaned amounts equaling the value of one-third the property deposited.[1] Pawnshops came under close regulation, having to keep detailed accounts of transactions. According to a law passed on June 17, 1916, all pawnbroker sales and auctions had to be conducted by "an auctioneer appointed by the judge of the Hustings Court." Furthermore, the law forbade misrepresentation in public advertisements, upon penalty of $25–250 and/or between ten and sixty days in jail.[2] An ordinance, passed on January 6, 1919, prohibited pawnbrokers from trading in firearms.[3]

Some less-than-honest pawnbrokers allowed for the fencing of stolen goods.[4] Law officials periodically, often with stakeouts, made arrests of persons attempting to unload stolen loot on pawnshops.[5]

One sad story was that of A. K. Bratke, who had been a salesman for Pride Mercantile Company. Becoming sick, and with sales falling off, he was discharged. About the same time his wife became ill, and the two were unable to pay rent. He pawned company goods—curtains, clocks, silverware, and other household furnishings—amounting to about $250 in value. Arrested and arraigned, Bratke threw himself at the mercy of the court, telling the judge of his starving wife and explaining that he had since found employment at the shipyard; he even promised "redemption of the goods." The court, nevertheless, was bound to impose the minimum sentence: twelve months in jail.[6]

In March 1911, Richmond detectives finally cracked one of their most difficult burglary cases by arresting William A. Hammond, a sixty-year-old ex-convict and thief extraordinaire. For ten months he had successfully raided Richmond homes of the wealthy for silverware. He had a sophisticated method for determining whether or not residents were at home. He also had a clever method of treating plunder to make it less identifiable. He would place stolen silverware in a fire and leave it in the flames until it was blackened. With a file he removed traces of engraving with a knife, and with a mallet broke up items into smaller pieces. One night Detective John Wren followed Hammond into Gellman's pawnshop at 212 West Broad Street.

> "Hello, Billy!" was Wren's hearty salutation when he thought the psychological moment had arrived.
>
> Hammond turned and eyed the plains-clothes man searchingly. "I don't believe I have the honor of your acquaintance," he replied.
>
> "Yes, you do," replied Wren. "I met you thirty-three years ago when you were arrested for robbing a church." He followed it up by giving the burglar his name and telling him he was under arrest.

While searching Hammond's residence, various items were found that were identifiable as to the owner. There were also more than a hundred keys "of all descriptions" and assorted burglary tools. With the evidence against him and his having had served three terms in the penitentiary, it was expected that Hammond faced life in prison.[7]

Pawnbrokers operated under close inspection of law officials. Among those caught in the net of enforcement, in November 1894, was Samuel Bachrach, the "well-known Ninth-street pawnbroker." The Hustings Court convicted him of knowingly buying and receiving a stolen diamond ring from three small boys in exchange for a gun. Bachrach received fifteen days in the city jail and was slapped with a fine of $100.[8]

One way for pawnbrokers to invite trouble from federal authorities was to allow the pawning of second-hand playing cards not properly stamped with an Internal Revenue tax. Violation of the law brought a $50 penalty. A federal agent in Richmond discovered in 1908 that all the pawnbrokers in the city had illegally sold playing cards, of which the seals had been breached. All eight pawnbrokers insisted that they were not cognizant of the law. They dispatched pawnbroker Sam Stern to Washington, D.C., to seek Senator Thomas S. Martin's assistance in negotiating a compromise with the government. As a result, each offender was fined only $15.⁹ Other pawnbrokers had to stand trial for receiving stolen goods.¹⁰

With their miscellaneous merchandise of value, pawnshops were likely places to be robbed, not only for the cash brought in but the items themselves. In April 1902, Samuel Bachrach's shop was robbed for the third time, with the thief on each occasion breaking the front window and then "helping himself to the first things he [could] get his hands on."¹¹

An unusual heist involved cleaning out Kaminski's pawnshop on Seventeenth Street of four dozen revolvers, all the watches, and "all other things that were easily portable." The burglars accomplished a financial "coup," of sorts. Before the robbery, the thieves had pawned nearly everything they could lay their hands on and sold the pawn tickets to friends; thus, they doubly profited, gaining funds from the ticket transaction and then stealing back everything they had pawned.¹²

Junk dealers appeared as fences for stolen goods whenever the law happened to be looking the other way.¹³ The sixteen junk dealers in the city were legally required to submit daily reports of anything purchased, except for scrap iron, rags, paper, and bones. Failure to make a report could bring a fine of $5 to $10.¹⁴

Two fifteen-year-old boys, arrested for thievery, identified as a fence twenty-three-year-old drugstore clerk Asby Burruss. The arrest of the three ended a spree of robberies on West Grace Street. The boys mostly stole watches, and for each one they turned in to Burruss, they received $2.¹⁵

Second-hand clothiers could also act as fences. In May 1889, Frances Beasley, a black seventeen-year-old, was arrested while making the rounds of second-hand clothing dealers who abounded on Seventeenth Street. She asked for a ridiculously low price of $4 from one dealer for the whole lot, which included shoes, pants, dresses, a skirt, a sack coat and vest, and a chemise.¹⁶

Money-sharks (or loan sharks) pretty much had their way in Richmond. The city half-heartedly installed regulations, but since the clients of the loan sharks were usually poor and ignorant people, they had little recourse against exploitation. The city, however, did require a special license tax on loan-sharking of $500 to $800 a year.¹⁷ Loan sharks charged between 200 and 500 percent interest on loans.¹⁸

Occasionally, loan sharks were hauled into court for being considered a public nuisance, for which they could be fined $50.¹⁹ They always claimed that their exorbitant interest rates were owing to lack of security deposits and that the risk of non-payment was high.²⁰ One of the problems with loan-sharking was that the lender would often receive in his favor a judgment by default in court, with the court's decision irreversible after thirty days. Victims had little or no knowledge of the legal processes.[21] Even the general public, for the most part, did not know that the law prohibited usurious interest.[22]

Land agents committed fraud similar to the interest scams of loan sharks. A favorite way was to get someone to exchange property, and with the subsequent convoluted paperwork, an unsuspecting victim wound up having his property forfeited.[23]

Other forms of money manipulation sponged off unsuspecting persons. Fraudulent brokerage houses came under legal restraint. Such firms, known as bucket shops, were not allowed; all sorts of gambling in stocks

"No Doubt," read the caption of this political cartoon in the Richmond *Daily Times,* August 18, 1895.

and bonds were not permitted. The "pretended buying or selling of the shares of stocks or bonds of any corporation," either "on margin or otherwise, without any intention of receiving and paying for the property so bought" was prohibited.[24]

Obtaining money under false pretenses came under the bucket shop prohibition. Basically, a bucket shop dealt in futures, failing to deliver on

HOW TIMES HAVE CHANGED.

"How Times Have Changed," commented the *Richmond News Leader* on April 2, 1916.

orders placed on margin. In September 1911, detectives raided the "business" of Myron A. Smith who ran a bucket shop out of a rented room at 28 North Eighth Street. Smith had put an advertisement in a local newspaper, which brought "an abundance of patronage and resulted in his falling into the hands of the police." In this insert, Smith announced: "Why pay rent or keep a vacant lot? We will build for you anywhere, and build to your own plan or you can build yourself on your own lot, and we will furnish the money at 5 percent interest." One customer hurried down to Smith's office and said he would like to borrow some money. Smith asked for $50 as evidence of good faith. The applicant gave Smith a check for the $50, but then, becoming suspicious, he went to the bank to stop payment on the check and filed a complaint at a police station. Detectives arrested Smith and found that he had received numerous deposits of $50 from other customers. Smith was convicted of obtaining money under false pretenses and sent to the city jail. Meanwhile, word came that Smith had been sentenced, in absentia, to fifteen years in prison in Seattle, Washington, convicted of more than a hundred charges of fraud. Even though Smith had not completed his Richmond sentence, he was extradited to Seattle.[25]

7

Fakir Paradise

Fakirs (swindlers with showmanship) had a field day whenever people assembled at large entertainment venues, namely state fairs, circuses, carnivals, and even large-scale reunions. One noteworthy example of fakir activity happened at the Virginia State Agricultural Fair, sponsored during most of the period just outside Richmond's western boundary by the Virginia State Agricultural and Mechanical Society. The property, on West Broad Street, from 1897 on, owned by the banking house of John L. Williams Son, contained a race track, a pavilion, an amphitheater, areas for exhibitions, livestock, and agricultural products, and a midway for shows, rides, and concessionaires.[1] A variety of games of chance lured unwary fairgoers. To get to the fair, there was a choice of taking one of the special omnibuses or carriages or a ride on a short streetcar line from downtown Richmond, a half mile to the fairgrounds. Visitors to the fair came from afar, especially from North Carolina; railroads offered round trips at half price.[2]

A little more respectable than the fakirs were those street vendors who hitched on to fairs, who were often referred to as "fakers." "Lone-Hand" Riley was "a fair specimen of the nomadic band doing business on the amusement plaisance. He follows the fairs." At different times he sold "confetti," canes, and balloons; sometimes he operated a candy wheel, selling "chances at a dime for each paddle, giving to the winner among the holders of the twelve paddles a box of candy that costs him exactly eighteen cents." When there were big crowds, Riley preferred to stay away from the more open form of gambling. In dealing with novelties, he could make quick sales and accrue profits at as much as a hundred percent. A Gladstone bag was Riley's sole luggage; it contained catalogs and price lists from about a dozen big companies that supplied "practically all the fair workers, street-men, carnival men, circus and summer-park-privilege men in America with their goods and equipment."[3] One time Riley was asked if he had a system of accounting. "Nix," responded Riley. "I don't need it. When I buy $9 worth of junk and sell it for $218.25 I know I haven't lost anything."[4]

Not all fairgoers were attracted to the primary function of the fair: exhibitions by farmers and livestock raisers. But "country folk" did mingle among the stock-pens and stables. Large spaces were reserved for the display of "wagons, carts, sewing-machines, stoves, buggies, etc.," and various farm machinery and foods. Women favored the attractions of the "west wing," which contained the art, fruit, and flower departments. The horse department presented "fine thoroughbreds and standard-bred trotters." Huge bulls, "peers of their race, with pedigrees reaching back 200 or 300 years, panted with the heat as their owners slicked their coats and covered them with fly nets or blankets." Swine, sheep, poultry, pigeons, and "pet stock" were also exhibited.[5] Several hundred boys' and girls' farm clubs showed exemplary produce. Most notable of the juvenile presentations was that of corn; in 1919, 275 collections of ears of corn each were laid out on tables for minute inspection.[6]

For every five minutes "country folk" spent among the farm and livestock exhibits, they, like their city cousins, spent a half hour patronizing the "white toys" of the midway: the amusement and sideshows.[7]

The "midway shows" were "beyond the shadow of a doubt half the life of the fair." To "the country cousin the Circassian beauty and the Turkish dancing girl" were "far more attractive than the blue ribbon swine, the prize bull, the Percheron steed, the fancy chicks or the monster pumpkin." The midway was "a crooked lane, with a long line of tents, booths, stalls, platforms and enclosed spaces sprawling rakishly and riotously on either side." On the midway

> a babel of sounds, a jostling throng, a chaos of grotesqueries, a confusion of man and beast; the fanciful, the weird, the picturesque, the humorous, the pathetic, the repulsive, the unbeautiful in animals and inanimate....
> Drums are beating, trumpets, tooting, unearthly noises filling the air. Oceans of dirty white canvas are billowing on either side. Lungs, limbs and lingerie make the ballyhoo upon which the competing shows count to draw business....
> The biggest and busiest of the midway attractions have their business interests promoted by a barker, a spieler, a bumper and a noisy, spectacular ballyhoo....
> The ballyhoo is the free entertainment offered in front of the little show shop. It may be a dancing girl, a team of blackface singers and dancers, a vocal quartet, a trained animal, a troupe of acrobats or a hundred other things that attract attention, of the passing throng. The function of the ballyhoo is to make the crowd pause.
> "Wait, watch, listen!" he shouts in a strident voice. "The big free show is about to begin."

7. Fakir Paradise

Not Much Longer to Wait.

"Attend and be Happy: Virginia State Fair, Oct. 5–10, 1914," advised the *Richmond Times-Dispatch,* **September 15, 1914.**

But the free show doesn't begin. The spieler does. The spieler rattles off an alluring description of what is on exhibition inside. The spieler is a romancer, like the barker, who just keeps on barking the same call to the crowd, he being no orator like the spieler....

When the spieler observes that the crowd is growing impatient and beginning to move toward the next tent, he gives the sign or the word to the ballyhoo and the ballyhoo gets into action.

The ballyhoo is not kept in action. Just long enough to get the attention of the crowd concentrated. Then is the psychological moment.

"Beat it," the spieler says to the ballyhoo, and the performers duck quickly into the canvas. As the gaping audience turns to depart with disappointment in their faces, the barker sounds the cry: "Walk right in. The performance is about to begin. Hurry folks and get your tickets while there is yet time."

Which cry is the signal for the bumper.

The bumper is employed to mingle with the crowd in front of the entrance and jostle the people toward the ticket stand. Not one man in a hundred who finds himself suddenly pushed, prodded or elbowed toward the entrance of the show by

"The Kiddies Cut High Jinks Today," reported the *Richmond News Leader*, October 13, 1914.

a somewhat excited person, evidently intent only upon purchasing a ticket, harbors a suspicion against the bumper.

Fairgoers expected to "get with, drift down the crowded street of the midway" and let their minds "be flooded with the delightful anticipation and realization of the pleasures to be found within the confines of fakedom." Or, to put it this way: "Get the spirit of the midway! Roam with the Romans, and don't be outdone in pastiming by any others who may rub elbows with you in your ramble through the lanes of the labyrinth of mirth." One may be reminded of the pitch of a spieler at the 1913 Fair:

> Here y'are! Don't fail to see them dare-devils at the motorcycle motordrome.
> All ready! All ready now! Step right inside and see Mazeppa, the fire-fighting horse, put out a blazing, flaming conflagration with brimming buckets of sweet cider made on the grounds while you wait!
> Meander into the forest primeval and see *your* Pamunkey Indians capture Captain John Smith, while Oklahoma Bill's Boomerang Throwers from Oklahoma pursue Colonel Ferris' Wild Animals and chase them into the crystal maze!
> Test your nerves by watching Crazy Curran and his death-seeking dare-devils do the double pass in the marvelous and terrifying motordrome exhibition.
> Step up, ladies and gentlemen, get your tickets and pass in while the band plays! A little harmony, Professor!
> Get your tickets here, nobody has any use for a stingy man, and we need the money.

"Imposing ballyhoos" at the October 1908 Fair may be cited. The "Theo" show had a six-girl exhibit, accompanied by several troubadours.

> The girls, some of them old enough to be grandmammas, are arrayed in bespangled short skirts. They sing, dance and pose. An orchestration bellows weird, uncanny music while the terpsichorean and vocal revels are in swing. A fine flash is made at night by this show with its electrically illuminated front.
> The "High Class Vaudeville" also has a girl ballyhoo. There are four of the fantastically garbed and painted creatures, who exhibit their feminine charms.
> Next door is the "Fatima" show with five singing maidens, who contrive to hold the crowd a sufficient time to permit the spieler and the bumper to get in effective work.
> Further down the line the "Gay Merry Widow" show, with a company of eight performers on the front platform, is raking in a plentitude of dimes. The spieler at this place directs the free performance. He presents in turn a Spanish dancing girl, in appropriate costume; a cowgirl, who wears sombrero, woolen shirt, short tan skirt, buckskin leggings and carries a big Colt's revolver in her belt; a butterfly dancer, with the sweeping diaphanous skirts, and a French danseuse.
> A more dignified and respectable ballyhoo is that offered in front of the canvas of the "Mazeppa" show. It is a red-coated band of musicians. The band is attractive and holds the crowd until it begins to play. A flower-decked horse is trotted up and down the platform to further delight the onlookers.
> Captain Jack Smith, the pistol shot, has for his ballyhoo a huge Indian, in

warpaint and feathers. From the topmost feather to his beheaded moccasins he is the real, genuine name-blown-in-the-bottle child of the forest. Ever and anon the red man gives vent to a warhoop, dances a ghost dance and brandishes a tomahawk to prove his identity.[8]

There were plenty of freaks at the fair. The painted images of them are on all sides of you. Here is a fat man whom the barker solemnly assures you weighs 749 pounds. Here is a lady who weighs even more. Ten cents will let you look at them both. To your left is a man with a common everyday ape, which he swears is a laughing gorilla and he is so earnest about it that you believe him and give him another dime to see it perform.

There are seven or eight midgets, each smaller than the other—if you believe the ballyhoo men. There are an equal number of giants, and there are five mermaids, whom the barker tells you were "captured alive." …

Let's keep on walking down the lane. Past a "girl" show, where they do Oriental dances we go, past a big tent where a bunch of darkies who sing plantation melodies and give an imitation of the days "befo' the wah." Near them is a Wild West show, and facing this is a snake-charmer in the same tent with "wild Rose, the missing link."

Then comes a turn in the road. We go up toward the administration building, where there are some fat men and lean men and a trained horse and, finally, a flea circus. This last gets another one of our dimes. Inside we find fleas drawing miniature chariots, kicking footballs, twirling tiny dumbbells, juggling bread crumbs and doing all sorts of other stunts.

"And what do you do with that big microscope?" asks a sweet young thing.

"We use that to put gold collars around the fleas' necks," says the "Professor."

"How do you feed them?" asks another.

"On my arm," says the professor, and the crowd goes out laughing.

A little ways off is a cage of trained flies, which do all the things the fleas do, and a few more besides, and then there are other things, scores of them, all calculated to entice the wary dime from one's pockets.[9]

One sideshow "attracted great attention." Draped over the tent was the legend, "The only Cannibal now in Captivity." One reason why it attracted so much notice was that it was ornamented by what many took to be a lifelike representation of Billy Mahone [a U.S. Senator from Virginia and political boss] in full war paint. In one he is represented as about to brain an imaginary foe with the leg of some victim just devoured.[10]

One show, considered to be obscene, regularly had to be modified to avoid being served arrest warrants, but always bounced back to its risqué form. That was the "Houche Khouche dance." Various announcements by the barker out front included: "The great gentlemen's show; No ladies or children admitted"; and "this is the show that was suppressed on the Midway."[11] Scantily "attired sirens" were pictured on the outside of the tent.[12]

One kind of fraud employed by some women at state and county fairs was that of preserving fruits in jars containing wood alcohol, the "specimens looking 'perfectly lovely' and all that, but preserved in poison." Such exhibits would earn "premium after premium and gold medals, depriving other exhibitors of awards for which they had worked hard." The worst of it was that the same misleading preserved fruit could be entered into competition year in and year out.[13]

Fakirs presided over the numerous gambling stations. From time to time city and county authorities bore down upon the iniquity of chance, but the sleek conductors of betting games were always one step ahead. In one year, 1900, the Henrico County Court succeeded, starting at the halfway point of the October fair, in closing down completely all games of chance.[14]

Although the Virginia code was quite clear in its prohibition of all forms of gambling at the fair, with penalties ranging from two to twelve months in jail and forfeiture of all proceeds,[15] the law, it may be said, was honored in the breach. Fakirs, noted one reporter concerning the fair of 1891, have conducted "more unmitigated swindles than ever congregated in the same space anywhere in Virginia, and perhaps in the Union."

The fakirs operated various "swindling devices" that were nothing more than "bare-faced robbing." Among the games of chance that fleeced the unwary were the "Guillotine," the "Pyramids," roulette, and wheels of fortune.[16] Fakirs used men and boys as decoys to snare players.[17]

This drawing of a merry-go-round at the Richmond State Fair was originally published in George A. Scala's *America Revisited*, Vol. 2 (London: Vizetelly, 1882), p. 235.

The fairs featured horseracing at a racetrack and grandstand within the fairgrounds. The races were in the form of running dashes (a quarter or three-quarters of a mile), trotting (harness) racing, and, eventually, even a steeplechase.[18] A rather elaborate bookmaking operation existed for a while in a "gambling joint" underneath the grandstand at the racetrack. A raid in 1909 revealed not only a lot of money on hand garnered from a steeplechase, but also a "faro layout" and a roulette wheel. The city

An undated photo of Sig. Lawanda, billed as "The Iron Jawed Man" (courtesy the Valentine).

and Henrico County police, who had joined forces for the raid, seized some $400 from the take of the faro game and roulette wheel; among the sixty persons who scrambled away were "the bookmaker and his legionaries," who made off with "a wad of money that would have made Rockefeller sit up from his counting table."[19]

The confidence men, pickpockets, and other thieves who descended upon Richmond during fair time, often came as "a corps of organized thieves from northern cities." Besides mingling among the throngs at the fairgrounds, these predators also worked the hotels, boardinghouses, street and railway cars, omnibuses, and public meetings. These outsiders usually came with their chiefs, who "after surveying the ground," assigned "subordinates" their respective turf on which to operate. This was done not only to provide harmony, but also to make the best use of time and talent.[20]

Security at the fair was usually extensive. A detachment of city police customarily went to the fair "to look after the interest of the State and to see that her laws were duly executed."[21] At the 1888 fair, posted outside "all the time" were ten policemen and one sergeant. Inside the grounds there was a special police force under a sergeant, which group was in the employ of the fair's officials. As the fair ensued, sixteen more policemen were added to the internal security, which allowed for smaller beats.[22] In 1910, twenty-eight of Richmond's police force were on constant duty at the fair. Included were mounted policemen and sixteen bicycle policemen. A police patrol was kept on the grounds to convey persons accused of serious offenses to a municipal police station; minor wrongdoers received immediate judgment by magistrates assigned to the fairgrounds.[23] For the 1915 fair, most of the bicycle men from the First Police District, most of the mounted policemen, several "street sergeants," and a twenty-man patrol had duty on the fairgrounds; in all, about forty persons. In addition, six detectives took their turns working at the fair.[24]

In the 1870s a cadet corps from Virginia Polytechnic Institute, at Blacksburg, were brought in to assist the police. This proved to have more than one advantage, as their drills and dress parades posed as an attraction. As sentinels, however, the military students occasionally provoked an untoward incident, such as prodding a disobedient citizen at the point of a bayonet.[25] Starting in 1913, the Boy Scouts assisted fair visitors. They gave "first aid" when there were mishaps; helped police to control crowds; and provided assistance to the "various departments" of the fair.[26] Although there was some resentment from Henrico County authorities over Richmond's claim of full police power over the fair, which grounds lay within the county, the matter never reached the point of stern disagreement. A state law had given cities a one-mile jurisdiction beyond city limits.[27]

Some of the fairground's arrestees came to the Henrico County court for judgment. One case involved Harry Stoner, "an itinerant fakir." Some citizens made a complaint of gambling against Stoner to Henrico authorities. A county constable, T. H. Samuel, made the arrest.[28]

The fair employed persons outside the law enforcement community to prevent anyone from climbing over the fence and generally to assist in preserving order. Overzealousness of some of the civilian guards produced a number of unfortunate incidents. Consider Henry Gaines, who was twice shot by watchman John Carr after climbing over the fairground's fence. One pistol ball struck Gaines in the stomach and the other, the left forehead; fortunately for both men, the wounds proved not to be life threatening. Gaines, a plasterer by trade, was about thirty years old. He claimed that he had permission to enter the grounds to obtain some water, after which he intended to depart; he had no weapon at the time of the incident. Carr, a former saloonkeeper, had previously faced trial for having

This undated photo shows what was once commonly known as a street fair (courtesy the Valentine).

shot a Richmond woman, but was let go through the entreaty of the victim. Carr was arrested for shooting Gaines, and bail was denied.[29] Overall, the law enforcement personnel effectively drove out beggars and known pickpockets.[30]

Fakirs and snatchers alike were almost as common at circuses as they were at fairs. Crowding under the "monstrous canvas" were city and country people from a radius of 150 miles. The C. & O. and the R. F. & P. railroads brought in large excursion parties.[31]

Circuses that made their way to Richmond included: Forepaugh's Circus; Howe's London Circus; Cole's Great New York and New Orleans Menagerie and Circus; Bostock Wild Animal Show; Sells Brothers Circus; Coup's United Shows; the Great John Robinson and Franklin Brothers Show; Wombwell's British Menagerie; the Barnum and Bailey circuses (which merged in 1881); and the Ringling Brothers' World Greatest Shows (which merged with Barnum and Bailey in 1919).[32]

Also drawing large crowds from near and afar were the frontier-type entertainments, namely Buffalo Bill's Wild West Show; Sig Alascon's Wild West Show, a "pocket edition" of

An undated playbill for the Van Nest Circus and Hippodrome (courtesy the Valentine).

Buffalo Bill's display; and Pawnee Bill's Circus.[33] Typically, a Wild West performance started off with an exhibit of the life of a Pony Express mail carrier and its hazards, then perhaps a hold-up of an "overland coach, and then Indian scenes, including warfare."[34]

Many people eagerly anticipated the circus parade: "Thousands of little children and as many more grown folk" gazed upon the pageant as it wound its way from the Main Street train station up to Broad Street heading westward to the edge of the city where the big tent was pitched. Broad Street was thronged with men, women, and children, and every window overlooking the street "served as a frame for an animated picture."[35]

The menageries of the circuses were often huge, as an observer described Forepaugh's Circus in April 1877:

> Six elephants, three of great size and one but a baby (about as tall as a yearling bull); four large lions and lionesses, rhinoceros (splendid specimen), hippopotamus, two Bengal tigers, horse-antelope, sea-cow, sacred bull, musk-deer, zebra, axis deer, Chinese bear, white wolf, California lions, leopard, jaguar, striped hyena, South American panther, black tiger, cheetah, sea-hog, tracker, musk-hog, African wild-boar, cow-antelope, sable antelope, Palestine sheep, deer of various kinds, goats of several varieties, ibex, three camels, birds, monkeys, [etc.].[36]

Two thousand Richmonders attended nightly and at matinees for a week a "mid-winter Circus" in 1910. This jag of delight, sponsored by the Shriners, was held in the horse show building at the fairgrounds. The Rhoda Royal Circus, Hippodrome and Wild West show, as it was called, offered "good, clean, wholesome amusement." So "numerous and diversified are the attractions and so palpitant with nerve and vim the work of the performers the spectator must needs have a dozen pair of eyes fully to comprehend and thoroughly enjoy the kaleidoscopic display presented in the space of two hours." A special feature involved Omar, the "equine aviator." Omar, with

> a heavy little woman on his back, made an ascension in an airship, soaring to the dome of the building. The rafter lights and streamers of bulbs were extinguished while the horse and rider floated above the heads of the gasping thousands, and from the platform upon which Omar stood a pyrotechnic display was released. Horse and rider were tumultuously cheered when they descended to terra firma.

Following the circus performance were the Wild West and hippodrome races. In this latter section, some of the events were "the Virginia Reel on horseback, John Agee's wild and reckless riding, a race between cowgirls, a representation of prairie life, showing how a horse-thief is lynched by cowboys. The performance closes with a thrilling and exciting battle of the plains."[37]

7. Fakir Paradise

"Advanced Sales"

"Advanced Sales," read the caption of this cartoon from the *Richmond Times-Daily*, July 9, 1915.

As many as eight thousand persons in Richmond attended performances of the "P. T. Barnum New and Greatest Show on Earth."

> As the visitor goes in at the main entrance he beholds the automatical curiosities. These are arranged in a circle around the tent.... Here also is the portrait gallery ... identified with the history of the country.... After viewing the numerous attractions in this tent we pass to the second tent, in which is located the menagerie.

Among the more prominent animals are the hippopotamus, giraffe, zebra, wart hog, tapir, horned horse, lions, rhinoceros, seal, polar bear, royal Bengal tigers, elephants, camels, etc. There is also a fine collection of birds, monkeys, snakes, etc.

One of the greatest attractions in this tent, however, is Captain George Costentenus, the tattooed Greek.... Altogether there are 388 tattooed pictures on the entire body.... In the same tent may be seen Admiral Dot and the Circassian girl.

In the next tent—the circus tent proper—the grand arenic performance was given. The most striking features of the entertainment were the introduction of the living curiosities by Professor Smith; performances of the hippopotamus.... trick ponies ... magic Japanese tub act ... remarkable feats of the Carlos Brothers, the comic fiddlers; the Carlo midgets, youthful trapeze performers; Miss Amelia Carlo's hoop and scarf act on horseback; Jeanette Watson's daring pad act; Martino Lowande, justly termed the world's champion bareback rider ... a remarkably handsome and well-trained trick-horse ... two clowns, Jerry Hopper and George Clark.[38]

Circuses, like fairs, challenged law enforcers. As one observer pointed out in November 1903, "The local police and detective force are keeping

SCHOOL BOY: "The circus didn't come in Washington's time!".

"Where Were You Yesterday?," the *Richmond Times-Daily*, October 2, 1906.

a sharp lookout for crooks, pickpockets, second-story men and light-fingered gentry of all varieties who they fear have been left in the city since the breaking up of the Barnum and Bailey show." Customarily, when a circus disbanded, these people lingered in town and engaged "in nefarious trades until they derived sufficient revenue" to get back to the large cities from which they came. The police, from time to time, when a circus or other large-drawing event was in town, raided stands set up by "attraction men," who offered various games of chance.[39]

Young boys were tempted to run away to join the circus. One such lad was Robert Booth, who exited his home in Waynesboro, North Carolina, and joined the Forepaugh's Circus in the spring of 1877. He obtained a job, supplying buckets of water for the baby elephant. The only problem was that while he was asleep one night the circus folded up in Richmond and headed out of town, leaving Robert behind. Richmond authorities persuaded a railway company to carry the runaway back to North Carolina.[40]

The Grand Reunion of Confederate War Veterans occasionally met in Richmond. In July 1896 it drew 75,000 persons to the city. Some of the

An undated photo of Ford's Hotel on Capitol Square (courtesy Cook Collection, the Valentine).

visitors were lodged at the fairgrounds or slept in parks, free of charge; others stayed in private homes, hotels, and boarding houses, paying their own way. It was estimated that the veteran affair brought an infusion of $500,000 to the city. Saloons and soda-water fountains were busy day and night. Fortunately, there was little drunkenness, and pickpockets were held in check. City police rounded up suspicious persons from out of town, who were deemed likely criminals, and required them to hit the road.[41]

Periodically, fairs were set up on blocked-off city streets. These events, offered free to the public, had many of the booths, stands, and tents one would find at the typical state fair. "Street fakirs," the usual out-of-town "sleight-of-hand" gentry, made their presence known. Again, authorities were successful in exiling newcomers who were profiled as "suspicious persons."[42]

Plenty of fakirs were on hand for the great street weeklong "Exhibition" held in mid–May of 1900. It was said to be "unlike anything Virginia and Carolina people have seen." Booths lined the sidewalks from Jefferson Street to the "carnival arch" at Tenth Street.[43] Free shows were presented on street corners, including a high-rise rope walk, bicycling on a sixty-foot tower, and diving from a seventy-foot tower. A "King of the Carnival" and his court appeared. The fakirs did "a land-office business," and "the side shows were patronized to such an extent as to frequently cause them to close their doors on the crowd." The fakirs sold "everything, from the inevitable circus balloon to collar buttons—from rubber balls to pure linen handkerchiefs, six pairs for a quarter."

At the 1900 street fair there were many exhibitions, not the least of which included a snake-handling display, among the collection being pythons, puff adders, anacondas, and boa constrictors. The major presentations were held at a canvas-covered "amphitheater," on the corner of Broad and Jefferson streets. The twenty-three round and knockout blow of the Corbett-Jeffries fight was viewed on film at a show at Fourth and Broad streets. All but two of the shows had admission of only ten cents. A gypsy camp, with its palmists and fortune tellers, was located on the south side of Broad and Jefferson streets. Wombwell's British Menagerie held forth on the north side of Second and Broad streets.

The "Streets of all Nations" could be seen at a corner of First and Broad. On the "streets" one would pass a sacred white camel and Leo "an old elephant, said to be almost as large as the lamented Jumbo."

"It is wonderful to have such crowds on our streets and so few disorderly persons," noted a police report of the time. Pickpocketing and

7. Fakir Paradise

A cartoon of a group of kids leading a Shetland pony in a circus parade, from the *Richmond News Leader*, July 5, 1916.

petty theft were almost non-existent, largely due to the positioning of one to five "big fellows" at corners to help "move the crowd along."[44]

The following year, President Theodore Roosevelt addressed a crowd for the opening of a street carnival on October 7, 1904. Thousands of Virginians and those from out of state attended the event. There were many free shows and exhibitions, including a "trick" bicyclist and hundred-foot high dives. A merry go-round was another major attraction. Very few fakirs were present, the absence of which was regretted by many members of the public who liked to be "humbugged." The street carnival concluded on October 17.⁴⁵

Carnivals, a sort of small-scale combination of fair and circus, came to town sporadically. These events purported to be entirely child-friendly, with the emphasis on rides and morally uplifting shows. The carnivals were usually held at the baseball park on West Broad Street, at Lombardy. At a carnival at this location on September 1920, "Peggie" Ewell, an Oriental dancer for the carnival, was arrested and fined ten dollars in Police Court for being "disorderly in the street." Dressed in feminine attire, he was confronted by a large police officer as he was leaving the carnival grounds. Ewell said that he failed to change out of his costume because there were no dressing-room facilities. A crowd of boys were following Ewell when the policeman arrived. The twenty-four-year-old crossdresser was from Guilford, Virginia, and had been on the carnival circuit for ten years.⁴⁶

8

"Shoving the Queer"

"Shoving the Queer" (passing counterfeit money) was no less a problem in Richmond than elsewhere in the country. The counterfeiting profession was looked down upon by other criminals. "They lack honor among themselves," noted a former "all 'round" thief while in prison. "I would rather be tried for murder than for handling the queer," he said.[1]

There were two kinds of counterfeiters: those who made and sold paper money; and those "who make, sell, and shove hard stuff (coin)." There were, it was reported, always "plenty of suckers willing to purchase counterfeit money." At least Richmond did not measure up to a community in Lehigh County, Pennsylvania, where "there was more 'queer' in circulation than genuine money."[2]

In the 1890s there were five kinds of paper money in circulation: U.S. treasury notes (greenbacks); gold certificates; silver certificates; coin certificates (representing silver coined each month under the Bullion Purchase Act of 1890); and national bank notes of less than one dollar (also known as "shinplasters)" secured by U.S. bonds purchased by banks.[3]

Making paper money required colored ink, antimony, paper, zinc, photographic supplies, presses, copper plates, drawings imitating little red and white fibers, and skilled engravers.[4]

Bogus coin—principally twenty-five and fifty-cent pieces—made their way into circulation in Richmond. Counterfeit items generally were brighter in color and lighter in weight than the real money.[5] Also, genuine coins, when dropped on a hard surface, would ring, while spurious pieces did not. Requirements for producing metal coins included a furnace, melting pot, molds, ladles, and plating batteries.[6]

Several operations for manufacturing bogus coins were discovered in Richmond. Most unusual was the discovery of a "complete counterfeiting outfit" in a cell at the penitentiary. The coins made there were "perfect as to size, figures, milling and thickness, but the feeling" was "a little 'greasy,'" and the weight was "against the penitentiary-made goods." The dubious scheme came to an end when a convict getting change from another prisoner received a five-cent piece "of the proper make" and two ten-cent pieces "that did not have the proper ring to them." An ensuing argument between the two men exposed the operation. Molds were found in a cell. An investigation revealed that the metal came from melting down the tin and lead from canned goods; some of the lead was smuggled in from the shoe shop.[7] Elsewhere, dubious coinage was made from melting down a mixture of tin and antimony.[8]

In 1877 a reporter noted that counterfeit coins abounded and "no man can certainly know a coin to be good." To meet the problem, the West, Johnston, and Co. marketed a surefire mechanical device that detected bogus coins. It consisted of a "metal disk, with three openings or slits for halves, quarters, and dimes." A coin slipped into the device caught on "an arm moving on a pivot and weighted at the other end." If the coin inserted was of proper metal and weight, it forced down the arm and fell through. The detector was small enough that it could be placed in any cash drawer.[9]

It was relatively easy to apprehend persons "shoving the queer," more so than ferreting out the manufacturers who carefully kept their doings secret. In February 1896, because of a rash of counterfeiting across the country, Richmond store cashiers received warnings to be on the lookout for fraudulent two-, five-, and ten-dollar bills.[10]

Instances of the "shoving" of paper money upon the public included, in July 1894, the brief operation in Richmond of a gang who arrived by train from Norfolk. These counterfeiters immediately set about funneling bad paper currency into saloons and stores. A favorite scam was to "short change" a customer; for example, exchanging two bad five dollar bills for a ten-spot.[11]

A former saloonkeeper, Anthony Schwane, accused by one of his former employees of passing a counterfeit dollar on to him, was arrested in Hoboken, New Jersey, in 1896. Extradited, Schwane wound up in the Richmond jail. Schwane had run away from Richmond, where he had been heavily in debt. With the help of an old friend he had known in the "old country," who was now "a big New Jersey brewer," Schwane worked as a barkeep in a "little saloon" in New Jersey. Schwane had a wife and nine-year-old son. Schwane denied that he was aware of passing a bad dollar bill. In tears, Schwane told his story to a *Times* reporter, declaring that all he was trying to do was clear his debt. A friend engaged H. M. Smith, a prominent Richmond lawyer, to defend him. The outcome of the case is unknown, but probably little, if any, punishment resulted, despite the cost of bringing Schwane to trial. He professed to be through with "keeping bar-rooms"; instead, he planned to return to his original trade: brewing beer. If Schwane could secure such employment, he explained, his salary would be substantial enough to pay all his bills and "take proper care" of his wife and son.[12]

Some counterfeiters were so bold as to try to entice persons of good standing to participate in a bogus money operation. In 1897, a Richmond councilman received a letter from an anonymous sender. The writer introduced himself as "an expert engraver," a twenty-two-year-old former employee of the U.S. Bureau of Engraving in Washington, D.C., and, for twelve years, superintendent of one of the largest bank note companies in the nation. The writer said that he made "perfect duplicates" of one-, five-, and ten-dollar bills. The councilman, he suggested, would be wise to put up an investment of $500. All communication, it was added, would be by telegram. The epistle was signed by the "Oldest Steel Plate Engineer in the United States." A response should be sent to A. B. Crum, Pocantico Hills, New York. The councilman did not accept the invitation.[13]

A favorite tactic of counterfeiters operating in Richmond was simply to find ways to increase the value on otherwise good greenbacks. Most commonly, two-dollar bills were raised to the ten-dollar level. In 1898, counterfeiting in Richmond consisted primarily of changing the face of George Washington on two-dollar bills to that of Daniel Webster and also redoing the figures on both sides of the bills. The work was accomplished in Indian ink by an obviously expert penman.[14]

On March 4, 1907, Richmond police seized G. L. Andrews out of bed at a boarding house and turned him over to federal officers for raising two-dollar silver certificates to the level of twenty dollars. Andrews had cut out "light naughts" of white paper and had pasted them to the right of each "two" on the bills. Andrews was remanded for trial in a federal court. Interestingly, his counterfeiting had been quite inferior and, adding to the poor reproductions was the fact that there were no twenty-dollar silver certificates in circulation.[15] To a lesser extent, five-dollar bank notes were upped to ten dollars by pasting rearranged numbers on the notes.[16]

In 1878, D. J. McCormick, an ex-justice of the peace and a restaurant owner in the city, was arrested for passing counterfeit five-dollar bank notes at local markets. The notes were "cleverly executed, but lithographed on a dirty-looking, greasy paper"; they were on the First National Bank of Hanover, Pennsylvania.[17]

National bank notes, produced by a highly skilled counterfeiter, made their way to Richmond in 1916. Chiefly, the bogus notes were of a twenty-dollar denomination. The fabricator would tear off two ends from a real twenty dollar note and paste them to a five-dollar bill, from which the ends had been removed. What remained of the mutilated twenty-dollar bill was taken to a bank and exchanged for a new bill.[18]

"Shoving the Queer" for coins rivaled the problem of passing bogus paper money. In January 1888, Timothy Sullivan was arrested for giving a counterfeit half-dollar to the doorkeeper at the Theatre Comique.[19] In May 1899, police picked up two Italians, Carolos and George (alias Carlos and George Semesat), and a woman named Emile Fast for "shoving" silver dollars and half-dollars in the city. Federal authorities took over custody of the prisoners. It was established that the accused had received the spurious money from counterfeiters; that the coins had been wrapped in rolls indicated an extended operation.[20] Secret Service officers, in cooperation with local detectives, arrested two more Italians, August Traine, a cooper, and Vincent Cardozo, an oyster shucker, along with their wives, for passing counterfeit coins in the city. There were indications that these individuals were connected with a counterfeit gang uncovered in New York.[21] One young man, who went before the Police Court for entering two bogus dimes into a card game, was suspected of being a front for a gang of counterfeiters.[22]

Even the passing of a few counterfeit coins could turn into a major felony case, as one Italian family discovered. On May 5, 1899, George Fasi and his fifteen-year-old son, Carlo, were arrested for passing bogus half-dollars in Richmond. George gave his real name as Shememshop, and said he had worked as a shoemaker, fruit seller, and helped out in a butcher shop. His wife, a registered nurse by the name of Maddelena Moscari Fasi, was also nabbed. The Fasis had immigrated to the United States three months before, settling in New York City.

The arrest of the Fasis stemmed from Carlo having entered a flower shop and a hardware store on Broad Street and passing the phony money. At the hardware store he had bought a five-cent package of tacks, paying with a bogus silver half-dollar. The proprietors of both stores, becoming suspicious, followed Carlo as he went to meet his father, who was standing at Seventh and Broad streets. A policeman was summoned, and Carlo was arrested before reaching his father. The elder Fasi fled, but was soon picked up after running for a few blocks. George had $28 in rolls of counterfeit half-dollars. Carlo had on his person counterfeit bills and coins.

The counterfeit coins carried by the Fasis were very lightweight and were of "aluminum composition," bearing dates from 1875 to 1899. The father had $8.37 in good money on him, and the boy, $2.35. George had a receipt for a month's rent of a room at 1429 East Franklin Street. The police searched the lodging but found no additional incriminating evidence. Mrs. Fasi had, tucked away in her purse, $340 in good money.

Testimony in the case, tried in the U.S. District Court in Norfolk, revealed that the elder Fasi had met a stranger at the corner of Baxter Street and Park Row in New York City; Fasi reluctantly gave a $10 note in exchange for $38 in counterfeit money. Father and son were convicted; Mrs. Fasi's case was dismissed. The court ordered that George pay a $10 fine and spend three years in federal penitentiary; Carlo, also a $10 fine and one year in the same prison. Both convicts were conveyed by a federal marshal, via the C. & O. Railroad, to the federal facility in Columbus, Ohio.[23]

In April 1909, the U S. District Court in Richmond tried a major counterfeiting case. Walter Turpin and Thomas Seybold had been caught with coin-making paraphernalia at the Methodist Mission House at Nineteenth and Main streets. Convicted, both men received sentences at the federal prison in Atlanta: Seybold, for five years; Turpin, four.[24]

Counterfeiting of another sort surfaced, including unauthorized Virginia state bonds which were presented for payment, chiefly at Boston and New York City banks. The certificates had been engraved by the Kendall Bank Note Company. As the Virginia government had not put in an order from that firm, measures were taken by the state Sinking Fund Commission to discover those responsible for imposing the spurious bonds on the public.[25]

Even the United States Postal Service was not immune to counterfeiting schemes. Bogus pink two-cent postal stamps appeared in Richmond and across the country. All the lines on the real stamps were even and regular, whereas those of the counterfeits were ragged and blurred, and the coloring too light. The production of the fake postage was traced to the Canadian Novelty Supply Company in Hamilton, Ontario.[26]

In 1904, an unidentified African American man from North Carolina was held responsible for targeting several Richmond merchants with fake postal money orders. The perpetrator of the scheme simply raised the amounts presented on the money orders, and so cleverly was the scheme executed that detection was almost impossible. The criminal presented the money orders as payment at Richmond stores, including the purchase of clothing at the store of Burk and Company and shoes at B. Samuels. The perpetrator used orders payable at offices other than those in Richmond. Typically, he changed an order for fifty cents to that of fifty dollars.

All that was known of the criminal was that he was a tall, black man, wearing blue overalls. Presumably he was never caught, and the affected merchants had to bear their losses. The crime was very bold. Rarely did one tamper with a federal postal money order. "The danger of detection is great, and the punishment is heavy and almost sure." The crime entailed punishment for forgery, uttering a forgery, receiving goods under false pretenses, and violating postal laws.[27]

The infamous "green goods men," who posed as agents to entice citizens (particularly those in rural areas) through the mails to purchase or invest in fraudulent items, entered into counterfeiting schemes. In one instance, three young Virginians received in the mail from New York a letter offering $7,500 in counterfeit money in exchange for $600 in good money. Summoned to New York, they arrived there and were informed that only one of them could be led to where the "goods" were. After passing through various places that required a password, the young man from Virginia put up the $600 and demanded to be given the full amount for which he had contracted. The green goods man opened a package, which contained $2,000 in apparently good money. As the intended victim insisted that all of the counterfeit money be delivered, the green goods man took the package of bills and managed to slip it through a hole in a wall to a partner who switched it for another bag, this one containing sawdust. The green goods man himself then made a quick disappearance.[28] There were similar counterfeit schemes in different parts of the country, some of which were reported in the Richmond newspapers.[29]

Probably the most far-fetched example occurred in 1906, when Samuel Corbin, an "old colored man," who lived on River Road just outside the city, was approached by a man who showed him a money-making machine. The stranger said that he was about to finish making another such contrivance, which he would sell Corbin for $200. The two men went to Corbin's home, and the $200 was paid. Corbin was told to go the next day to a "negro saloon" on West Broad Street to claim his machine. Of course, the stranger was a no-show.[30]

9

Larceners

A number of burglaries in the city were prearranged through some clever planning or trickery. The boldest and most successful of breaking and entering to commit larceny involved the coordination of several or more persons. Burglars sought entry into buildings through stealth, avoiding noise or any destruction that would attract attention. They preferred entering and exiting at the rear of a building or from a roof or second story. Mainly, they avoided the exposed front.[1] Professional burglars preferred downtown stores.[2] An unusual robbery occurred at the City Small Pox Hospital, located between Hollywood Cemetery and the Reservoir, in November 1885; nearly everything portable was taken.[3]

In December 1915, almost the entire stock at the store of A. G. Yarid, which specialized in Oriental rugs, linens, and novelties, was stolen by burglars who entered from a skylight. Some $5,000 worth of goods was lost. The plunder consisted of laces, pillow covers, scarfs, silk kimonos, embroidered negligees, bed spreads, napkins, and handkerchiefs; fortunately, most of the Oriental rugs were left behind. The robbers scaled a drain pipe at the rear of the building. Once on the roof they lowered themselves with a rope made out of a clothes line and pieces of a curtain pole; burglar tools, which included a jimmy, a wood chisel, a screwdriver, and two candles, were discovered in the store. Using the rope, the thieves opened the skylight and lowered themselves into the second story. The intruders only had to descend a stairway in the rear of the second floor to reach the stock on the first floor.[4] For other skylight-entry robberies, the thieves had other improvisations of rope, such as that fashioned out of sections of clothing, counterpanes, or sheets.[5]

Richmond's policemen were constantly on the lookout for gangs of thieves operating in the city. The department was proud that "when the enterprising burglar goes-a-burglaring," the police force "always bring to grief such gangs by arresting one or more of them, the rest leaving Richmond at once."[6]

While syndicated crime organizations did not take root in Richmond, the city played host to a variety of gangs of thieves in its midst, often those who made a circuit of Eastern cities.[7] In summer 1878, a regularly organized gang of young thieves existed "with headquarters in the lowest dens of several sections of Richmond" and kept the police busy for a while with a flurry of robberies of stores.[8] A similar situation appeared in summer 1886.[9] One gang of thieves resided on an oyster boat.[10]

Some of the gangs operating in Richmond were out of the ordinary. The "Hall-Thieves Brigade," for example, specialized in gaining entrance into the hallways of residences and buildings and stealing coats and other wearing apparel. The gang usually operated on alternate nights in Church Hill and Shockoe Hill. All booty was taken either to one or two second-hand clothing stores, located at Seventeenth and Broad streets or Seventh and Cary streets. Police recovered a large number of overcoats, hats, umbrellas, ladies' cloaks, and shawls.[11] In 1910, two gangs of dog thieves operated in the city. This crime increased about the time that hunting season began. Valuable pointers and setters were stolen and shipped out of town. It was an easy matter to lure an animal from a backyard.[12]

Three men, who appeared to be "dope crazed," calmly entered the Richmond Billiard Academy, at 828 East Main Street, about 10:30 p.m. on May 11, 1918, and then quickly lined up the patrons against a wall and relieved them of all their valuables, worth more than $6,000. A fourth man guarded the front door and helped his cohorts make a fast getaway by car. The robbers were armed with "big automatics." The wild look of the assailants, which had first given the impression that they were drug users, was enough to terrify the victims. Early the next morning police dispatched search parties, carrying riot guns and pistols, and scoured the roads leading to the city. The "stick up" men made good their escape, last being spotted near Atlanta, Georgia.[13]

More often than not, it seemed that criminal gangs in Richmond had members who were African American. In 1896, police broke up "a negro Jesse James gang of worthless but dangerous young fellows." The group had serially robbed and ransacked stores. The gang "had its rendezvous under the Second-street bridge, where they lived and kept their plunder." Six of the twelve members were immediately caught. They went to jail for six months, and Hester Fowler, "a mulatto girl" who had been living with the gang, netted sixty days in jail as a "suspicious character."[14] A gang of six teenaged African Americans who specialized in robbery of lead pipes and gas fixtures held sway for many months before being arrested in 1899; they received two-to-five-year sentences in the penitentiary.[15] In 1901, five young blacks, considered an organized gang, went to jail for robbing residences and stores in the East End of Church Hill.[16] Other gangs of African American thieves were rounded up from time to time.[17] In August 1901, Richmond detectives "succeeded in unearthing one of the most notorious gangs of colored crooks in the country." Besides Richmond, the six thieves had also operated in Baltimore, Washington, D.C., and North and South Carolina. Although they were known for robbery, individual members of the gang were adept as "expert card sharpers," and their leader, Henry Napier, was a master of the "lock and knife trick." Four members of the gang were apprehended; Napier was sent to jail on a charge of conducting a confidence game.[18]

Richmond had its share of young children, often in the nine-to-fifteen age bracket, who tried their hands at burglary.[19] As previously stated, offending children were tried in Police Court along with the adults. Sometimes the youngsters were so small that they were hard to keep track of in court. Little Aleck Clarke, a "ten-year-old colored boy," was so small that he had to be placed ten feet from the justice's desk so the justice could see him. Aleck and another boy were charged for doing "a professional piece of work" at a tailoring shop at 506 East Broad Street. At 3 p.m. on August 5, 1903, the "little darkies began to tear away" the plastering around a bay window and remove the lathe behind it. They made a hole big enough to crawl through when a policeman came along and apprehended them. Aleck's aunt was present in court. The justice asked her the whereabouts of the boy's mother. "In New York," said the aunt. Aleck was remanded to the "colored reformatory."[20]

Two "little negro boys," arrested for theft, "made things lively" at noontime at the Second Police Station on September 6, 1896. They told a guard that their cell was being flooded with water. When the guard entered the cell, the boys rushed out of the door. One of the boys was found hiding in the bell tower of the jail, while the other jumped fifteen feet from a window on to a stone pavement. No injury ensued except for skinning his legs. A passerby caught the boy and brought him back to the station.[21]

In summer 1889, the city endured a series of robberies by a gang of "small negro boys," whose "business was to rob every store when they could see a chance." Usually, the loot was of minimum value and grocery related, such as cans of sardines, jars of jelly, cans of beef, and even champagne. All of the thieves, "big and little," wound up in the city jail.[22] A gang of white boys in summer 1907, who lived in the neighborhood of the penitentiary bottom, preyed upon local grocers.[23]

In burglarizing stores and homes, boy thieves stole such items as clocks, watches, pistols, hardware items, and grocery goods (especially

A representation of what was dubbed "The New Juvenile Impersonation Artiste," as seen in the *Richmond News Leader*, February 27, 1911.

eggs and butter), liquor, and money. The items were those which could be pawned or sold to unsuspecting persons. Jail time usually amounted to thirty days to six months.[24]

Shoplifting seemed to be the misdeed of women, with the crime becoming very extensive during the winter holiday season. Pinkerton and local detectives, joined by women gumshoes, went undercover among the retail crowds to ensnare culprits. Penalties varied from two weeks to eight months in jail and/or a fine up to $100.[25] One device used by shoplifters proved very successful. This was the French muff which was a framework of wire covered by fur. Inside, instead of containing cotton, the space was vacant, into which stolen goods could be stuffed. At the bottom of the muff was a slide, which, when pressed, sealed the muff.[26]

Surprisingly, at Christmastime 1916, a sort of amnesty was tried to curtail snatching of goods at retail stores. Pinkertons and the city's "shoplifter's squad" busily rounded up the culprits.

> As rapidly as women are detected stealing they are escorted to the office of the manager of the store, where they are requested to give up the articles they have been seen to take. In addition to returning the stolen goods, every shop-lifter, in the presence of witnesses, signs a confession.
>
> The number of women detected daily is said to be large and there have been lively scenes in several of the stores when the purloiners of articles were tapped on the shoulder and asked to visit the office. The identity of those detected is closely guarded, and in the absence of court proceedings will always remain a secret.[27]

Women and girls accounted for some of the burglaries. Several were formidable desperadoes. Tennessee Jackson, a "colored woman, brawny, buxom and bad," accused of burgling residences, "exhibited a reckless boldness rarely seen in a woman criminal." Operating mainly in the city's West End and adjacent Henrico County, Jackson made three larcenous forays in one night, mainly carrying off groceries and confections. One night as she was breaking a window to a store, a railroad man, on his way home from work, spotted her and gave the alarm to the police She was charged with a felony and had to stand trial in the county court.[28]

"One pair of brass knuckles, one bulldog revolver, a bottle of knock-out drops, and many pawn tickets" were discovered by detectives belonging to three women in a Richmond house on Thirty-second Street; the women were from Chicago, Evansville, Indiana, and Memphis. Their crime spree came to an end through the efforts of one Captain Delaney. He was riding in the same streetcar as the three women. He overheard their conversation.

> There ain't any money in a job of that kind," said one of the women. "I'd rather have the hard cash than the best clock that ever was rung. Give me the long green. But, of course, when you can't get that, a stone or a clock ain't to be overlooked."
>
> "What did you get on that stone Jack sent you?" asked another.
>
> "He was just wasting time on it. It was full of flaws, and the clock was a filled super," was the answer.

Delaney left the streetcar when the women did, and followed them as they entered a house. The next day, the captain and several other men went to the women's rooms at the house, but were refused admittance. After they threatened to break down the door, it was opened.

"Well, what do you want?" said one of them.

"You," said the Captain.

"Git up," said the woman, derisively. "We're on to you, and there ain't anything here."

The three women were taken to a police station. Their rooms were then searched, with an "assortment of articles brought to light." Clippings found told of robberies in the West.[29]

Lizzie Shelton, Gladys Robinson, and Marie Coles, "colored girls, age 11, 12, and 13, respectively, were responsible for three 'daring robberies'" over a three-day period in June 1910, and for a "long list of thefts committed in Richmond within six months."

> The youthful trio have absolutely upset all traditions in the annals of local criminology. The knowledge which the girls possess of the proper time and methods to employ in committing a robbery is almost unbelievable. The situation which they occupy in the eyes of the police is distinctly unique.

The thefts occurred at stores and residences during the night. The loot included children's clothing and jewelry, especially diamond rings and gold watches. All three girls had been abandoned by their parents. When finally caught, they were incarcerated at the Industrial Home for Colored Girls in Hanover County.[30]

For almost ten months, Richmond police sought a woman who was styled "the slickest and most daring female sneak-thief" to be arrested in the city for many years. Lillie Hamilton, "colored, nineteen years old," was arraigned on some twenty charges of theft. All the robberies had been committed between 6 and 9 p.m. on Saturdays. At her home police found stolen articles, which included "a mass of handsome clothes, a great collection of handbags, several articles of jewelry" and "one of the finest assortments of skeleton keys yet captured from an alleged thief." One of the pieces of jewelry consisted of "a very handsome rosary while other articles were gold powder boxes and similar trinkets." At the thief's house were found nearly fifty pillow slips, taken from beds of the robbed houses and used to carry away the booty. In one instance she stole almost the entire wardrobes of several actresses along with "a number of dresser articles." Lillie said that she and her mother took in washing, and it was probably through this means that she first gained access to the houses she robbed.[31]

City residents experienced many instances of breaking and entering. Summertime provided the greater frequency of this crime, as citizens were prone to leave windows opened or unlocked and rear doors unsecured.[32] Climbing to second stories from porches also provided easy access into a home.[33]

9. Larceners

This was purported to be "a Good Cure," according to the Richmond *Daily Times*, August 8, 1897.

Professional burglars had a favorite mode of operation. It was something like this. Two men would "cruise around until they found a house the occupants of which are not at home." Then "one of the men goes into the back yard and begins to cut up wood in the most industrious manner, in order to delude the neighbors into the belief that he is employed there"; his accomplice meanwhile enters the house through a door or window. The thief then goes leisurely through the house selecting items that are most valuable.[34] Richmonders who spent time away at the seashore or other vacation spot usually failed to have someone to provide a continual watch over their residence.[35]

Because robbers limiting themselves to houses thought to be vacant and moving clandestinely, residential and store burglars often had a long crime stint before being apprehended by the law. Fingerprints and footprints left at the scene of the crime provided one means for making arrests.[36] As in the case of the "barefoot burglar," Clarence Sales, one way to apprehend a house thief caught red-handed was to lock him in the room where he was found, and then call the police.[37]

Then there occurred a situation of a burglar coming up against more than his match. When Mrs. V. S. Carlton confronted a thief in her home, the intruder "doubtless thought she would scream and thus allow him to make an easy getaway." Consequently, he "was literally paralyzed with astonishment when Mrs. Carlton grabbed him none too gently by the coat and demanded what he was doing in her house." The thief replied that a man had sent him after clothes to be cleaned. "Terror was written on his face." Mrs. Carlton said that she did not believe him and proceeded to shake him briskly. She searched his pockets and found that he had nothing of hers. When she diverted her glance from him briefly, he "simply tore down the stairs to the street."[38]

Boarding houses provided great opportunity for robbery of personal belongings. In February 1908, Julian T. Lane faced a dozen larceny charges. He was arrested after being spotted wearing clothes that he had pilfered. In three weeks' time he had robbed eight boarding houses. His method of operation was to be lodged in a room along with one or more men, and after living there for several days he would depart with everything of value in the room. His take included wearing apparel, razors, watches, shoes, and even streetcar tickets. The main evidence against Lane came from pawnshop items ticketed to him.[39]

Nothing seemed to be safe if left in backyards. Thieves, often little children, relentlessly pursued any items left unattended. The children "trespass upon premises on the pretext of picking over the ashes or taking away the garbage, but before they are out of sight something of more or less value is missed." Besides chickens, also in great demand were coal and wood. Household articles, including druggets, rags, and children's toys could be found among the contraband. Many blacks, old and young, "slink through the alleys of the city day and night peering into backyards and sneaking in to commit all sorts of petty thefts and depredations." Some citizens installed locks and bells on their gates.[40]

Since the city contained so many poor and hungry people and a small cadre of the homeless, it was not surprising that any livestock and fowl was fair game for snatching. Cows and oxen went missing from time to time. The best way to catch an urban cattle thief was when he brought the stolen animal to the slaughterhouse.[41] Horse thieves would visit farmers of Henrico County (adjacent to Richmond) and go off on horses, which were sorely needed for the farm work. In spring 1907, vigilante committees cropped up in the country because of the horse thieving, and there was even talk of lynching if the perpetrators of the robberies could be caught.[42]

9. Larceners

The city had a proliferation of hen houses and chicken coops, not to mention wandering fowl in backyards. Chicken stealing proved a temptation for the young and old, and gangs of chicken thieves were to operate in the city. Irate citizens were known to wait in ambush to pepper chicken snatchers with buckshot, or worse.[43]

Some chicken snatchers operated boldly, fearless of capture. On September 22, 1906, a "chicken thief with the name of Jones Edwards" was sentenced to twelve months in jail for the theft of four chickens, the property of John T. Duval, a farmer. One morning Duval was at an "eating house" near the Second Market when he heard the birds "cackling for help." He ran to his wagon and a "negro peddler" said he had seen Edwards steal the chickens.[44]

One night in July 1907,

> Just as the hands of the clock in the city hall pointed to the witching hour of midnight and as the moon rolled behind a bank of clouds in order not to see what was going on, Walter Merrit percolated through the palings of Cornelia Madison's back fence, passed through the dark and stealthily entered the house occupied by Cornelia's pride and joy, the big dominica rooster which has long been the envy of the epicures of the ward.
>
> For weeks Walter's mouth had been watering over thoughts of succulent stews in which the dominica was to take the leading role, and as his scrawny fingers closed—with the deftness only acquired after long practice—around the yellow legs of the rooster and his other hand sought the neck to prevent a cackling giveaway, he could not help humming over to himself the snatch song ... "A thousand dollar bill for the chicken that can roost too high for me." One twist and the head was gone to cackle no more and another movement and the dominica was under his coat.
>
> Then Walter hied him lightly through the palings again and wrapped in visions of succulent morsels he made his way homeward and his spouse to put the kettle on. In a shorter time than it takes to tell the one time pride of his mistress's heart was under the cover of a kettle and was boiling away, every simmer telling of the delicious morsel for breakfast.
>
> Such is the story of the dominica and such is the story of Julia Harvey's three frying-size chickens which disappeared so mysteriously last week, and such is the case of Willis Martin's three white leghorns which have been eaten and forgotten by the epicure, Walter, and his spouse....
>
> As soon as he had gotten into bed to dream of the feast in the morning a Nemesis sat upon the lid of the kettle and the police did the rest. A shadowy botch in the alleyway resolved itself into the person of Policeman Palmer and a darkness moved showing the well-remembered form of his consort Belton. With stealthy tread the two approached the raider's stronghold and in a few minutes affected an entrance.
>
> Feathers, chicken and simmering pot gave Walter dead away, and in a few minutes he was in the strong arm of the law and was riding merrily toward the station house.

Walter was sentenced to six months in jail, "where he will get nothing that even looks like a chicken and where a cackle is as rare as the teeth of a hen."[45]

Thievery of jewelry presented opportunity for both sharpers and snatchers. A clerk's attention could be diverted so that a person could pick up a ring or pin from a display tray. In more extreme cases, a burglar would smash a showcase and then flee.

One enterprising jewel thief was D. Morgan, a suave individual who passed himself off as an advance agent of Hoyt's theatrical company. In the course of one afternoon in January 1891, he visited three jewelry stores, and, after casual conversation, during which he examined various items, having laid his handkerchief on top of the showcase, he would then pick up the handkerchief, put on gloves, and depart. A ring or a scarf pin would then turn up missing. Morgan, found to be in possession of the stolen jewelry, was arrested; in court he received a sentence of six months in jail for each robbery.[46]

Three little boys, two of them ten years old, burglarized the jewelry store of W. T. King on West Main Street in April 1913. Two of the lads posted themselves as lookouts at the front of the store, while Emmet Toney climbed over the transom over the alley door, and, upon entering, grabbed "his choice of the more inexpensive jewelry which had been left out of the safe." He exited with rings, watches, and pistols crammed into his pockets. Acting upon a "hint" provided by an informer, detectives arrested the boys; the loot had been stashed in a hole under the Seventh Day Adventist Church and also under a woodpile.[47]

A true bunco artist, of course, preferred to avoid the high-penalty crimes of direct robbery, preferring instead to stick to trickery and clandestine methods. But sometimes distinctions were blurred.

10

Footpads

Footpads (sometimes designated as highwaymen) robbed persons on streets and roads. Typically, a footpad would dart out from the shadows of an alley or from a low-lying building. He would shout, "Hands up!" or more elaborately, "Hold up your hands and keep quiet or your brains will be blown out." The victim, usually facing a revolver cocked in his face, would then surrender all the money or valuables on his person.[1]

Prominent citizens were often inviting marks for highwaymen. One well-known Richmonder recounted this ordeal. Aaron Greenwald left his store at the corner of Henry and Broad streets on a Saturday night about 11:30 p.m. and stopped at a restaurant nearby. After dining briefly on some oysters, he went down Belvidere Street and then up Grace to Harrison, coming within a few doors of his home. Two men sprang up from the shadows. They ordered the victim to "give up what you've got." Greenwald said he would, but then one of the men pressing a pistol against his head told him to hold up his hands. The footpads took Greenwald to a house at 826 West Grace Street, where he was pushed up against a wall. While one of the robbers kept a pistol against his head, the other rifled through his pockets. Greenwald had to give up all his money, a watch, and a tie pin. The two robbers tried to force their victim through a gate, but fearing that he might be physically harmed, Greenwald successfully resisted. The robbers then backed off to the street, making "a dead run" toward Shafer Street.[2]

Giles B. Jackson, noted black lawyer and director of the Jamestown Tercentenary, likewise was robbed by two men on September 28, 1903. Having heard that Jackson had just raised $50,000 for a charitable event, the robbers pursued him from the street into a saloon and then outside again. Failing to reach his car in safety, Jackson went back into the saloon. Upon the arrival of policemen, the two holdup men fled. They had been heard earlier in the saloon to say that if their intended victim had "fifty thousand now he will not have it in the morning." Jackson, after his ordeal, commented that he never carried the $50,000 and "if I had that much money I would go into a bank."[3]

There were others who were able to elude footpads. Two white "thugs" accosted Richard H. Mead as he walked down Franklin Street, near Fifth Street. The two ruffians held Meade by the neck and went through his pockets. He decided to fight back. Though his arms were pinioned, he "kicked viciously at his assailants, and finally landed a prodigious blow in the stomach of the man who was rifling his pockets." With several pedestrians arriving at the scene, the attackers were frightened and fled.[4]

Two hours before the crack of dawn one Sunday morning in January 1897, George E. Sangster headed home from his job as a composition man at the *Times*. The city was deserted; only a stray dog and a passing cabman were seen. At the corner of First and Duval streets, he noticed two tall white men who were trying to conceal themselves in the shadows. When these footpads approached him, Sangster pulled out a revolver, and the two departed. Sangster commented later that there was something desperate about his would-be assailants, and that "their movements were cool and defiant."[5]

A person crossing a bridge seemed especially vulnerable to being robbed, if for no other reason than being distant from quick help.[6] One of the more unusual suspects involving street robbery was a young woman dressed as a man; she was arrested after being seen darting among trees. Her explanation was that she was "on the trail of her husband."[7]

One of the more enterprising footpads was Richard Hawkins, an African American who had come up from North Carolina. For nearly a month in the summer of 1890, he systematically raided the vessels docked at the city, removing the "wardrobes of the jolly tars," including trousers, suspenders, shoes, and shirts; he also lifted watches, which he then took to the pawn shop. It was estimated that Hawkins stole from all the ships lying in the docks. During the daylight hours Hawkins was "something of a dude"; he would change clothes several times a day, dressed in the stolen garments. That was what did him in. A warrant was issued and his living quarters were searched, revealing a stash of the sailors' missing clothes.[8]

Often the street robbers resorted to assault. Some victims were beaten with clubs or bricks.[9] J. E. Anderson, a concrete contractor, was felled by blackjacks wielded by three "thugs" at Fifteenth and Franklin streets.[10] Angelo Bonucelli, a confectioner, was also waylaid by a blackjack-wielding assailant and robbed.[11]

Even children tried their hands at street robbery. "Throw up your hands!" shouted a youthful bandit "as he pointed a big revolver at Annie Jones, colored, of 511 Henry Street, when the woman passed Jefferson and Franklin streets on her way home." At the same time three small boys "stepped out from a hiding place and announced they were prepared to relieve Annie of her valuables." The woman exclaimed, "Every one of you needs a good spanking," as "she boxed the ears of the youth holding the pistol and then resumed her walk."[12]

Before the city became mechanized on wheels, citizens needed to be on their guard against horse thievery. Typically, in June 1879, a horse was stolen from W. N. Tyler, along the canal a few miles west of the city. Tyler, with R. W. Allen, gave pursuit, covering nearly twenty miles. Tyler fired his revolver several times at the "Dick Turpin" (the name of a notorious highwayman in England), slightly wounding the fugitive. Eventually, the highwayman ditched the horse and jumped into the river, swimming to the other side, making his getaway.[13]

Little children sometimes entered into the ranks of horse thieves. Nine-year-old Harry Gentry, one July morning in 1907, spotted a horse hitched to a grocery wagon standing in the street, the driver having left it to make a delivery. The boy mounted the seat of the wagon and drove off. He went all over town and even several times stopped and sold vegetables from the wagon. He tried to sell the horse and the wagon as well, but no one would buy them. Harry's stepfather found him and brought him home, where the boy was whipped. The wagon and horse were sent back to the owner, a Mr. Fetig. The boy's mother thought the stepfather had beaten her son too severely and had the stepfather arrested. Mr. Feitig, in the meantime, had Harry arrested for incorrigibility. When the case came up in Police Court, the mother requested that the boy be sent to the reformatory. Justice Crutchfield, however, thought the boy deserved another chance and dismissed the case, sending the boy home.[14]

A similar but more farcical case involved Jessie Brown, a "delicate little boy, six years old," who was charged with "stealing a horse and buggy from a negro named B. F. Turner." Jessie was probably the "most diminutive prisoner" that ever appeared before the judge. The case became the "subject of no little ridicule by the people at the court." It was decided that Jessie, who had been playing nearby, had climbed into the buggy, and the horse walked off. At Seventeenth and Main, Jessie merely left the team, being "doubtless much gratified to get out of the buggy." Justice Crutchfield, remarking that Jessie was the youngest person to be tried in his court, dismissed the case with "a jocular smile."[15]

"Fifty-Fifty"—so reads the caption of the political cartoon from the *Richmond News Leader,* **January 6, 1917.**

In the early 1900s, Richmonders realized they had to deal with a new major crime—auto theft. In 1915 the city had 115 automobiles reported stolen. The "majority were driven off by persons who used them for joy riding purposes for a few hours and then abandoned them in an unfrequented place in the city."[16] In 1919, two detectives were assigned to the regular traffic squad that handled speeders and "other careless and reckless drivers." The new assignees were provided with "a high powered car," from which they could "keep a weather eye to the windward for automobile thieves while on the lookout for traffic violators."[17]

Reminiscent of the Wild West days, road bandits, sometimes masked, forced the stoppage of vehicles for the purposes of robbery.[18] On August 20, 1919, Percy Dowell, twenty-seven years old and a white chauffeur for Thomas L. Moore, was stopped on the roadway by an unmasked man, while driving his employer's automobile, a seven-passenger Cadillac. The two other men, wearing "handkerchiefs over their faces, with eye holes punched in them, stepped out of the bushes, each flashing a revolver." Dowell was bound and gagged and left in the shrubbery beside the road. The three highwaymen then drove off in the car into the city, abandoning it on Grace Street between Fifth and Sixth streets. Dowell was freed when Mrs. Grover C. Dula happened along in her car and untied him. Police looked for the culprits, described as neat, young men.[19]

In November 1912, Richmond police had to search for a "brand new kind of crook—the pay-as-you-enter robber." On November 11, just before midnight, a man boarded a trolley car of the Broad and Main Line and robbed the cash box containing five hundred tickets and $10 in cash. Greatly aiding the robbery was the absence of any other passengers in the trolley-car; when the conductor turned his back, the thief removed the glass cover over the tickets and coins. Grabbing the loot, he quickly stepped from the vehicle and hurried down Hancock Street. A reporter commented on the event that "in former days, bandits made a practice of boarding trolley cars late at night and relieving the conductor of his cash at the point of a pistol. The introduction of the pay-as-you-enter cars temporarily ended this form of depredation and, until last night, conductors felt reasonably safe from highwaymen."[20]

By the turn of the century, the northernmost end of Church Hill had become infested with "gangs of negro rowdies, who congregate on corners, indulge in disorderly conduct, play crap games, fire pistols and otherwise disturb the peace." These ne'er-do-wells frequently transformed into footpads, waylaying, beating, and robbing passersby. Some effort, but not enough in the eyes of many citizens, was made to break up the gangs of "worthless roughs" who "hang out and exclusively occupy street corners."[21]

Being a highwayman brought its occupational risks. Consider the case of a lone African American bandit in October 1913. The would-be assailant accosted Robert O. Bell, president of the Bell Book and Stationery Company, and his wife, just after they had left the State Fair Grounds. At a spot in the road amid dense undergrowth and trees on either side, the bandit pushed a revolver up against Bell's head, saying, "Don't go a step further, don't go a step further!" As the two men grappled, Mrs. Bell let out a scream that could be heard all the way back to the midway. Bell managed to draw a revolver from his pocket while the robber had him by the throat; with the pistol barrel pressed up against his attacker, he fired. At the same time, the robber fired his revolver, missing its mark. "With a loud shout that sounded above the cries of the fear-stricken woman, the robber leaped to his feet and sprang out into the darkness. Bullets sped after him." Bell, himself bleeding from the struggle, ran to his wife's side. Two policemen arrived, and, after a ten-minute search, discovered the assailant about two hundred yards from the road, with his head in his arms. He was still living, but upon being dragged back to the road, he died. The body was taken to county police headquarters in the city in a police patrol wagon. As the vehicle was driven down the midway of the fair, a large crowd followed. Bell, *pro forma*, was arrested, but subsequently granted immediate bail of $500. The highwayman, identified as Otto Brown, had been discharged from employment at the fair a day or so before. Bell surrendered his revolver, a .32-calibre Iver-Johnson; the assailant's pistol was an "old fashioned one."[22]

Penalties for highway robbery varied greatly, depending largely on whether it was a compounded crime, such as assault plus robbery. Probably the greatest discrepancy between crime and the punishment was that meted out to Joe Price, a "burly negro," for taking nineteen cents from a small boy on Brook Road. His ten years in the penitentiary was owing to the impression on the jury of the comparison of the "size of the negro" and the "small stature of the boy." It was Price's first felony conviction.[23]

At least no Richmonder during the period under consideration was executed for highway robbery. Such was not the case elsewhere in Virginia for convicted criminals. One particularly brutal assault and robbery led to death by electric chair for a Surry County man.[24] Penalties for highway robbery in Richmond, in federal or state courts, normally ranged from twelve months in the city jail to sixteen years for combined assault and robbery.[25]

11

Cracksmen

"The safe breaker does not associate with those who 'crack' a store for the purpose of stealing bulky goods." He "represents the aristocracy of the profession, and uses force only when absolutely necessary."[1] Richmond had its share of cracksmen (safe breakers).

Safe breaking called for professional skills. One way for robbing a safe was simply through use of the combination of the lock. This might involve "removing the dial of the combinations, fitting a sheet of tinfoil over the latter, and replacing the dial." The "legitimate opening or closing of the safe makes the impressions of letters or numbers on the soft foil." At another visit by the robbers, the "dial is readily removed, and for the expert one glance at the foil is sufficient to apply the combination which opens the safe with force." The cracksmen usually preferred, after a robbery, to disorder the combination, so that "a safe cannot be opened again for hours," thereby gaining time for escape.[2] Some cracksmen were successful because of the custom of some businessmen to leave safes partially unlocked. This meant that after the door of a safe was shut and the handle turned, the combination, instead of being thrown all the way, is moved only the fraction of an inch, just sufficient to prevent the door from opening when the handle is tried." For someone familiar with "the manipulation of combination," it was an easy matter to open the safe.[3] Of course, someone hanging around an establishment could eventually learn a safe's combination, and in the after-hours make a robbery.[4]

The "mechanical" cracksman relied upon a wide variety of tools. Such safe robbers carried a "kit." A complete kit contained "an air pump, putty, powder or dynamite, fuse, sectional jimmy, steel drills, diamond drills, copper and steel faced sledges, lamp and blow pipe, jackscrew, wedges, syringe, brace with box slide, feed screw drill, steel punches, small bellows, skeleton keys, nippers, dark lantern, twine, and screw eyes."[5] Sometimes a huge wrench, as long as two and a half feet, might be used to break the inside frame of a safe.[6] Boring holes, particularly to break combinations, seldom brought success. Battering a safe with a hammer, hatchet, axe, or even an automobile axel usually also failed to produce any booty, and were considered the efforts of amateurs.[7]

Professional safe crackers were apt to use explosives and carefully plan their larceny. On Monday, March 15, 1886, at about 8 p.m., a man entered the grocery store at the southeast corner of Broad and Fifth streets. Going to the rear private office of the owner, Hermann Schmidt, the stranger asked to see the city directory. Given the directory by a clerk, the stranger asked if anyone stayed at James C. Smith's ice-house at night, and said that he was looking for an H. M. Smith, a shoemaker who once worked in Washington, D.C. While the stranger talked, Schmidt noticed that he was glancing all around the store and especially eyeing the iron safe. After the stranger left, Schmidt reported the visit to the police, the result being that the suspicious character was placed under surveillance.

On the morning of March 17 at about 3 a.m., two policemen heard an explosion at Schmidt's grocery store. The back door had been forced open, and burglar tools lay nearby. The combination lock of the safe had been blown off from a powder explosion. The burglar was still at work on the safe when the police arrived and fled before he could open the doors of the safe.

Captain James B. Angle brilliantly figured out that the burglar was a member of a theatrical company then performing in the city. It was learned that the troupe had recently been performing in Baltimore and Norfolk, at which places cracksmen had blown open safes. The name of a suspect emerged: Charles Shaw. As the theatrical group was about to board a train for Washington, D.C., Carl Wippermann was brought to the scene and pointed out Shaw as the person who had previously cased the grocery store. Wippermann accosted Shaw, who broke away, drawing a pistol. In the ensuing pursuit, the fugitive was wounded, as was Sergeant Robert J. Brooks; shots were also fired at Sergeant Alexander M. Tomlinson. The fugitive managed to cross the river; later, he re-crossed it, appearing at the village of Manakin. As he made his way toward a train depot, he was captured. Shaw's case was first heard in Police Court, from which it was remanded for trial in Hustings Court. Shaw was charged with four counts: wounding Sergeant Brooks with intent to kill; shooting at Sergeant Tomlinson; entering Schmidt's grocery store with intent to commit robbery; and possession of burglary tools (including having placed white powder [explosives] in holes bored into the store's safe). A major piece of evidence against Shaw was that he was found in possession of a diagrammed map of the premises of the grocery store; he was also fingered as the person who had surveyed the crime scene beforehand. A jury convicted Shaw, who received a sentence of eight years in the state penitentiary.[8]

Gangs of traveling cracksmen proved elusive to catch. Often, these criminals timed their heists with the departure of a freight train; they preferred small towns for their operations. The cracksmen departed from a job before the country constable could "find his boots," and were soon five miles away, on "the blind baggage, counting the spoils." The "rich season" for safe cracking was the fall. It was then that there was enough of a chill to keep windows closed, thus helping to "smother" the sound of an explosion; it was also important that there was no snow on the ground, lest footprints would give them away.

The arrest, in November 1903, of several members of a roving cracksmen gang rated as a major accomplishment. Ernest Layton, who hailed from Clifton Forge, "Cockney Tim" Madden, and Fred Davis were taken into custody in Richmond; the head of the gang, however, avoided capture. These men, traveling with hobo burglars for many months, were said to have "reaped a rich harvest" in "cracking safes and robbing post offices in many Southern towns and villages." The criminals used nitroglycerin and modern tools. The arrests came quickly after the cracksmen's most recent haul from the safe at the post office in Columbia, Virginia, about fifty miles west of Richmond.

In Richmond's Police Court, Layton, "a shifty-looking fellow," laughed when accused of cracking the Columbia safe. "I wouldn't crack a chestnut," he said to Judge Crutchfield.

"Perhaps not," the judge retorted. "It would be hardly worth the trouble."

Tim Madden, conducting his own cross examination of witnesses against him, contested a witness's testimony that he had seen two men run from the post office after the explosion. Madden said it was too dark to recognize anyone. He called for a calendar; when one was furnished, it was found that the moon on the night in question was almost full, and therefore the witness's testimony was deemed truthful. Madden and Davis had been arrested "in a haul of hobos caught roosting" in an abandoned house on Cary Street. It was assumed that the house had been the headquarters for the gang in their ventures out of Richmond and also for robberies within the city. Layton had been arrested at a dive on Broad Street. The Police Court remanded the cracksmen for trial in U.S. District Court.[9]

In the summer of 1900, a well-known "safe blower," Joseph R. Evans (who went by the alias Joseph Rapley) and "Topeka Joe" were arrested as leaders of a gang of bank robbers who blew open a bank's safe in Williamsburg and lodged in the Richmond jail to escape detection. The ever-wiry "Joe" escaped from custody on September 3.[10]

Not only to prevent the dangers of fireworks display but also to give some deterrence to cracksmen, Richmond's police chief, B. F. Howard, in July 1900, ordered a prohibition of the sale of large torpedoes and firecrackers within the city limits. The interdiction included all dynamite and nitroglycerin torpedoes and firecrackers. The only "powder" crackers allowed to be sold in the city were those of size No. 5, or less. The city code had proscribed any sale of fireworks of large size and any that had nitroglycerin as "a constituent part"; penalty amounted to a fine in the range of $20–$100.[11]

In Richmond, even young children tried their hands at safe-cracking. In 1908, for example, ten-year-old William Crittenden cracked safes at two banks. When a banker would temporarily abandon his post, William, wielding an axe, would crack a safe "just as well as if nitro-glycerin had been used." With the loot, William bought all-day suckers and peppermint drops. When arrested, William was "too small to deal with, and the skinning process was resorted to."[12]

At 3 p.m. on December 16, 1912, two boys, age fifteen and seventeen, in short pants, entered a wholesale grocery store, where they proceeded to act like professional robbers. They stalled for a few minutes to "get the lay of the land," telling employees that they were searching for work. They then waited outside until all but one of the employees left for a late lunch. The boys then went back inside. One of them drew the sole remaining worker, Miss Bernice Pollard, into conversation. Miss Pollard was told that the boys had come back to obtain the telephone number of the bank.

> While the boy was doing this his confederate had noiselessly slipped behind a railing and was kneeling before the safe, the door of which stood open invitingly. He hastily gathered up everything in the way of cash that was in sight. The haul was not up to expectations, amounting to only $4.12.
> The boy who had rifled the safe returned to the desk, where his companion was conversing with Miss Pollard, and nodded to him. It was their signal that the "job had been finished and both took their departure immediately."[13]

12

Dips

"The Light-Fingered Gentry," otherwise known as pickpockets or dips, found a compatible environment in Richmond for their sneak-thievery. Wherever there were crowds, there were dips aplenty. Even on the streets among passersby or in places of business and residences, persons might be accosted by a dip. Often, these pickpockets networked with each other, traveling from city to city, wherever opportunity beckoned.

Some of the best-known crooks in the country were wont to descend upon Richmond. When the Confederate Reunion was held in the city in July 1896, police arrested such dips as William Moore, alias "Black Jew" of Pittsburgh; George Woods of Philadelphia; John Johnson of St. Paul; J. Wolff of Cleveland; Kid Tisdale, a race track thief; William Myers of New York; William Ford, alias Molincant; William Doer, alias Dutch, alias Nobb Myers; John Burton, alias Jimmie Bryant; Edward O'Connor, alias Jimmie Connors of Chicago; and Samuel Harvey, alias Sam Jackson. Two of the "bad 'uns" who got away were Billy Bird and Daniel Nugent, both of Chicago.[1]

Many famous dips followed aviation meets, and at each event they were "augmented by local amateurs," who kept "sharply on the lookout for innocent skygazers." The "task of sneaking out the fat roll of the man whose attention is fully occupied with watching the maneuvers of an aviator wheeling and circling hundreds of feet in the air with the whirr and buzz of the propeller in his ears is like taking candy from a child compared with pulling off a job in the ordinary crowd."[2]

Trains and railroad depots provided abundant opportunity for dipping. Dips regularly showed up at the Main Street Station and the Chesapeake and Ohio Railroad Station.[3]

A gang of pickpockets, consisting of eight men and two women, stalked presidential candidate William Jennings Bryan in 1896 as he brought his campaign to Virginia. The two women were Fannie St. Clair, a pretty brunette, and Lillian Armstrong, a stately blonde. They signaled out victims and took care of the stolen money. Richmond detectives assisted in the arrest of these dips aboard a train as it reached Petersburg. Among those taken into custody was "Denver Ned," who "cried like a child," claiming that he was the sole support of his widowed mother. Since a crime had not yet been committed, Ned and several of the other dips were jailed as suspicious characters.[4]

A favorite situation for dipping was to mingle with groups standing around post-office delivery windows. Two such postal dips stood out. One, about thirty years of age, was clean shaven, with light hair, wearing a close-fitting brown suit and a brown hat; his face showed signs of dissipation. His accomplice was about twenty years old, wearing a gray suit and a light fedora. They were said to smoke large cigars and to converse freely.[5]

Persons mingling and going in and out of theaters and the Virginia Opera-House experienced dips brushing against them and stealing their wallets.[6] Dips could even be found fleecing emotional attendees at prayer meetings.[7]

On railway passenger trains and in train stations, pickpockets readily culled valuables from victims. Richmond detectives were fairly successful in pursuit of pickpockets detected red-handed as they fled from stations or jumped off trains.[8] Streetcar riders were fair game as they were jostled by dips, chiefly when getting on and off cars.[9]

The Virginia State Fair in Richmond always came with "a horde of pickpockets, burglars, and thieves of every description to ply their vocation on the unsuspecting and rural strangers." The detective force was enlarged for the occasion, and plainclothesmen moved through the crowds. Usually, there was a sign warning fair visitors that "the closest watching is necessary." No one should take any money on his person other than that intended to be spent at the fair; "in case you are 'touched' you will not be out much."[10] Besides greenbacks, pocket watches were frequently lifted by pickpockets.[11] Dips caught at their game in Richmond could usually expect up to twelve months in jail.[12]

Of course, a "countryman" visiting the city for a night of "doing the town" provided the ideal mark for a dip. All one had to do was to nudge against the victim at a bar or follow him closely as he left to go outside.[13] Dipping on the street also proved profitable.[14] Sometimes, an encounter with a dip involved assault. At 7:30 p.m., on November 19, 1903, a man and a woman caught up with R. L. Jenkins on Nineteenth Street between Franklin and Main. The intruding man grabbed Jenkins about the neck, and as the victim raised his hand to defend himself, the woman yanked a pouch from his pocket, containing ninety dollars (four twenty-dollar gold pieces and ten dollars in currency). The woman ran toward Franklin Street, and the man disappeared in an alley. Sergeant Werner managed to arrest the woman, Lizzie Morris, also known as "Sixth Street Liz." The male assaulter managed to evade the police.[15] A similar dip assault occurred in October 1906. W. J. Ford was waylaid on Nineteenth Street by a man and two women. The assaulters were identified as Eddie Jones, Hannah Johnson, and Henrietta Wankin, all African Americans. Jones had used brass knuckles in knocking down Jenkins; the women rifled through the victim's pockets, seizing a watch. Ford was disfigured by a scar across his right cheek. All three assailants were apprehended and bound over for trial in Hustings Court.[16]

As would be expected of any resourceful urban crime community, Richmond had its youthful pickpockets. There were encounters such as that of May 5, 1878, when a woman, walking along Fourth Street between Broad and Marshall, dropped a handkerchief which a black boy picked up and, in so doing, picked her pocket when he handed it back.[17] At 7:30 one Saturday evening in March 1881, three black boys—Richard Ward, Daniel Page, and Thomas Allen—were leaning against a tree near First Street. Mrs. Allie Graham passed by. One of the boys approached her, and she thought he was begging; instead, he grabbed her pocketbook. Page was caught with nine gold pieces identified as having belonged to Mrs. Graham. For some reason, a grand jury declined to indict him on a felony count.[18] In May 1899, a fifteen-year-old boy was arrested for pickpocketing at an auction sale.[19]

One afternoon in July 1911, a farmer living near Richmond, F. B. Lucas, was loading wood at Tenth and Marshall streets, when a boy accosted him.

"Say, Mister, don't you need somebody to help you?" asked the boy, stopping to gaze at the perspiring Lucas.

The youth had a winning smile. Although the farmer didn't really need any help, he gave him the job. They were carrying wood into the root cellar of a house in barrels.

After struggling manfully with a couple of barrels, the boy stopped and took off his coat. "Better take yours off, too," he said. "You'll be cooler without it."

Lucas took off his coat. Right there, Fate played him an ugly trick. He took $34 out of his trousers' pocket and put it in the coat, which he hung up on the fence....

When the farmer descended into the cellar with the next barrel, the boy waited outside. He hung around for a few minutes then hurried away.

Of course, when Lucas put on his coat after all the wood had been carried, his money was missing. Lucas called a policeman, and they unsuccessfully searched the neighborhood for the culprit. "Dang it all," Lucas later said. "I had to work hard for that money. I tell you now I'd be willing to go to the electric chair just to fix that scoundrel and get my money back. I ought not to have given him a job, I suppose, but he was such a nice talkin' little feller."[20]

"A touching little incident" occurred on Main Street near the post office one day in July 1898. A man was standing on a corner when he felt something touch him. Turning around, thinking that some friend had approached him, he saw a small boy running away with a five-dollar bill in his hand. The man quickly thrust his hand into a pocket to check on a five-dollar bill he had there, and it was gone. The man caught the boy by the arm, sat him down, and began talking to him. The boy was not listening because his sobbing drowned out the voice of his captor.

> "Mister, please don't have me arrested," begged the boy in such a pathetic way that it touched the heart of the good man who held him.
>
> "No," said the kind man. "I am not going to have you arrested, but I simply want to talk to you and before doing so we will step into this soda fountain and get a glass of soda water."
>
> This was a great treat to the little fellow whose pennies were hard to earn, for it was by selling papers that he got them and it was not often that he had such luxuries as this.

The man asked the boy if his parents had taught him to steal, and the reply was in the negative. The little boy said he had learned to pickpocket from some bad boys, but that he would never do it again.

> "Now," said the gentleman, "here is five cents, not to pay you for taking the money, but to reward you for being sorry for having done wrong. I want you to go to Sunday school next Sunday and then as you come along here on Monday morning you will find me around here and if you will show me a card to prove to me that you have been, I will give you another nickel and will continue that each week so long as you will bring me the proof of you having attended Sunday school the day before. May God bless you and make you a good boy. Good bye."
>
> This was no doubt the happiest boy in Richmond that day but no more so perhaps than the man who had returned good for evil.[21]

Some dips, instead of sliding a hand into someone's pocket in search of cash or a watch, deftly went for the exteriorly carried purses (pocketbooks). Women were advised to carry their purses in their hands rather than let them dangle from a strap. Purses were snatched openly on the street or at a store or marketplace. As did their counterparts, the pickpockets, purse-snatchers worked crowds on trains and streetcars. It was not uncommon for victims to be stalked after leaving a store. Sometimes, delivery boys could not resist the temptation of grabbing a purse at a residence.[22]

"Boasting that she was the best pickpocket in Virginia," Lou Charity, a black woman who was long under police surveillance and had previous arrests, was nabbed for good in July 1910. The arrest occurred at Cohen Company's Store, at 11–17 East Broad Street. Policemen and detectives had, for quite a while, been stationed in Cohen's store hoping to catch Lou. At the time of her arrest there, she was carrying under her arm a pitcher, into which she had dropped three stolen purses.[23] Men's pocketbooks could just as well end up in larcenous hands.[24]

To clamp down on pickpocketing, city police kept a sharp eye out for all suspicious persons. Policemen were on the alert to arrest "all men interesting themselves in the affairs of others."[25] Richmond authorities, from time to time, received notices from other jurisdictions to be on the lookout for professional dips known to be headed by train toward Richmond.[26] Sometimes out-of-town lawmen showed up in Richmond in pursuit of dips. For example, in July 1896, sleuthing in the city were detectives John Murray of Philadelphia; J. T. Connors of the Pinkerton Agency; H. J. Witte of Cincinnati, and B. T. Rhodes of Washington, D.C.[27]

With what seemed an overwhelming presence of snatch thieves in the city, some civic leaders called for harsher penalties. Whipping for all kinds of theft, particularly relating to blacks, had been a frequent remedy, sometimes along with a prison sentence, throughout the state during the Civil War. But, by 1880, the use of the lash had lapsed.[28] In November 1877, a white purse-snatcher wound up at the "whipping post"; the culprit had "only clutched a moneyless book, but his guilt was as great as though it had been filled, and he got justice."[29] A year later, Stephen Campbell, an African American, stole a purse and received a sentence of three months on the city's chain gang and thirty lashes.[30]

A *Dispatch* editorial, of November 14, 1877, called for renewal of the whipping penalty regarding pickpockets. An anecdote was presented to readers:

> Two pickpockets—very gentlemanly-looking white thieves—were once arrested at a Fair in this city and sent to the penitentiary. In the penitentiary they acknowledged that when arrested they were making a tour of the States in pursuit of "business." They went down the Mississippi and through the Gulf States, and along the Atlantic coast as far as Virginia before they were stopped. They said they passed through North Carolina without attempting to rob anybody, "because that was a barbarous State, where they whipped people for stealing." They "could stand the penitentiary—that was a gentlemanly punishment," but they "could not run the risk of being whipped."
>
> Exactly! The rogues cannot stand the whipping-post. The State owes it to society and to these wretches, who might be deterred from crime by it, to make the act of pilfering from the pocket punishable by whipping.[31]

Justice Crutchfield had an even more vengeful assessment. Upon remanding alleged purse snatcher James Graves for trial in Hustings Court, Crutchfield commented that "if Virginia juries got in the habit of hanging for a couple of years, this sort of thing would stop soon enough." Graves, "a vicious and brutal-looking negro," had attempted to grab the handbag from the hands of Mrs. L. C. Tucker. The lady "held tight to the chain handle, and the negro, in a vain attempt to rob her by force, struck her in the face." Crutchfield cited a Virginia law still extant: "If any person commits robbery by partial strangulation, or suffocation, or by striking or beating, or by violence to the person robbed, or sought to be robbed, etc., the penalty shall be death." Graves had a long police record but had never before been convicted of a felony. To ensure that he stayed in custody until his Hustings Court trial, Crutchfield sentenced him to twelve months in the city jail.[32]

13

Suspicious Characters

Strangers and other "queer-looking" persons did not go unnoticed in downtown Richmond. Like other small cities, anyone out strolling was expected to be accountable, and at the very least to be a resident or, if an out-of-towner, to have a legitimate reason for visiting the city. Anyone just hanging around, especially if that individual bore an unusual appearance—whether that meant someone who had fallen on hard times, or if the individual possessed one or more stereotypical characteristics associated with those of criminal tendencies—was subject, according to the city's ordinances, to be swept off the street; upon appearing in Police Court, he or she could be compelled to hit the road or jailed, or both. The city's restrictions against vagrancy and begging fit into this prohibitive mold. Similarly, the city had its anti-tramp regulations. Of course, there were the bunco-type persons who tried to smooth-talk the authorities into overlooking their predicaments. The modern racial-profiling is but an extension of the long-standing practice in American life to be distrustful of outsiders coming into a community. Sadly, arrests of persons simply for arousing suspicion violated the age old principle in common and constitutional law of the right to habeas corpus. But even in the earliest colonial times, if you did not belong to a community, it was best to keep on moving.

Suspicion of a person as a thief was enough cause for arrest; the accused might resemble a "wanted description" from another jurisdiction, possibly a robbery suspect who may be responsible for that or any other crime. Such was the situation of a young black man, John Ellis, who was confronted in downtown Richmond by a stranger toting a heavy bag.

"Hello," said the stranger.
"Hello" said John.
"See dat air bag."
"Yep."
"Got sumpin in hit wurth money."

"Huh," said John.

"Now you help me to carry dat air stuff to a junk shop, an' I'll gib yer half wot I gits."

"Well, I reckon," said John, as visions of the price of a crap game entered his head.

The man with the bag took two railroad brasses from the bag and left two in the bag and then John took up the bag and the two started toward a junk shop, whistling a merry tune as they went along.

At the first corner the man who had the bag when John met him said: "I gotter go up did yere way, cause a fren er mine libs up dare; I'll meet yer at de shop," and then he disappeared up the street.

John went on his way and ran across a police officer who arrested him as a suspicious character. "The tale he told" in court did not affect Justice Crutchfield, and John went to jail for sixty days.[1]

Suspicion of thievery, but not being convicted, could bring a jail sentence up to twelve months.[2] Persons were incarcerated up to ninety days on general principles of being "suspicious"; usually the sentence was in the form of asking for security for good behavior, and being unable to pay the amount (approximately $100), the accused went to jail for default of payment.[3]

Two white boys, Ded Willson and Jack Williams, went to jail for a year, being charged as suspicious persons and carrying concealed weapons. The punishment applied only to the concealed weapon charge, and the boys were remanded in Hustings Court for trial as suspicious persons, an unusual decision as such an allegation was ordinarily considered a misdemeanor.[4]

Alleged flimflammers were hauled in as suspicious characters.[5] In February 1918, three New Yorkers: George Poll, age thirty-five, a peddler; Hermie Cohen, age thirty-four, a salesman; and Leon Horwitz, age thirty-eight, a junk dealer, were arrested at a Richmond rooming house for having in their possession Dutch gold ("sheets of thin brass of little value") and "several pounds of small pegs that looked as though they might have been removed from sets of castoff false teeth." In addition, on the way to the police station upon being arrested, the trio threw away a small box of bogus diamonds. Justice Crutchfield allowed a rare instance of habeas corpus in his court and the three men went free, there being no evidence of intent "to make any use of their Dutch gold."[6]

"Loafing around places" for no reason led to arrests. Children in particular were apprehended as suspicious persons on this account.[7] Sometimes the punishment was rather severe. A black youth, caught "loitering" at the rear of a hospital, received thirty days in jail as a suspicious character.[8] Another black boy, found hiding in an alley behind boxes at a hardware store, with the back door open, although nothing was stolen, drew three months in jail.[9]

Two "black and ragged little niggers," in a hallway of a building on Franklin Street, were arrested as suspicious characters. The boys had been

"Mr. Jack" was a popular comic strip in the *Richmond News Leader*, **August 18, 1908**

in trouble with the law before. They were punished by a whipping under "the supervision of the Court." The boys readily expressed preference for corporal punishment rather than going to jail.[10] Waverly Bates, acting suspicious when found loitering in an alley, was sentenced to thirty days in jail.[11]

To be poor and down-and-out in Richmond was a crime. An 1867 city ordinance provided for the arrest of anyone without "ostensible means of support" and who recently entered the city. Such persons would be held in jail until they could be sent to where they came from, and, if that was unknown, to somewhere out of state.[12] A later amendment called for the penalty for being a vagrant a fine of $2.50 to $100, and in default of this, ninety days in jail.[13]

A non-resident could be arrested as a vagrant or a suspicious character, or both. A child with no home could be sent to the reformatory.[14] Men drifting into Richmond because of the state fair could be regarded as "vags" (vagrants) or suspicious persons. Such a group were the five men who arrived on October 26, 1891, on a freight train.

> They said they were neither tramps no crooks and they pulled out cards enough to show that they were entitled to Jay Gould's private car, but still they came in on a freight, and when the train arrived they were securely sealed in with boxes of starch, soap and canned fruit. They evidently came to the Fair, and it was difficult to tell them from crooks as it was to distinguish between the different branches of Methodists at the Ecumenical Conference. The town is gathering a right good contingent of suspicious-looking citizens and these were warned to leave town by 12 o'clock.
>
> "Every gust of wind brings a shower of falling leaves,
> Every rumbling freight train brings a gang of cunning thieves.
> As the dropping of the leaf will strip the branches bare,
> So the average Northern thief the unwary at the Fair."[15]

One major problem that was hard to address was the presence of "loafing gangs," often referred to as "Johnnie squads." This undesirable element consisted of youngsters "who filled the sidewalks with their feet and the air with smoke and vulgar talk." These ne'er-do-wells were usually reasonably well-dressed and could not rightly be regarded as vagrants or tramps. Nor could they properly be considered suspicious characters. The police eventually got around to breaking up the gatherings because the youths blocked access to retail shops and were a nuisance to theatergoers.[16]

Two "negro boy vagrants, as black as crows under the ashes which covered their skins, and regular ragamuffins" were brought into Police Court. The two young vagrants declared they had "no whar to stay and nuthin' to do." Moreover, it seemed that near to where the boys had camped out, chickens disappeared. The boys were sentenced to fifteen days in the city's chain gang; they went to their cell "in great glee at the idea of three square meals a day."[17]

"I'm going to scour Richmond clear of every scrap of humanity that looks like a vagrant," Justice Crutchfield declared one day in November 1906.[18] He made good on his claim by ridding the city of a variety of homeless persons. There were the tramps, who were inclined collectively to camp out on the fringes of urban areas.[19] A published notice tells of the travail of a "family of vagrants."

> For several days the wife, two daughters, and a little son of James K. Livingston *alias* Van Ness, have been in the city depending upon the charity of the public for subsistence. Yesterday they were all committed to jail for ten days as vagrants in default of security.
>
> The mother and children are neat, respectable-looking people, but have a peculiarly free-and-easy and bold manner, probably acquired by the wandering life they have led.[20]

One person dragged before the Police Court on charge of being a vagrant was William Walby, who claimed to be a Methodist minister from Pennsylvania. He said he was looking for work in Richmond. It seemed likely that the person in distress was not a "regular Preacher," although he showed the court that he was a "lively exhorter." Walby was ordered to exit the city immediately, and "with his little bundle under his arm, and his face radiant with joy he departed from the court-room in double-quick time."[21]

Not all unfortunate vagrants hauled into Police Court silently endured a lambasting from Justice Crutchfield. When Crutchfield told E. R. Dennis to get out of town or he would be sent to the "rock-pile," the vagrant "shook a forefinger over the desk as long as a trolley pole and declared that there was a higher law than that of Crutchfield's "which demanded that the weary stranger should be succored and not persecuted." Dennis then "regaled the Great Dispenser with Scripture texts by the yard with a vehemence that made him jump up and down like a milk-shaking machine at a soda fountain." Dennis was ordered to be held for ten days for psychiatric evaluation.[22]

Beggars could be treated as vagrants. Penalties ranged from ninety days in jail or a fine of $100[23]; an obscure revision in a state law made pandering punishable from one to ten years in prison and a fine up to $500, if the offender had been convicted of "accepting any money or other valuable thing from a fallen woman."[24]

"My Dear Boy, I'm Busted," was the caption of this cartoon seen in the *Richmond News Leader*, June 12, 1908.

The "begging game" constantly unfolded in Richmond as it did in other municipalities. A reporter obtained a "confession" from one who had been posing as a blind man on the city's streets for three weeks. This beggar revealed not only his tricks but also some of the techniques of other kinds of panderers. The "blind" beggar's mode of operation was as "ridiculous" as it was simple. He never asked for money nor wore a sign saying he was blind. He made "no outside pretensions" whatever. The goal was "the big game"; keeping his mouth shut, he made big money, between five and ten dollars a day. The interviewee commented on his tactics:

> My game is simple. I put on the glasses, take my stick in one hand and feeling before me with the stick, walk down the street.... I go slowly into the middle of a street, feeling my way with a stick, allow myself to get in the path of a heavy wagon or something coming toward me, and betcherneck, I know how far away it is. Of course, always at the proper moment, I move. Meanwhile some half a dozen men will rush out from the sidewalk to save the poor blind man.

Then when someone asked where the "blind" man was going, the reply was a place which "I know to be a mile or so away." Then he would say he had no money for a ride or that a boy he had paid to guide him had gone off.

The interviewee offered comment on three other 'begging games." The "deaf and dumb game" which required "a great deal of care and training" because of "always being liable to look around at any sudden noise" or to speak or indicate understanding. The "cripple game" sometimes involved considerable pain since a person had to hold his hand or leg in a certain position for a long time. The "Child game" was a good one, but it was hard to find a child with "enough sense to work it"; usually it was "a story of hunger and sick mother and medicines and things."[25]

Indeed "the city is overcrowded with able-bodied men begging," noted one observer, because they were too lazy to work. "To give help means to keep them here, to refuse means to cause them to seek riper fields."[26] Some street beggars falsely claimed they had been veterans of certain Civil War battles.[27] Begging while pretending to be deaf and dumb or a cripple normally brought a thirty-day jail sentence.[28] Pretending to be hungry was a favorite scam. C. J. Murphy, "an insolent soak, who blew in from somewhere, panhandled Broad street by day and lapped suds by night in a negro bar."[29]

Justice was quickly served to beggars in the Police Court. Thus, Justice Crutchfield asked of George Dempsey,

> "Where are you from and what are you doing here?"
> "I was from Washington originally, but I have been here for some time working at the printing business. I got out of jail yesterday, where you sent me about thirty days ago. I took two drinks which went to my head."

"Well, I will give you sixty days this time."

This had a bad effect on Dempsey. He pleaded with the Justice, and told him if he would let him off he would get out of town immediately. The Justice decided to let him go on condition that he shake the soil of Richmond from his feet forever.[30]

There was no end to the kinds of personal problems and physical disability dreamed up by beggars. One man falsely claimed his tremors were from St. Vitus's Dance and his crippled leg from a recent paralytic stroke.[31] Even merely being old was used as an excuse.

"I'm an actor, your honor, and I should be grieved beyond words if you found it necessary to incarcerate me," said Charles Tremaine, 60 years old, of Boston, when arraigned today in Justice Crutchfield's court on a charge of begging.

"What kind of an actor?" sharply asked the Judge.

"A dramatic actor, your honor," replied the old man.

"Mostly bad actors find their way into this court; I simply wanted to be sure," said Justice Crutchfield.

"I can assure you that I am not bad in the criminal sense," Tremaine hastened to say, "and the critics never applied that offensive adjective to my acting. ... I've never had my name in electric lights over the entrance to a Broadway theatre, your honor, but until I became ill a year ago I was always working and was considered reasonably successful. I've been an actor for thirty-five years, but I guess I'm down and out now...."

Tremaine told how he made audiences "sit up and take notice" when he played in "Ingomar" from coast to coast, and how the folks in Kalamazoo and Keokuk applauded his acting in a fast part in "The Blue Mouse."

At mention of "The Blue Mouse," Justice Crutchfield showed more interest in the prisoner ... "If my memory serves me, that was the name of a show that we refused permission to play here a few years ago," he said. "I reckon if you were fast enough to travel in swift company like that, you've still got enough speed left to get out of town immediately. You're discharged."

Tremaine bowed in elaborate fashion and disappeared through the door of the courtroom. "When I played in Peoria..." he was heard to murmur in fond recollection of the halcyon days.[32]

In winter, extreme cold and heavy snowfall compelled poor, homeless men who walked the streets, "benumbed and chilled," to seek out food and shelter. But even such a situation, as community leaders were wont to point out, begging was unnecessary, given the availability of aid to the "outdoor poor." Of several city agencies who assisted indigents, the City Mission had by far the most extensive role. It reached a large number of people in issuing food, clothing, bedding, ice, coal, and small amounts of money to destitute families.[33] The mission maintained soup kitchens for the poor.[34] The city also provided several settlement houses.[35] In April 1893, the Society of Associated Charities (later becoming the Community

Chest and then the United Way) was formed.[36] The Richmond Almshouse took in the homeless of all ages, but it had limited capacity. At Fourteenth and Franklin streets the Associated Charities turned the old Ballard house "into a comfortable, homelike retreat for the beggar on the streets."[37]

Of the possibly 100,000 gypsies of all kinds scattered in the United States, 30,000 were nomad gypsies. Gypsy bands, always on the move, particularly during harvest time, periodically came to Richmond and made camp at the outskirts of the city. Normally eschewing outright begging, they had a number of tricks to work on local people. "One of the largest, if not the greatest, gypsy bands in the country, the Harrison-Hoalder gang," in a cross-country trek, laid in at Richmond in May 1903. The band of some thirty members was governed by Agnes Williams, who "queens it over these people, and old Bob Lock, a Glamorganshire Englishman, is their high priest of sorcery and horse trading."[38]

The gypsies were a mystery to Richmonders as they were to other people among whom they traveled throughout the world—in North America, Africa, Asia, and Europe. Originally they came from India. Their language was that of Romany, a form of Hindustan. The unity of the gypsies was a marvel. Yet, they had no religion to bind them together, although at times members professed variations of Christianity and Islam. They had no literature and no national history. Gypsies, however, did share a common physiognomy. They had "a general attitude of lawlessness toward all other races" and "fixed standards of morality and honor among the Romani race."[39] In July 1876, eight gypsies were arrested in Richmond for working on citizens "the feather-bed trick." This chicanery involved approaching strangers and convincing them to receive several stuffed beds with geese feathers as security for a loan, supposedly of far less worth, only it turned out the feather-beds were worth far less than the amount of the loan. The gypsies, of course, quickly fled.[40]

With so many swindles being committed in Richmond and hucksters at the ready to dupe persons for illicit gain, the authorities, perhaps, should not be begrudged for employing preventive measures.

14

"American Nobility"

"Tramp, Tramp, Tramp! The tramps are marching, Richmond is infested with them and housewives will do well to guard their silver," reported the *State* in November 1893. "The frosty winds of autumn that have been sweeping through the streets for the past week have ushered in the city an alarmingly large detachment of the great army of tramps." Richmond had "always received its share of the 'American nobility' with good grace and the police have sheltered the visiting tourists night after night without a murmur," but "when they invade the town in legions as they are now doing the line must be drawn."

With this infestation, officers received complaints from all over the city, and particularly from citizens who lived at the outskirts of the city. The tramps came from "every point of the compass "in duos, quartettes and herds." Not since the winter of 1877, when "the tramp crop yielded such an abundant harvest that they had to be stored two or three deep in the cells at the police stations, has there been such a remarkable influx of the knights of the turnpike." Many of these intruders were neatly dressed; they were mostly men "thrown out of work in their own towns on account of business depression."[1]

The tramp had a calling that was fundamentally American:

> In America the tramp has a broad field for his operations. He can go upon a tramp 3,000 miles wide and 1,800 miles long from North to South. Cat-a-cornered he can take a trip much longer. He can accommodate himself in all seasons and to all zones. Dry latitudes can be visited by him in damp seasons and cool climes in August. No globetrotter with millions in his pocket can outdo the tramp in variety. We see him everywhere.[2]

Camps of tramps could be found all along the perimeter of the city. Such sites included one near the Virginia-Carolina Wheel Works; at the Lime Kiln; Byrd Island, a "fortified camp on the river, near Belle Island"; and on the south side of the river Bankard's sawmill; pump house in Manchester near woods; a vacant lot in Manchester; near Maury Street and

Southern Railroad tracks; and in the woods near Chesterfield County Court House.[3]

On the average, there were fifteen camps on the outskirts of Richmond. In all, they contained a hundred or more tramps. Most numbered about eight to ten men; one always stood guard while the rest were away. Tramps usually appeared to be "of the lowest order of humanity and intelligence," although many had been in the professions or trades. Most tramps carried knives, and a few had pistols. As soon as one band of tramps moved out of a camp, they were replaced by another group, having just come out of railway cars.[4] Each group of tramps usually had a dog, which accentuated the problem of the city having too many stray dogs, numbering about 10,000.[5]

It was somewhat mystifying how tramps obtained money during their long tours. By interviewing them it was found that 25 percent worked for what they needed. The least amount a tramp could live on was one dollar per week, which included the cost of food, drinks, clothing, and shoes. Thus, at most, a tramp had to work one day a week. Approximately 25 percent of tramps "beg and steal what they get." The remaining 50 percent depended on friends or relatives for their income. In any event, it was the leisure time that formed the habits of tramps. Tramping mainly was not for the young. It was estimated that only one tramp in a hundred was under age twenty-one; fifty out of a hundred were over age thirty-five; and twenty-five percent were over forty years old. It is said that "there are no old tramps; they die or become city vagrants at sixty."[6]

The more honest tramp steadily looked for work. This minority of men had their own union: The Brotherhood of Railroad Tramp Association. Edward Stillwell, in the 1890s, served as the group's representative in Richmond, with its headquarters was in New Orleans, with annual dues of ten cents.[7]

For those who professed to be seeking employment but were unable to find it, there was little sympathy in Police Court. Tramps, like anyone else who seemed to be up to no-good, appeared before this venue. One time in court,

> Charles Morris, a strong, healthy-looking youngster, leaned up against the throne to rest himself.
> "Where are you from?" asked the Great Dispenser.
> "York State."
> "What do you want down here?"
> "Looking for work."
> "Want a job?"
> "Sure."
> "Fifteen days with Sugar Bottom Jones [chain-gang]."[8]

Here, according to the editor of the Richmond *Daily Times*, is a "Sample Group of the Tramps," as seen in the March 4, 1899, issue.

Two tramps came before the Police Court, for "the second time in the past day and a half."

"Thought you fellows wanted to get back to New York," said he of the Napoleonic features.

"We did," they said.

"Why didn't you go?"

"Well, sir, we have grown accustomed to the delightful pleasures that are experienced by strangers, when they come in contact with real gentlemen, and so attractive are the features that emanate from that ecstatic old Virginia hospitality, that we would fain tarry in your midst for yet a while longer, or until the bluebirds 'gin to sing, and the buttercups show their beautiful heads among the shrubbery that covers the landscape hereabouts, while the turbid waters of James river rush on toward the shipyard and thence the great Atlantic."

"You may tarry just thirty days longer, at the expense of the city, and under the eye of 'Squire Sugar Bottom Jones,'" said the Great Dispenser.

And they did.[9]

As if lured by a pied piper, boys went off with tramps, or sometimes they were compelled to do so.[10] Sometimes boys hung out with tramps at their camps at the edge of the city. Some boys tramped on their own."[11] John Alley and J. D. Hupp, both teenagers originally from Richmond, threw on the air brakes of a C. & O. train near Pemberton Station, because they simply wanted to get off there; the sudden stop forced the caboose off the track, seriously injuring the brakeman and conductor.[12]

Female tramps appeared in the city, and unlike their male counterparts, they traveled alone. They were usually not very cooperative with efforts to establish their identity, and it seemed also that they were likely to be mentally unbalanced more so than the men. One such female wanderer was Augusta Wright, who was picked up while walking barefoot down Broad Street. She "presented a dilapidated appearance, dressed in a faded calico dress and her hair streaming down her back." She said she was from Wisconsin and had traversed the whole country. Her last walk had been from Washington, D.C., to Richmond. For being unable to put up security, she was sent for a spell to the city's jail.[13] Another female tramp who walked from Washington, D.C., was Annie Flasher. Not knowing where to go and braving cold weather, in mid-October 1902, the sixty-year-old woman went to the First Police Station and asked for shelter. Upon questioning, her "story was but the oft-repeated tale of a wife following a good-for-nothing and drunken husband."[14]

One female tramp, who gave her name as Jane Orr but who was thought to be the missing Annie Orr from a well-to-do family in Bridgeport, Connecticut, was arrested in Richmond as a suspicious character, while dressed in male attire. Jane, however, insisted she was from Marion, Indiana, and was on her way to Florida to work, picking oranges.[15]

Tramps were distinguishable from vagrants in that they formed into groups, were always on the move, and could engage in severely aggressive behavior. Tramps were known for trickery in eliciting sympathy. For example, some of them put "bugs" (pouring on croton oil to produce sores) on their arms.[16]

Railroad security guards constantly sought to ward off tramps. The railroad companies faced sanctions from municipal authorities for allowing tramps into urban areas. Richmond had a city ordinance that levied on railroads a $25 fine per tramp brought in, or a requirement that the railroad return a tramp to where he had come from.[17]

Tramps were prone to injury. Farmers and townsmen alike set dogs on them.[18] Freezing to death was a hazard during winter.[19] Riding the rails presented plenty of mishaps. Along the tracks of the Richmond and Petersburg Railroad was "a sort of cemetery for tramps," chiefly of those who fell off cars and were mangled.[20] Sleeping in boxcars filled with freight could be the cause of death when parcels shifted.[21]

Tramps passing through Richmond became involved in thievery. They would stroll into establishments, and while no one was looking would make off with various items, including wearing apparel; houses were also broken into.[22]

Violence sometimes ensued in encounters with tramps.[23] Gangs of tramps fought with railroad guards. At the battle of Kirby Station near Richmond, in March 1897, a Seaboard Air Line crew and a band of tramps fired on each other, with one tramp killed.[24] Two tramps, eighteen-year-old George Patterson and Joseph Bradley, were arrested for the murder of a railroad worker.[25]

Tramps and vagrants could receive assistance primarily from two sources. Despite being financially hampered, the Associated Charities claimed it never turned anyone away and that there was no need to beg in the streets. Transients were housed in three large dormitories on Franklin Street.

> Bed, board and lodging are given to all who ask. Every man is required to take a bath before he goes to bed, and his clothes are fumigated while he sleeps ... the Associated Charities ... has ... a kitchen, which is going all day, and a dining room, where the men may sit down in some comfort for their meals. Plenty of soup is provided, with bread and coffee.[26]

Richmond's three police stations also served as a receptacle for destitute, cold, and hungry men. More often than not, the tramps and vagrants voluntarily applied for lodging in the jail. The police department kept a "tramp register." During all of the year 1893, the "hospitalities of the stations were extended to 1,708 weary pilgrims." During this period, birthplaces of those assisted included England, Ireland, Scotland, Wales, Australia, France, Italy, Germany, Switzerland, Sweden, Arabia, and Denmark. All these countries sent "recruits to the Great American Army of Tramps, that meets the house-dog in deadly fray, storms the hen roosts of the suburban resident and adds a heavy burden to the life of the farmer."[27]

In August 1878,

> a small, emaciated, middle-aged man presented himself at the First police station and asked for rations. He had a weary and unhappy look, and, in broken English, explained to Capt. Pleasants, who happened to be seated at the desk, that he was a Frenchman, and being unable to obtain work or assistance, he applied to the city for something to eat. He said he had not eaten anything "for two days full." "If

14. "American Nobility"

The above was said to be a "Severe Shock," according to the Richmond *Daily Times*, July 11, 1897.

that's a fact," said the Captain, "you must be hungry, sure 'nough. We don't keep a boardinghouse, and you can't expect to come here regularly at meal times for your victuals, but if you haven't had anything for two days, you may have 'one good square meal.'" Then the Captain, turning to his colored butler, said, "Go over to Mr. Frischkorn's and tell him to send a big dinner for a starved man." In a few minutes a big dinner, steaming hot, came in on a waiter. As the hungry individual sniffed the aroma from the soup and chops, and saw the waiter moving towards him, he could hardly believe his senses. But when the repast was spread before him he took in the situation in a hurry. He was a half-starved man and no mistake. There was no discount on his appetite—no dyspepsia; no hesitation. A corn-dodger went down at a single gulp—soup, chops, vegetables and pie were devoured in the twinkling of an eye. The bystanders looked on, glad to see a fellow escape the throes of starvation. The contempt usually felt towards tramps was forgotten in this case, for no one with a spark of humanity in him but would rejoice at seeing charity bestowed upon a hungry man.[28]

Other wayfarers, descending from boxcars, "starved and almost dead with cold," availed themselves of the hospitality of the police stations.[29]

Not out of the ordinary was a request in Police Court:

> "I'm weary of knocking about the country. I need to rest up a bit. Can you give me a jail sentence?" asked William Layton, 50 years old, of Justice Crutchfield.
> "Certainly, I'll oblige you; ten days," said the judge.
> "That won't be time enough. Make it thirty."
> "Thirty days; take him back."[30]

One factor that made it easier to obtain lodging at a police station was a new ordinance in 1899 equating treatment of tramps the same as vagrants.[31]

Stopping off at a town, tramps were up against people who already harbored prejudices against them. Some destinations differed as to leniency, bordering on acceptance to outright hostility. Richmond veered back and forth between the policies of forcing hobos to keep on the move and offering them charitable assistance. More often than not tramps faced a punitive response: put up money as security for good behavior (which, of course, a tramp did not have), go to jail upon default of the security, or be run out of town. Many tramps had an affinity for stealing, which resulted in incarceration.

The infusion of tramps varied as to numbers. In spring they headed northward, and in the fall, southward. Certain events also accounted for the flow of these "tourists." For example, hobos returning northward from the Atlanta Exhibition in December 1895, came in large numbers to Richmond. The city police at this time attributed a swell of robberies to this Hegira.[32]

Tramps taken into custody could be charged simply with trespassing, begging, vagrancy, or as suspicious persons.[33] Just being a tramp (or vagrant) could bring thirty to sixty days "on the rock pile."[34] Begging incurred fifteen to sixty days' jail time.[35] Sleeping on a park bench could bring a fine or jail time.[36]

Being considered a "suspicious person" could result in confinement. Patrick J. Mack, a "white man who fills the dual role of tramp and fakir," convicted as a suspicious character in his effort to sell eye glasses with brass rims, received ten days in jail.[37]

Willie Wilson, described as "white, in spots where the skin shows," glided into court as if he wore roller skates, and it was evident that he had never done a day's work in all of his life." When asked of his means of support, the reply was "umbrellas to mend." But Willie offered no evidence to back up this claim. When Justice Crutchfield recommended that "a spell on the rock-pile would do him a little good," Willie "fainted dead away." Upon being revived, Willie said he had come from Baltimore and that he "never could a come 'ere if the boys had let me know dat dere was a rock-pile." He added: "Gimme five minutes to get out of de state and you'll never see me again unless the rock-pile is suspended." The Justice gave Willie five minutes to take his leave, and threatened him with a life term in segments of thirty days if he came back.[38]

As for another suspicious person, when a tramp/vagrant came before the Police Court, Justice Crutchfield asked,

> "What's your name, sir?"
> "Why-ti-ti-sis-ti-ti-ti-t," he replied.
> "What is that?"
> "Ti-ti-sis-ti-t-t-t."
> "What's the man charged with, Sergeant?"
> "He looks like he is charged with soda water," replied the Keeper of the Exchequer.
> "Well, just give him fifteen days."[39]

Boy tramps could not expect much leeway from the justice system because of their youth. David Deputy, the "little white tramp, who was arrested ten days ago for being a vagrant, was sent back to jail to spend days more, while a home is hunted for him."[40] J. M. Cronin, a "white boy, arrested while in company with a gang of tramps, claimed that he lived in Washington." There was no such address as the one he gave, and "he was put under security for 30 days."[41] Similarly, Ded Wilson and Jack Williams, two white boys, were "placed under $100 security and sent to the city jail for a year" for being suspicious characters and carrying concealed weapons. After the court pronounced sentence, Justice Crutchfield said,

> "Tell me, just for curiosity, what did you boys want with pistols?"
> "If you could see the graves in the California deserts along the railroad tracks, where tramps have been thrown from moving trains by the conductors and killed, you would see," one of the boys replied.[42]

Some tramps were ordered to leave town instantly, despite a custom of spending one night at the police station before hitting the road.[43]

In December 1876, George Morris, "a champion tramp," in Police Court, stepped

> out of the pen as nimble as a cricket, and upon arriving in front of the Justice he made a profound bow, and started out at a rattling rate to give a history of his life. He stated that the home of his childhood was in Jersey, where his life had been one

of happiness; that upon arriving at the age of seventeen he took up the honorable profession of machinist.

A few months ago he was strongly impressed with the idea of spending the winter in the orange groves of Florida, but not having wealth he started to foot it. After crossing the Potomac, he "met up" with a fellow-traveler, and the two journeyed along peacefully until they entered the beautiful capital of the Old Dominion—a State that has furnished presidents and statesmen. His reception here was a cold one, having to sleep on a hard bench in the police station. The Justice here knitted his brow, and with an angry scowl, cried, "Hold, I have heard enough!"

Morris: But, your Honor, please allow me. I was going to conclude by saying...

Justice: Stop sir. Then pointing to the door said: Do you see that hole left by the honest shover of the plane when this edifice was erected?

Morris: Yes, your Honor.

Justice: Well pass through it at once, and if you are found in the city again, you will be furnished lodgings in the Valley Inn.[44]

Four tramps, who were caught trespassing on the property of the C. & O. Railroad, came before the Police Court. The defendants declared that they had left the North to come South to look for employment. Justice Crutchfield told them that the only work he knew available in the city was cleaning out Shockoe Creek, but that job was not ready to start, and, therefore, he could "give them board and lodging until the time rolled around." The tramps replied that they would rather leave town. Justice Crutchfield then said: "Git! If I catch either of you again it will mean twelve months."[45]

In August 1897, George Roberts, a tramp, was picked up on a Richmond street. He "had a face that looked like a fried egg covered with liver gravy." He "was a real tramp. One foot was encased in a boot and on the other he wore an old low-quartered tan." The Justice asked the defendant what he was doing in Richmond. "Wall, see here. I wants ter tell ye, see. I jest dropped inter town, an' I was on de hog. Not a sou in me pocket. I needed a little hash, see? So I braces de first mug I meets for er is ter it," said the tramp, trying to act nice. The Justice ordered the tramp to leave town. "Just let me see you in town in an hour, and to the rock pile you go."[46]

15

Narcoticists

Government—federal, state, and local—belatedly faced up to an ever-increasing narcotics use by some members of the public. The most significant step-up in attempting to stem drug trafficking occurred at the beginning of the twentieth century. Until the new laws went into effect, narcotic use had been treated as a misdemeanor. Most law enforcement relating to drugs involved personal injury, including death or robbery.[1]

It was estimated in 1918 that there were 1,500,000 drug addicts in the United States.[2] Three narcotics caused the most havoc, as noted in 1914:

> Cocaine is an alkaloid from the leaves of the coca plant and is most frequently used in the form of hydrochlorate, a white powder which is "snuffed" up the nose. Its temporary effects are a sense of greatly-increased bodily strength and mental power, enabling the person who uses it to perform unusual or prolonged physical or intellectual labor. It is habit-forming and results in a most disastrous collapse of the nervous system.
>
> Morphine, which is one of the oldest of the habit-forming drugs, is an alkaloid form of the opium of the poppy. It is a narcotic, produces the typical "opium dreams" and soon establishes such a hold on the victim that its cure is extremely difficult. A morphine habitué is in many respects the most complete nervous wreck with which science deals.
>
> Heroin is a diacetic cater of morphine, in the form of minute crystals. It is an anodyne and sedative and is used in regular medicine, in minute quantities, to quiet coughs. It is a relatively modern habit-forming drug, which has recently been acted upon by drug-fiends and is somewhat similar in its action to morphine.[3]

Selling and dispensing cocaine in Virginia first became a felony with the enactment of a law in 1908 that provided a one- to five-year sentence in the penitentiary.[4] The federal government entered into pervasive regulation of narcotics with a law of February 9, 1909, prohibiting the importation of heroin prepared for smoking and the selling of opium. Penalties were a $5,000 fine and two years in prison.[5]

In addition, unlicensed persons were liable to a misdemeanor charge if "selling, giving away or dispensing drugs, poisons or narcotics of any description." Thus Charles Robinson, the "negro caught by Sergeant Amos," in Police Court for selling trianol, was fined $100, and "in lieu of $300 security for his good behavior was sent to jail for twelve months." Futilely, at the time of his arrest, Robinson had declared, "You cain't do nuttin' wif me, Mr. Amos, dis ain't coke, dis am trional, an' de knock-outenest stuff yo' eber see."[6]

Cocaine dealers made "enormous profits." They collected as much as $600 a day. A coke peddler could buy an ounce of the drug for $5, and, mixing up the coke with other substances, could sell the resulting product for $65 an ounce—a profit of $60.[7]

Despite great difficulty in nabbing coke vendors, Richmond police did nail "Cocaine King," C. L. Hancock of Newport News, who did business in Richmond. Picked up at Foushee and Broad streets as he stepped out of an automobile on August 15, 1913, he had $1,000 worth (at retail price) of cocaine. He received a one-year jail sentence.[8]

The milestone for federal regulation of narcotics came on December 17, 1914, with the passage of the Harrison Narcotics Law. Unlawfully selling and dispensing the harmful drugs brought a minimum $2,000 fine and one to five years in jail. All persons legally manufacturing or selling narcotic drugs were required to register with the Collector of the Internal Revenue Service and to keep detailed records.[9]

From 1850 to the 1890s consumption of opium multiplied in the United States seven times as fast as the population. In Victoria and elsewhere in British Columbia, Canada, "cook houses" usually manufactured up to a million pounds of opium, of which three-fourths came to the United States.[10] Maintaining supply and distribution of opium in Richmond became the almost exclusive province of the city's small but substantial Chinese community. Raids by revenue agents and U.S. marshals turned up unstamped cans of opium in the city's Chinese restaurants, groceries, and laundries. Many well-known white Richmonders patronized Chinese "opium joints," which contained "cots of rattan settees and pipes and other paraphernalia."[11]

By 1900 Richmond experienced a flood-tide of cocaine use. Drug stores reaped immense profit simply by selling cocaine in ten-cent boxes. An ounce of cocaine brought $2.35. Even after the passage of the stern anti-narcotic laws, drug stores were not held liable for filling prescriptions.[12]

Cocaine could be found in many popular items, including soda pop, medicines, cigarettes, and ointments. Burnett's Flavoring Extract supposedly prevented hair loss.[13] A newspaper commentary in 1895 noted:

15. Narcoticists

Coca-Cola is one of the popular soft drinks of the day, but if it does what it is claimed to do, or even is what it is called, it is very injurious to the system. It is claimed to be a remedy for nervousness and mental and physical exhaustion.... From its name, it contains cocaine, which is quite as detrimental as opium. On being taken for the first time it has a far from pleasant taste, but a very insinuating one, which is said to grow until one who has once started, drinks nothing else at a fountain.[14]

Cocaine dens dotted Richmond's downtown area. Such places could be found on College Alley, a "rookery" near Broad and Seventh streets, pool rooms, and even at the Maternity Hospital on East Clay Street. African American men increasingly used it in place of liquor.[15]

King of Richmond's "dope fiends and cocaine vendors," at least for a while, was a six-foot-tall Italian with a black mustache. This individual was a wholesale cocaine dealer, with his headquarters (or den) on Franklin Street. Dope vendors came to this place for their supply. For several years he operated with impunity. One person who had kept an eye on the place reported:

> Haggard girls, with scarcely energy enough to drag themselves to the door of the miserable hovel, would come out after several hours in high spirits, and as pert as crickets.
>
> In time, and after watching from a distance for a while, I became bolder, and one night determined to see for myself what was going on inside. Immediately in the rear of the room in which the cocaine, whiskey and other drinkables are sold, there is a shed, and upon this I crawled to the window, and through a tiny peephole, I saw the most ghastly spectacle my eyes ever glanced upon.
>
> There brooding over a room filled with his followers, stood the grim-visaged proprietor dispensing the death-dealing drug. The room was encircled by shelves, lined with packages of various shapes and sizes. Some of the miserable wretches had fallen asleep, after having drunk in to their heart's content the cherished dreams which only cocaine can create.
>
> On another occasion, I succeeded in getting inside the hell-hole and there I saw for myself sixty gallons of whiskey, fifty crates of beer and a barrel nearly filled with cocaine. The barrel of the drug must have been worth two or three thousand dollars. On Sunday the Italian conducts an illegal barroom, in connection with his dope joint.[16]

In 1909, a new craze helped to ameliorate the severity of the drug situation. Somewhat taking the place of "coke" was a concoction of equal parts of quinine and common soda, which was not harmful or costly.[17]

Laudanum, the medicinal drug of choice during most of the nineteenth century, still held sway. Though not taken for pleasure, there was the continual problem of easy overdosing. A common means for suicide, the drug, which was a stricture of opium, could be used in commission of crime, merely by administering it to an intended victim. Such was the

"First Aid," the *Richmond Times-Dispatch*, December 31, 1914.

case of George Kelly, a streetcar motorman. While passing a lumberyard late at night, Kelly was overpowered by three men who forced laudanum down his throat and robbed him. Fortunately, after gaining consciousness, Kelly vomited, which was said to be a factor in saving his life.[18]

Other narcotics made a limited appearance in Richmond. For example, a man died from having taken fruit-flavored acetanilide, a compound of gas tar.[19] Cannabelloca, originating in British India, made only a scant appearance in Richmond. "Diluted with water it has the taste of rice whiskey and it is intoxicating."[20]

Richmonders, it was estimated, consumed one-fifth of all the alcohol and malt liquors dispensed in Virginia.[21] Druggists were required to have a license to sell medicines with a "booze" basis.[22] In 1904, medicines necessitating a license included: Atwood's LaGrippe Specific, Cuban Ginferic, DeWitt's Stomach Bitters, Dr. Bouvier's Bucha Gin, Dr. Fowler's Meat and Malt, Duff's Malt Whiskey, Gilbert's Rejuvenating Iron and Herb Juice, Hostetter's Stomach Bitters, Kudros, Peruna and Rockcandy Cough Drops.[23]

As to alcoholic beverages, Virginia went "bone dry" on July 1, 1917, in accordance with the Mapp Prohibition Act of November 1, 1916. Virginia's interdiction of booze received reinforcement by the beginning of national prohibition on January 18, 1920. All intoxicating beverages could not be imported into or sold in Virginia, with the exception for scientific, sacramental, medicinal, and mechanical purposes.[24] The first arrest after Richmond became "dry," occurred on September 16, for the manufacture of "ardent spirits." Cody Hatcher, a twenty-eight-year-old black man, answered to the charge of producing "peach brandy," a mixture of corn meal, peaches, yeast, and "plain James River water."[25]

While Prohibition did not alleviate Americans' thirst for alcohol, legislation against the drug traffic did lead to a reduction of the number of "dope fiends" in Virginia. In December 1916, a Richmond newspaper reported (perhaps inaccurately) that since the enactment of the Harrison Act of 1914, prohibiting the "use of habit-forming drugs" in Virginia, the number of "dope fiends" in the state had fallen from 2,000 to twenty or thirty.[26]

One positive effect of the crackdown on drug trafficking was the lessening of narcotics use among children. Before the Harrison Act, some druggists engaged in the "indiscriminate sale of cocaine to young boys." This led to the young users to become "emaciated in body and sluggish in mind." They would "steal anything and run any chances to get money to buy the stuff." The cocaine was taken with a syringe, or swallowed. It also, it was reported, put the victim in a semi-trance.[27]

Many of the young addicts became hooked on cocaine by hanging out at the foot of Oregon Hill at Pine and Belvidere streets. There they fell under the influence of "Hobo" Leighton, who taught the boys how to take cocaine in powder form, "snuffing it in the nose in small pinches." The boys could get a dose for ten cents that afforded three "shots." Leighton eventually wound up in the federal penitentiary.[28]

On the night of March 31, 1906, Richmond police raided "a dope joint and gambling den" at 701 Church Street and arrested twelve white boys and two women. Presiding over the den of iniquity was Mark Armstrong, a "one-legged and one-armed white man" and "a confirmed cocaine fiend."

The crippled Armstrong answered the door at the raid and proceeded to drink a full quart of whiskey, then falling into unconsciousness. At the station house it took a physician several hours to revive Armstrong. "The dive is the worst that I have ever seen in Richmond," commented an arresting officer regarding Armstrong's "dope joint."[29]

Some girls, mostly involuntarily, came into contact with narcotics. E. E. Fagan, a junk dealer, and Frank Armisted faced charges of enticing fourteen-year-old Bessie Clark to drink whiskey and take drugs, then attempting to assault her.[30] In May 1906, Lottie May Foster, a little black girl, and two others were said to have been "enticed into a dope house." Lottie May later became sick from taking morphine. Two fathers rescued their daughters from the drug den; the woman who ran the disreputable site then disappeared.[31]

Richmond police considered themselves able to profile drug users from among the general populace. Body searches usually yielded incriminating evidence.[32]

Occasionally, leading citizens found themselves snared in the net of drug enforcement. In 1914, Robert H. Childrey and Judson Cunningham, both downtown druggists, were arrested for trafficking in heroin and cocaine. Cunningham was a member of the city school board and sang in the choir of Leigh Street Baptist Church. Since the two men were managers and not owners of drugstores and therefore did not stand to profit individually, they were left with the light fines of twenty-five dollars each.[33]

In 1914, Dr. J. Williams, a seventy-five-year-old physician, although a specialist in treatment of victims of drug use, faced charges for prescribing "habitual cocaine" to users.[34] Dr. Boyce D. Brooker, a physician, a year later, was indicted by a federal grand jury on thirteen counts for unlawfully dispensing cocaine and heroin. The chief witness against him was William Williams, a twenty-two-year-old piano player for a cabaret in nearby Hopewell, Virginia. Convicted in a U.S. District Court, while out on a $2,000 bond, Brooker fled, purportedly going to England.[35]

16

Kidnappers

To cause someone to disappear was not only the province of a magician. A kidnapper could do the same and actually transfer a person to a different location. Kidnapping charges ranged from abduction to being an accessory. Most abductions were of children. A relative (or someone posing as one) taking charge of the victim was a common mode of operation.[1]

One case involved a woman trying to regain custody of her eight-year-old son. The mother, an ex-convict, was regarded as a dubious character. The child for several years had been cared for by Patsy Smith, whom the mother, Betty Brown, sued for custody. In hearing the suit, Judge Wellford ordered that Patsy should keep the boy. One day, the boy was sent to get milk and did not return. After setting out on a search, Patsy located the boy, dressed as a girl, at Roseberry Moses's place on the corner of Seventeenth and Marshall streets. Patsy fetched a policeman, and, after further investigation, found the child in a room above a shoe shop next to Moses's place. Patsy, Betty, and the boy were persuaded to go to a police station. There the two women acknowledged to the police captain that a judge had granted Patsy custody of the boy. The captain responded by telling Betty, "Clear out of here," and, pointing to Patsy, told her to take the boy along. The captain then warned Betty that if she should get a warrant against Patsy, the judge would send Betty to jail. Betty left, swearing vengeance.[2]

One kidnapped Richmond child was restored to his parents simply as a result of his photograph being published in the *News Leader*. Fifteen-year-old Courtland Moon, of 134 South Cherry Street, met a stranger at a local theater. The man promised Courtland money, good clothes, and a chance to see the world. Courtland could not resist the temptation and agreed to go. In Washington, D.C., the stranger bought a newspaper in which the boy saw his picture and a story of "how the entire police force of Richmond was searching for him." He began to cry and said he wanted to return home. The stranger, fearing arrest by the Washington police, hurried with the boy to board a train back to Richmond. When the train "stopped at the siding near Acca, young Moon was put off by the 'traveling salesman' who told him he would see him again soon." According to the boy, the stranger caught a train back to Washington. Courtland steadfastly refused to divulge any information that might have led to the abductor's arrest. He did note that he had been lured away when the stranger came within a half block of his home in a taxicab and whistled for him to go with him. Upon his return, Courtland hugged his mother, declaring that he would never leave home again.[3]

"Mystery surrounds the identity of the well-dressed man who invaded the house at 113 North Nineteenth Street" on the night of January 6, 1911, and lured away eight-year-old Abraham Brown. The stranger appeared at the workshop of the boy's father, Joseph Brown, on the first floor. Samuel Zimmerman was there, working at a sewing machine while singing at the same time. The intruder said that Zimmerman's voice sounded like that of a child and inquired if Brown's son was nearby. Zimmerman summoned the child from the basement where he had been playing. Zimmerman could understand little English and did not fathom what proceeded next. The stranger picked up the boy without informing any member of the boy's family, who were in another part of the house. The captor and the boy visited a saloon, where the man purchased a drink, and after visiting several other locations, finally wound up at a grocery store at 1608 East Franklin Street. "Thoroughly frightened," Abraham, at the first opportunity, dashed out of the store and ran home. The man, realizing that the boy had fled, soon disappeared. The father said he had no known enemies and could not offer any theory on the intended kidnapping.[4]

Occasionally, a false kidnapping was reported. In April 1906, quite a stir resulted from information that four-year-old Ruth Anderson Lockhart, supposedly the daughter and heiress of the $100,000 estate of C. D. Lockhart of Pittsburgh, had been kidnapped. It was thought she had been whisked away by Jessie Russell, alias Mrs. J. S. Foushee. The story was picked up by the *New York Journal*. That newspaper did a little investigation on its own and discovered that the child's mother was living in Richmond and was the daughter of an Atlantic City, New Jersey, barber; the father was a salesman for installment houses. Actually, the child had been removed from her home by the Children's Home Society. The real story was that this institution was holding the girl while awaiting payment of $100 due for the child's board.[5]

16. Kidnappers

In 1909, fear gripped Richmonders that the Black Hand (an early name for the Italian Mafia) were involved in a scheme to kidnap children of wealthy parents in Richmond. Letters, supposedly from members of the Black Hand, were sent to three affluent businessmen, threatening to kidnap their children if ransom was not paid. Richmond police and postal inspectors investigated, but no clues surfaced. The houses of the intended victims were staked out by police. Nothing further of the plot appeared, and the scrutiny had to be abandoned.[6]

Certain groups allegedly kidnapped children. In 1875, John Shield, manager of the Theatre Comique in Petersburg, was accused of luring away children. On a charge of "abducting and secreting" seventeen-year-old Adalaide Hutchings of Richmond, he was acquitted at trial.[7] In 1907, Mother Frances Turner, of the Church of God, was arrested and charged with abducting four children of Samuel Dabney, of Barton Heights (in Richmond). Turner planned to deliver the children to an orphanage in Baltimore. A magistrate in Richmond, however, did not certify the charge for trial, but instead warned "Mother Turner" not to proceed, and dismissed the case.[8]

Traffic in infants at "baby farms," unlicensed homes or hospitals from where the children were sent out for adoption, invited a crackdown by authorities. Mrs. Sarah Kelly ran a "baby farm" at 211 North Twenty-eighth Street. She had been denied a license by both city and state officials. Brought into Police Court, she was fined $25 and warned that another appearance in court would necessitate a jail sentence. Sarah had taken in seven babies; two died, and two more died after they had been removed. Investigation revealed that other such establishments in the city had deplorable conditions similar to that offered by Mrs. Kelly. All had insufficient financial support from patrons to afford healthy and competent care.[9]

The Virginia Maternity Home, at 100 West Clay Street, came under censure for sending infants to persons who gave improper care. In particular, the Home dispatched seven female babies to a Mrs. Gudgeon in Tampa, Florida. Mrs. Gudgeon herself was childless and illiterate. The age of the infants ranged from six weeks to six months. It seemed that Mrs. Gudgeon planned to broker the adoption of the babies. Two persons from the Home in Richmond went to Florida when word came that the babies in Tampa were found to be starving, improperly attended to, and living amidst unsanitary conditions. The infants were too sickly to bring back to Richmond, and, therefore, a Florida county judge assigned six of the babies to the Tampa Children's Home and allowed for the adoption by "a private family" of the seventh.[10]

Concerning instances of an adult detaining a child not his or her own, two similar cases had an unusual twist—of fleeing with a child into the woods. In March 1907 a man abducted a white girl of about five or six off the street in the neighborhood of Marshall and Twenty-sixth streets. The abductor was about fifty-five to sixty years of age, gray-bearded, and wearing a long black coat, dark trousers, and a slouch hat. Holding the girl by one hand and a cane in the other, the man descended into a ravine at Thirty-sixth and Marshall streets. A search party spotted the fleeing couple some one hundred yards away in the woods, but no one wanted to fire for fear of hitting the child. Eventually the man and the child "disappeared as completely as if the ground had opened up and swallowed them." Witnesses said that they had heard the girl pleading to be allowed to go home to her mother. Unbelievably, no one reported a missing child, and, apparently, no further details were forthcoming.[11]

Similarly, in November of the same year (1907), fourteen-year-old Asby Spears, a Henrico County school boy, was grabbed near Dumbarton School by a black man who was wanted for a holdup. Apparently the abductor had been hiding in the nearby woods for several weeks while searchers looked for him. With the boy in tow, the criminal took a long trek through the dense woods. Several times during the lengthy walk, during which the man spoke not a word, the boy heard voices, but escape was prevented by dashing further away. When the two fugitives at last came to a spot in the woods near Glen Allen Station, where "the underbrush is thickest and where man is seldom seen," the fugitive went through the boy's pockets and relieved him of his overcoat, cap, collar, necktie, collar button, and the lunch he was carrying to school. Then the thief headed from the woods toward railroad tracks over which a slow freight train would soon pass. After this ordeal, Asby made it back home.[12]

One form of kidnapping was to lure young women and girls into prostitution. Richmond had some 500 to 600 active prostitutes at the beginning of the 1900s, and from 1905 to 1915 it had a legally sanctioned red-light district on all of Mayo Street (encompassing several blocks). The city's main problem with prostitution concerned the white slave traffic, particularly bringing in and holding in bondage young women emigrating from abroad or from the countryside. The federal Mann Act of 1910 prohibited the bringing of persons across state lines for the purpose of immoral conduct. The Virginia Code of 1904 stated that no one should detain any woman or take charge of a female under sixteen years of age as concubine or prostitute upon penalty of three to ten years in the penitentiary; any accessory in such crime faced two to five years' imprisonment.¹³ From time to time, collusion between police and other officials and the white slave traffic surfaced.¹⁴

For a while a main source of obtaining young girls for prostitution involved the "so-called maternity homes," which operated under a state charter. These places, often presided over by "disreputable women," were actually "assignation houses," where children might be disposed of by being given to some person of ill-repute or even sold into "the New Orleans whore house market."¹⁵

A favorite way to bring young country girls into prostitution in Richmond was to lure them to the city with the promise of employment, usually in one of the millineries or tobacco factories. Once alighting from the train, the victim would run across a person who would show her around, ending up in a house of ill-repute.¹⁶ Or, a girl could be a resident of Richmond and face the same situation. Thus was the case of one particular fifteen-year-old girl, described as "pale and fragile" and an employee of a tobacco factory. Her mother, who sewed for a living, said of the girl that she never had any interest in boys or young men." Leo Kidd, twenty-two years old and regarded by police as a "menace to every girl allowed to run the streets of Richmond without a guardian," picked up the girl outside a theater, where she had been waiting to meet the actors. The man offered to take the girl to supper. Instead, the pair showed up at a local brothel. In court, Kidd wore "a loud white and black overcoat," an "ascot tie high in color," and a white vest; he carried under his arm "a fluffy, little French poodle. He was as self-assured as if he was on a Broad Street corner, in all his regalia, ogling passing women."¹⁷

One "sacrifice" to the white slave trade was that of twenty-three-year-old Olaa Thaxton, who was lured from North Carolina "by a worthless rake who deceived her and kept her in a miserable joint on 18th Street." She escaped. Found sleeping in a lumber yard, she was brought before the Police Court, which sentenced her to ninety days in jail. She caught pneumonia and died. The body was dispatched to a pickling vat at the Medical College. A local woman gave money to allow the body to be sent to Thaxton's home in North Carolina.¹⁸

Local procurers were constantly on the lookout for girls loose on the street to be enticed into houses of ill-repute. The quarry responded to offers for a sleeping place, employment, or a gift, such as candy or money.¹⁹

Except for the period when Richmond had its legalized red-light district, 1905–1915, police sporadically made raids on alleged brothels. Frequently the denizens of these places had ample warning and avoided arrest or obtained dismissal of their cases. Sentences included putting the accused to work cleaning cells at police stations, vacating the premises of a brothel, or, most likely, some jail time and a fine. Typically, in the 1880s, penalties were a fine up to $25 and three months in jail; security up to $300 was also required, with failure to pay this sum resulting in jail time of six to twelve months.[20] Men, as well as women, had charge of brothels. In 1876, John Fick, found guilty of running such a place, was convicted in Hustings Court and fined $50 and jailed for thirty days.[21]

The legalized red-light district came to an end after a decade for a variety of reasons, as determined by a vice commission:

> 1. The segregated district did not segregate. Three times as many prostitutes were carrying on their activities outside the district.
>
> 2. Local vice interests had corrupted a number of respectable hotels and boarding houses located in various parts of the city, and taxicab chauffeurs and messenger boys were being used to solicit.
>
> 3. White girls were living in certain disorderly houses which were managed by Negro proprietors.
>
> 4. Much procuring was going on.
>
> 5. Most of the prostitutes in disorderly houses were mentally subnormal.
>
> 6. Unnatural vice was being fostered for commercial purposes and was a growing evil.
>
> 7. Narcotics were in some of the houses.
>
> 8. Certain members of the police force were receiving graft from disorderly houses.[22]

Closure for the red light district came in February 1915.[23]

From time to time, children went missing, most likely while on an errand or on their way to or from school.[24] Notices were posted for boys who simply wandered off. In August 1888, a Richmond newspaper published a letter from the Rev. E. Anderson, a Methodist pastor in Tryon City, North Carolina, to the police chief of Richmond:

> Dear Sir,
>
> My son Frank left home July 24, and we have not heard from him since. Although we have searched, written, and telegraphed in different directions, we can get no trace of him. He is thirteen years old, rather small for his age; light complexion, and light but coarse, stiff hair; he wore gray knee-pants and calico waist, straw hat, and was barefooted. His clothes were considerably worn. If you will make a thorough search in the machine shops and among railroad hands and elsewhere you may find him. He may change his name. Please do this great favor for me and let me know at once. If found take care of him till I get there.[25]

16. Kidnappers

Ten year-old Edward F. Thurston, in December 1883, followed an organ grinder and his monkey toward Hollywood Cemetery, near which he met another boy, who had had cigars which he said he was on the way to deliver. Ned went off with this boy. They wound up on a railroad track twenty-seven miles from Richmond. They slept in an empty boxcar, and existed on green apples and blackberries. After a week, during which time his father placed notices in the newspapers and at Sunday schools, Ned returned home.[26]

Girls also wandered off, most likely to elope.[27] Boys and girls, as "wanderers," who went from Richmond to another large city, were held in detention, usually by an aid society, until provisions could be made to send them home.[28]

Juveniles inclined toward criminality were candidates for running away. A "small negro boy," in 1894, wanted for robbery and assault, fled. When caught, unable to obtain security for good behavior, he was sentenced to thirty days in jail.[29]

Elley B. Runyon, a Richmond boy, teamed up with Julian D. Whichard, a boy from Atlanta, for a series of robberies in southern cities from Atlanta to Washington, D.C. Once the boys were caught, Runyon's mother came up from Richmond to the nation's capital, whereupon Runyon was declared mentally incapable and sent to the Boys' Republic, near Annapolis, Maryland. While diving with other boys in shallow water, Runyon damaged his spinal cord, and was paralyzed. At St. Luke's Hospital, Runyon exhibited a "dual personality, a condition attributed to some strange pressure on the brain." It was concluded that while "in the grasp of this evil self," he had become a thief.[30]

Some juveniles ran away in the hopes of entering show business. On January 11, 1887, a Richmond newspaper noted:

> The little negro Monk who left here in the fall of 1885 with the Chanfrau has been heard from. Police Justice Richardson received a letter from him this morning, in which he said that he was stranded in Chicago; that the manager of the [theatrical] company had left him in the city without any funds and he was dead broke, with no prospect of securing another engagement. He says he has gotten his fill of show business and wants to come home.[31]

Ruth Mallory, of Richmond, a fifteen-year-old, was arrested as a runaway in October 1910. She had joined a juvenile traveling troupe, the Peerless Minstrels, as a singer. Little Dennis O'Neil, "the boy vocalist," led the group of three boys and three girls. They performed in vaudeville shows. Awaiting a court appearance, Ruth stayed at the Associated Charities building.[32] Several Richmond youths went missing, having set out to link up with a moving picture company.[33]

Adventurous children who left home, becoming disappointed, like the "Prodigal Son," returned. A newspaper item of June 1879 declared that

> two youngsters from Cowardin avenue, who have been absent from the city some time, and have travelled throughout the South in search of a fortune, returned here a few days ago, and are deeply impressed with the fact that there is no place like home.[34]

Warren Cousins, missing for a month, "ragged, weary and forlorn," returned to the "open arms of his widowed mother, who had given up hope of ever seeing him again live." While in Baltimore, Warren's money had run out. Unable to find a job, Warren hired out on a barge to earn his passage home.[35]

While on his way to school, ten-year-old Frank Strang disappeared. He teamed up with George Lavender, an army infantryman recently discharged from the service. Frank became "very much attached" to the former soldier. George took a job as a policeman in Hopewell and had to leave Frank with his mother in Danville. Mrs. Lavender notified Richmond police, but said that she would not part with Frank unless she was sure that the boy would be returned to his parents. Mrs. Strang journeyed to Danville to bring Frank home.[36]

For a child to disappear, either by abduction or running away, was less feasible than in modern times. Before the explosion of all forms of communication in the twentieth century, and of relatively sparse population, one found escape more limited. Someone fleeing, whether by railroad, boat, wagon, horse, or simply walking, was more noticeable than exiting by automobile or aircraft and mingling among vast crowds on the move.

One form of kidnapping had a similarity to bunco—steering-shanghaing. Youths were lured aboard a ship at dock and forced to become part of an enslaved crew. In October 1906, Joe Burruss and Charlie Wells, both eighteen years old, went off on an oyster boat. Wells quickly escaped and returned to Richmond. Burruss endured his ordeal until January 1907 when he escaped by rowboat off Crisfield, Maryland. He had actually been paid $15 a month and had no complaint about his treatment while on the oyster boat except that he was not allowed to go ashore.[37]

"Weak from exposure and the lack of food," William B. Keene, an African American sailor, after an absence of more than two months, reappeared in Richmond. He had been shanghaied, and eventually made good his escape. According to Keene's story, he had been approached by a man offering a good salary as a cook aboard the *James E. Wells*, a "regular trader" at American ports. Keene decided to investigate the offer, but once aboard, the ship immediately weighed anchor. The captain said he was short-handed. Most of the rest of the crew, consisting chiefly of foreigners, had also been shanghaied. Keene and the crew experienced great hardship, having very little food and insufficient clothing for inclement weather. The vessel was frequently hailed by police boats, whereupon the crew was locked up below deck among the illicit cargo. When the *James E. Wells* pulled on to a wharf in Norfolk, Virginia, almost totally disabled, the captain disappeared, and Keene managed to escape.[38]

17

Fugitive Felons

Prison escapees and outlaws on the loose, fending for themselves, had to be every bit as cunning as bunco artists finagling unwary citizens. Richmond and Henrico County's enforcement officials kept a sharp lookout for criminals who had escaped custody in the city or from jurisdictions far and wide.

Most fearsome of fugitives were those hard-timers who broke out of the state penitentiary. Even to be around ex-convicts caused uneasiness. At a neighborhood just west of the city (called Harvie) residents armed themselves for protection. A newspaper notice warned of potential danger from the "colored ex-convict birds."[1]

The penitentiary had its share of spectacular escapes. In March 1882, two brothers, James T. and Albert G. Batton, absconded from the penitentiary. They and their younger brother, O. W. Batton, had been sentenced to eighteen years each for the murder of their father. At the time of the homicide, in 1878, they were twenty-two, twenty, and eighteen, respectively. James and Albert, confined on the upper floor of the prison, cut through the slate roof, and from there descended into the outer yard by way of a lightning rod. They had with them a rope fashioned from a blanket which, at its end, had a hook made from pieces of a bedstead. The prisoners threw the hook over the wall, latching on to the parapet. From the top of the wall they lowered themselves into an open lot and made good their escape. Freedom was short-lived; the escapees were caught in Princess Anne County, shackled, and returned to the penitentiary.[2]

"The wildest excitement prevailed in the vicinity of the penitentiary" on the afternoon of July 12, 1885. Hugh Nixon and Edward Green, "two of the most desperate convicts in the prison," had scaled the fence enclosing the prison grounds and entered the adjacent Hollywood Cemetery. A large crowd of men and boys went in pursuit. Both escapees were soon captured—Nixon being wounded by birdshot. The two prisoners had effected their escape "by filing the wrought-iron bolts in the top of the iron grating and forced the grating outwardly, bending it down on its bearings." Then, with a rope made from strips of bed ticks and blankets, they lowered themselves to the ground. They placed a ladder, made from the boards taken from their bunks, on a woodpile in the corner of the prison yard and, from there, climbed over the wall.[3]

Most other attempts to break out of the state penitentiary were also foiled at the point of the convicts gaining freedom. Escapees used tools of their own manufacture, such as saws made from knives, ropes from blankets, and imitation pistols of wood covered with tinfoil.[4]

In March 1916, after thirteen years on the lam and a "terrific fight with North Carolina officers," C. W. Bouldin, a "badman" was brought to the Virginia State Penitentiary. He had escaped from the state farm, an adjunct of the penitentiary just west of Richmond. Bouldin had "roamed practically over the entire country." He thought he was immune from arrest as long as he stayed out of Virginia. He had returned to his "old haunts" in North Carolina.[5]

Breaking out of the old, dilapidated Richmond jail posed fewer risks than did escaping the state penitentiary. Three hotel thieves exited the Richmond jail on the night of November 28, 1878, and managed to hitch a ride on a C. & O. freight train. At Hanover Junction, the three men jumped from the train and into the woods; subsequently, they made good their escape.[6]

Despite being understaffed, guards at the Richmond jail managed to thwart well-laid schemes to escape. Such was the situation of Henry Byers, a black "accomplished jail-breaker." Arrested and lodged in the Exchange Hotel, he escaped handcuffed, but was captured. Next he was confined at the station house. One morning guards discovered that he had "dug a big hole in the brick wall of his cell." At first there was no indication of how Henry was able to cut through the brick wall so quickly. What he had done, it was finally determined, was first to scrape the cemented plaster from the surface of the bricks and then dislodge them. Henry had mapped off, "with geometrical precision," the lines for the cutting. Officers found in Henry's vest pocket a small satchel-key only an inch long, which was the tool he used to cut "by perseverance and muscle" through the bricks.[7]

While the majority of escapees were caught, some jailbirds managed to break free. On Saturday night, September 12, 1885, James Maxwell, a sailor in jail for stealing a ship's compass, and J. H. Robinson, imprisoned for housebreaking, escaped. They obtained a piece of scantling about four feet long, which they used to bend the bottom end of the iron door of their cell, and crawled under it, into the corridor. Getting outside, they jumped from a porch into the jail yard, at the northwest corner of which was a woodpile stacked up against the outer wall of the jail. It was easy then to scale the wall. Robinson was captured several days later, but Maxwell remained free.[8] Six months later Frank Renfrew and Charles Williams, two burglars awaiting trial, made good their escape by using wood planks from the cell floor to bend outwards grating on the cell door; rope supplied by visiting friends further aided the escape.[9] In November 1888, Morton Riley, a diamond thief, and George Monta, who had burglarized a restaurant, easily exited from the jail. They simply hid in a closet outside their cells and scaled walls by using a rope fashioned from a blanket, which had a board two feel long attached at each end.[10]

William Jefferson, alias "Indian Bill," in jail for default of a security bond, and Scott King, alias Tom Walker, in April 1889, took advantage of being employed in the jail's kitchen to escape. The two prisoners had been working in the evenings and had full access to the jail yard. They went to the laundry, where they picked up a rope. At the Marshall Street wall they let themselves down to the ground outside by means of the rope. This seems to have been but one of a rash of escapes from the jail in the short period of several months. Besides the escape of Riley and Monta, mentioned above, the other escapes were

> the champagne and cigar thief, who committed a big robbery at the Exposition, who escaped together by hiding behind the water closet when the prisoners were drawn up in line to be counted, and being left out climbed to the roof of the jail by means of a rope made of blankets, and jumped into Jail alley; W. C. Bryant, a fugitive from justice from Danville, and charged with carrying concealed weapons, who acted as jail carpenter, and walked away in broad daylight; William Blackwell, the Kentucky thief who deftly disappeared, and two youths who neatly got away about Christmas.[11]

More embarrassing was an escape from the holding pen at Police Court by a prisoner waiting to be called before the presiding justice. In 1895, Charles Johnson, arrested as a suspicious person, escaped while guards were distracted by the proceedings of the Police Court, by climbing over the open top of the pen. The "openings to the pen were covered with wire netting after this incident and nothing bigger than a humming bird could gain exit through the same way."[12]

The Henrico County jail, located in downtown Richmond, had a mass jail break during the night of December 10, 1916, when two black prisoners overpowered the sheriff, Harry G. Heckler. The leaders of the revolt, Percy Gaddy and James Young, "two giants," after seizing Hechler in the corridor, took the sheriff's keys and went about "liberating the prisoners, opening one cell after another and commanding the inmates to come out and accompany them." Young had obtained the deputy sheriff's revolver from the downstairs office. The sheriff was tied up but soon freed himself. Seven prisoners calmly walked out of the jail and onto Main Street. Two later voluntarily returned. Within a half an hour after the escape, forty city and county policemen were in pursuit, and police of nearby towns were alerted. But the escapees had made a clean getaway.[13] A month later four of the escapees were still at large.[14]

Women prisoners at the state penitentiary had an easier time escaping than did the male convicts. The female department of the prison consisted of several frame buildings situated in a yard enclosed by a wooden fence, separate from the penitentiary proper. In the yard, a guard stood duty day and night. An escape, en masse, occurred in the female department in August 1878. Two white women—Amelia Roussell and Jennie Beatty, the latter known as "Irish Jennie"—shared a room together on the second floor of the middle building. They cut a hole through the plaster partition and crawled through it, out into the hall from which they walked into the yard. The three black women—Susanna Collins, Columbia Collins, and Mary Hall—occupied a cell together in another building; they burned a hole through the wooden door of their cell, and, unfastening the hook, made their way into the yard. Susanna and Columbia were mother and daughter. Susanna had her eight-month-old baby with her when she escaped. The women joined together, and by simply prying open a wooden door in the fence surrounding the yard, they gained their freedom. The escape was not noticed until the following morning, when a guard made his rounds to feed the prisoners. The escapees were tracked down Westham Road to a gypsy camp, where dogs were sent toward the escapees, who then disappeared. The three black women were captured after several days of freedom; the white women, however, evaded arrest.[15] Interestingly "Irish Jennie," a convicted murderer, in July 1874 had enjoyed a brief stint of freedom by walking out of the penitentiary in men's clothes.[16]

Lizzie Dodson, a nineteen-year-old black girl, already serving a second confinement at the penitentiary, escaped during a breakfast break in December 1900. Stepping up from a bench in the yard, she scaled a twelve-foot fence. She had clad herself in men's clothing. Lizzie was apprehended near her old home in Fairfax County the following April. She seriously wounded one of the police officers who arrested her by using a pistol she had concealed under her shawl. It was now expected that Lizzie would serve the rest of her life in prison.[17]

On New Year's Eve 1907, two black women, Ida Owens and Jennie Strange, made an easy escape from the Henrico County jail in Richmond. They went through a window, a "tier of cells," and through three doors, all of which had been left unlocked. They walked through the sheriff's office and left through a side door. "Store-keepers in the neighborhood saw them walk leisurely down Main Street to Twenty-first street, where they turned towards the river."[18]

Richmond police picked up fugitives from other jurisdictions. Among out-of-state escapees arrested in Richmond were those fleeing from Patterson, New Jersey (1876); New York City (1878 and 1897); Kentucky (1888); Baltimore (1888); West Virginia (1897); Philadelphia (1899); and Ohio (1900).[19]

One "all-around outlaw," Stanley Williams, managed to live "in outlawry for many months, camping in the suburbs of the city, and defying the officers." He was wanted for "sundry offences," including assault. On one occasion he escaped from a police station by jumping out of a second-story window. He was finally arrested while standing on the corner of Sixteenth and Marshall streets.[20]

Probably the most notorious and long-sought-after fugitive by Richmond authorities was Joseph Rapley, alias "Topeka Joe." According to a newspaper report, Topeka Joe was

> a notable figure in criminal annals. He is known from one end of the country to the other as a desperate man, and he has achieved note as a bank burglar of nerve and pluck. He has never served time in a penitentiary, but has been arrested many times. He always succeeded in getting off at the trial.

For a decade Topeka Joe was associated with a "hobo" gang, consisting of John Butler (alias "Frisco Slim"), Edward Carney (alias "Hutch"), Sylvester Collins (alias "Dashing Billy"), John Hamilton (alias "Brooklyn Johnny"), John Gilchrist (alias "Providence Slim"), and others known by their aliases only: "Michigan Red," "Shenandoah Red," "Child Jack," and "Denver Harry." On July 23, 1900, Topeka Joe was arrested in Portland, Oregon, by Pinkerton detectives and city police for the robbery of the Peninsular Bank of Williamsburg, Virginia, on May 4, 1900. This was one of the most daring robberies in Virginia's history, netting $5,000 in cash and $3,500 in other valuables. The robbery was accomplished by blowing open the safe. Topeka was brought to the Richmond jail on August 13, 1900.

The following month, on September 3, 1900, Topeka Joe escaped from the Richmond jail. This was not surprising as the jail was in dilapidated condition. But the escape was a remarkable one because of the ease and speed by which it was accomplished. Topeka Joe had been able to make a wooden key and a sixty-foot rope made from bed ticking, with which "he scaled the inside wall without detection." The next time Topeka Joe was heard from was when he had been arrested with two cohorts for the robbery of the West Toledo post office, in Ohio. On the morning of July 30, 1900, Topeka Joe and several other prisoners made their escape from the Toledo jail by exhibiting two pistols they somehow obtained. A wide search by state and federal officials did not discover the ingenious "yeggman." A watch at his former headquarters, a saloon that he had operated in Baltimore, did not produce any results.[21]

Richmonders had a fascination with the famous outlaws of the time. In June 1903, the Younger and James Wild West Show, headed by two noted ex-outlaws—fifty-eight-year-old Cole Younger and sixty-year-old Frank James—gave performances in Richmond, at Main and Vine streets. The show could not obtain permission for a parade because of "the disturbed state of affairs" due to a full-fledged trolley-car strike. A newspaper report stated that "the careers of these men have been marked by a greater number of thrilling adventures than the histories of any other two living men." Frank James had been tried several times for alleged crimes of robbery and murder, but was acquitted in each case. Cole Younger, according to the Richmond print notice, looked "like a well-groomed, modestly attired lawyer or doctor." At a prison in Oklahoma he had been a preacher, giving "carefully prepared, excellent sermons of a character calculated to convince his hearers that when they regained freedom they should lead moral lives."[22]

18

Forgers

Check flashing, or forgery, frequently required tracking by law enforcement personnel—ranging from policemen to the Allan Pinkerton National Detective Agency. Of course, bank tellers often sounded the initial alert. Forgers, as did most bunco-artists, often operated under false identities.

Forgery usually involved signing someone else's name on a bank draft or check as payer or payee; endorsements were also put on bad checks. A common trick was to hike a check; a slight turn of the pen could raise the amount on demand. Among many instances of this practice in Richmond were upping amounts from $7 to $915; $7 to $70; $10 to $50; $15 to $50; $15 to $950; and $275 to $2,000 or $3,500.[1] It was relatively easy to change number amounts on checks. In one instance, for example, all but the first two letters of "thirty" were erased; then the word was made into "three"; with no line drawn from this word to the end of the line, the word "thousand" was added.[2]

Most forgeries involved individuals versus individuals or in cheating retailers while making purchases.[3] Some con artists would post orders with suppliers fraudulently billed to retailers.[4] Many forgeries were drawn on accounts from out-of-state banks, therefore increasing the amount of time before the crime was discovered.[5]

Forgers were known to visit Richmond, dump fraudulent paper, usually drawn on out-of-town banks and firms, and then quickly depart from the city.[6] In the investigation of forgers caught in Richmond, it was not unusual to find that the culprit was a fugitive for the same offense from other cities.[7] Virginia law did not allow for the extradition for any theft that did not measure up to grand larceny, normally $50 or more.[8] There were, however, exceptions. For example, there was R. H. Thompson, thirty-five years old and recently discharged from service in Richmond as a sergeant in charge of Marine Corps recruiting, who stole a mere $34 from Mrs. E. F. Webster, in whose home on East Franklin Street he had roomed. The Pinkertons were called in to track him down. Apprehended in Columbus, Ohio, extradition was granted to return him to Richmond for trial.[9]

Confidence men used forgery in the cause of supposed charity. In April 1893, J. Harvey Blair, a young "sharper," went to the office of a businessman and persuaded him to endorse a check, of which Blair promised to turn over "a goodly portion" to the Christian Endeavor Societies of the city. The businessman accompanied Blair to a bank, and vouching for the check, it was cashed. Of the $816.30 check, Blair gave $150 to the businessman to deposit with the charity. Blair then disappeared with the remaining $666.30.[10] In July 1911, Louis B. Phillip, an employee of the black mutual assistance organization, the Grand Fountain, United Order of True Reformers, was arrested for writing worthless checks on this group.[11]

An unusual case of forgery involved the name of a prominent society woman of Richmond, Mrs. Norman V. Randolph. Someone sent letters, "crudely written and couched in maudlin terms," to local merchants, soliciting funds and supplies in the name of poor people or charitable institution. Typical of the forged letters going to retailers was one that went out by a special messenger:

> Please excuse my taking up your time, but have heard you have one of the kindest hearts in the world and today we belong to a missionary society and have a case of the greatest poverty—a lady whose husband has been ill in bed for nineteen months and who had fore [sic] little children. We are trying to raise today the money for her rent, and if you will help us you will be doing the greatest charity. She hasn't a cent and is behind two months [in rent]. I would have called on you myself, but am sick in bed. We will never forget your kindness should you help.

With many good wishes, I am
Very Truly
(Signed)
MRS. NORMAN RANDOLPH[12]

Probably the youngest of Richmond's forgers was Jacob Baker, an eleven-year-old "colored boy." Jacob had gone to the store of W. W. Taylor with a forged order supposedly signed by W. H. Nelson for a box of Virginia cheroots. The boy professed that the order had been handed to him by an unknown man. Police had the boy seek out the unknown man in a stakeout, but the suspect did not appear, and Jacob was taken into custody.[13]

In February 1913, Wesley George, a sixteen-year-old white boy, was apprehended for "flashing" four worthless checks, with which he sought to purchase merchandise. At the police station, Wesley said that "I haven't a word to say. I've done all the talking I'm going to." Because of his youthful, innocent appearance, the boy (who was still in short pants) had easily persuaded the merchant to cash the checks. Wesley claimed to be from New York City and Columbia, South Carolina, but said he knew no one in those places. Efforts of the police to find his parents came to naught. It was surmised that the boy might be "the tool of a professional check flasher."[14] One African American girl found herself in trouble when she went into Pledge's Confectionary Store and presented the owner with an order: "Will you please send me ten ponds french candy, 5 ponds of rason, and charge it to Mr. John Purcell." The note bore Mr. Purcell's forged signature. The girl, Lizzie Anderson, seemed so guilty that the Police Court justice sent her case forward for trial in Hustings Court.[15]

There were some high-profile cases of check flashing in Richmond. In July 1874, a "man calling himself James K. Van Ness, having a gentlemanly appearance" and "about sixty-five years old, gray hair, side whiskers, and light complexion," represented himself as an agent for Commodore Cornelius Vanderbilt of New York, and said he had come to the city to purchase, for Vanderbilt, one or more flour mills and a large factory. He exhibited four $100,000 bank drafts, one for $150,000, and one for $200,000, drawn in favor of Van Ness. Negotiations proceeded to the actual purchase of "one large establishment" and "the conditional sale" of another valuable property. The president of a local Richmond bank, however, made inquiry of a correspondent in New York by telegraph, and received a reply that Vanderbilt did not know Van Ness. Detectives arrested Van Ness in his hotel room. Discovered upon the prisoner were twenty-five keys (seven of which were for safe-deposit boxes) and four pocketbooks, containing fraudulent drafts, signed C. Vanderbilt, for amounts of $2,700 to $50,000, totaling $160,000.[16]

Upon the death of the Reverend Jeremiah Bell Jeter, the executor of the popular preacher's estate discovered that some individuals and banks held negotiable notes endorsed by Jeter and Dr. Luther R. Dickinson, the publisher of the *Southern Planter and Farmer*. It was discovered that these notes were forgeries, bearing the names of Jeter and Dickinson, proprietors of the *Religious Herald*, and also Dickinson's brothers-in-law, the Reverend George B. Taylor of Rome, Italy, and Charles E. Taylor, a professor at Wake Forest College. The brothers-in-law connections facilitated the acceptance of the forged notes, which amounted to $28,000. Dickinson left Richmond to visit a sick brother in Louisa County, and then disappeared.[17]

In March 1895, Burnley Taylor, Commissioner of Revenue for King

William County, was arrested by Richmond police officers and brought to the city to be arraigned for forging a check of $192.50, fraudulently representing the cost of one year's board and cost of clothing for a lunatic, one Mary Young.[18] In 1918, the Pinkerton National Detective Agency was assisting Richmond police in attempting to locate N. L. Massey, who had skipped town after exposure of multiple forgeries coming in the aggregate to $36,000.[19]

One forgery case became a cause célèbre, despite the fact that the amount involved in two instances totaled only $120. Witnesses were called from the state's leading politicians; defense counselors were noted lawyers James Barbour, John S. Wise (son of a governor and himself a gubernatorial candidate), and Major General James G. Field (later a candidate for vice president of the United States). Colonel C. T. Crittenden, paymaster and doorkeeper of the House of Delegates, was charged with two counts of forgery. Pay certificates had been issued to the amounts of $18 each to J. W. Poindexter, an African American delegate from Louisa County, and J. L. Arthur, a delegate from Bedford County. The funds represented three days per diem at $6 for legislative service. The certificates were given to Crittenden to collect endorsements on the back of the checks. Crittenden raised the amount to $78 for thirteen days each and gave $18 to Poindexter and Arthur, pocketing the remainder ($60 each for the two delegates). Crittenden's receipt books showed that the two delegates had received the correct amounts, $18 each. Crittenden, examined in court, could not account for the extra $120.

General Field conducted a brilliant defense of Crittenden. He demonstrated that Crittenden's endorsement of the pay warrants did not prove that these certificates had been given to him. Furthermore, it was pointed out that Crittenden, within minutes of discovery of the forgery, admitted his responsibility and planned to repay the Treasury, but after his arrest could not do so "without incurring the suspicion of paying 'hush-money.'" The "magnanimity" in assuming legal responsibility, it was argued, proved his innocence. General Field said that

> he appeared not as a feed attorney, but as a friend bound to the prisoner by hooks of steel, having ... eat[en] with him, slept with him, fought with him, bled with and [fallen] with him.... Because Lucifer fell that was no reason other angels must too. Defense might by technicalities of the law have estopped conviction. That was not what they wanted. They desired honorable acquittal. The indictment with its several counts in it was described as a shower of grapeshot; in the hope that one would strike; whereas if the Commonwealth's Attorney had been certain of his case he would have fired one single rifle-shot. Crittenden had felt grape-shot before and had been stricken down. In this case he was wounded—sorely wounded—by

A cartoon of a convicted forger and his excuse, as seen in the pages of the Richmond *Daily Times*, September 19, 1897.

being held up to the gaze of the world as a forger; but he would recover. Yes, recover, even as he recovered from wounds received upon a more ensanguined field, and the chief regret of the people of this city in a few days would be that this young man had been incarcerated at all under so unjust a charge.

James Barbour, for the defense, presented an equally spirited argument. Among the many points he made, perhaps the most telling was that, as he said, "If the man in the Auditor's office had been worth 'a baubee he would have detected the errors within three days'"; the responsibility for overpayment belonged to the Auditor. On Saturday, May 5, 1877, after deliberating for only ten minutes, a Hustings Court jury brought in a verdict of "not guilty."[20]

Another high-profile forgery case occurred in the fall of 1891. William S. Dashiell, of the real estate firm of Dashiell and Cobb, was charged with forging the name of J. L. Ludwig on several notes involving the estate of the late William C. Ludwig, totaling the sum of $3,550. The thirty-six-year-old Dashiell had been the manager of the affairs of the four Ludwig brothers and was the executor for William's estate. A trial was held from October 22 to 26, ending with an acquittal.[21]

A "check flasher," considered the "smoothest of the smooth," was C. H. Doyle, who went by many aliases. He was caught while trying to swindle a hotel manager in Denison, Texas. Doyle had committed his many felonies throughout the country. He hoodwinked Richmonders with fake checks in 1906, in the fall of 1907, and in June 1908, using in his last appearance in the city the alias of N. C. Gates. Doyle's forged checks were issued under the name of a "specialty or novelty company," such as Cincinnati Glaze and Electric Company, Utica Fixture Company, Buffalo Specialty Company, Missouri Glass Company of St. Louis, National Supply Company of New York City, and Providence Glaze Burner Company. As his method of operation, he would start by going to a hotel and registering for a room. The next day, at the clerk's desk, he would ask for his mail, whereupon an envelope he had addressed to himself would be handed to him; this would contain a check, payable to whichever alias Doyle was using.[22]

William B. Pizzini qualifies as Richmond's prince of swindlers. A real estate broker, of Italian and Jewish extraction, for about ten years he managed to divert funds of his clients for his own use to an amount ranging from $800,000 to $1 million. A grand jury indicted him on nineteen counts involving forgery and grand larceny. Particularly, he defrauded four Richmond banks. On the night of Thursday, January 4, 1917, he boarded a train for New York City. With law enforcement officials and Pinkerton detectives looking for him in major U.S. cities and Canada, with nothing turning up, it was assumed Pizzini headed for Costa Rica, Honduras, or Panama, countries where he did not need a passport; he was fluent in Spanish. Pizzini's properties and that of his mother, Annie Pizzini, were attached. Several of Pizzini's creditors had a federal district court declare him bankrupt. This action automatically removed all legal proceedings against Pizzini in other courts to the federal court and placed all creditors on the same footing. Forfeiture involved his expensively furnished mansion as well as his mother's property; embarrassingly, the vast stock of whiskey and wine found in the mansion could not be disposed of, as the law considered it a "dead asset," prohibited from either being sold or given away. Despite being a devoted family man with a wife and five children, Pizzini remained at large. He was never heard from again, and eventually his wife sued him for divorce.[23]

Entrapment could bring in a check flasher. Albert Schwabacher, alias J. C. Knowles, had such an experience in September 1904. A newcomer to the city, he registered at the Jefferson Hotel as being from Ohio. Schwabacher went to the office of R. A. Patterson and Company, and introduced himself as a member of the firm of Schwabacher and Company of Seattle, Washington, which allegedly had done business with the Patterson Company. Schwabacher made arrangements with John Landstreet, vice president of Patterson's, to meet the next day about placing an order with the Patterson Company. Landstreet had been warned from Seattle to be on the lookout for Schwabacher. He, therefore, contacted police. Captain Tomlinson, of the Richmond police force, showed up at Landstreet's office at the appointed time. Schwabacher arrived, and requested that someone from the Patterson Company go with him to the National Bank of Virginia to vouch for cashing a check of $150. The bank clerk, being suspicious, hesitated to complete the transaction. Officer Tomlinson was constantly nearby. Schwabacher left and got on a streetcar, only to find officer Tomlinson sitting next to him. When the conductor asked for fares, Tomlinson said that he and Schwabacher would not pay and that they would disembark at the next stop. This was done, and Tomlinson booked his prisoner at the Second Police Station. When interviewed by a newsman, Schwabacher said that he had been on business "of a commercial traveler, who bought up job lots of stuff," which he "disposed of in leading markets." When asked where his headquarters were located, Schwabacher replied, "In all the large cities." Schwabacher was charged with "attempting to utter a fraudulent draft" and for being a "suspicious character."[24]

There was a wide leeway in sentencing for forgery, with the maximum of ten years in the state penitentiary. Lucile Moore, a South Richmond girl, was convicted in Juvenile and Domestic Relations court, in May 1916, for passing worthless checks of $20 each at eight different retail places. Lucile would make small purchases and have the goods sent to her home or to a false address, keeping the change in cash. She was sent to the reform school for girls.[25]

A bogus check given to a grocer resulted in a four-month jail sentence.[26] A young man by the name of S. P. Woodson was convicted in Hustings Court for going to the Exchange Hotel, and, representing himself as a traveling salesman for the Fidelity Wall Paper Company of Philadelphia, exhibited a telegram authorizing Woodson to write a check for $25; this was done, and the hotel clerk cashed the check. The check was returned from the bank, and it was determined that the telegram had been a forgery. Woodson would spend the next two years in the penitentiary.[27]

Alfred Hopkins was convicted of "forging a paper for subscription to Rev. J. W. Dungee's church," and was sentenced to the penitentiary for five years.[28] The maximum penalty of ten years was sometimes imposed.[29] Robert Henry Epps, a "crafty negro forger," charged on four indictments, pleaded guilty and left his fate to the judge. "You are an intelligent negro," said the judge in pronouncing sentence, "and I think you are setting a bad example for your race, therefore, I propose to give you the full extent of the law. You are sentenced to serve ten years in the State penitenitiary."[30]

19

Embezzlers

Embezzlers, like forgers, appropriated funds illicitly. Embezzlers stole from persons or institutions who had entrusted property or money to their care. Richmond had its share of this stripe.

First of all, there were those who defrauded government. William E. Smith, a state tax collector, was arrested for applying to his own use moneys he had received; the Auditor's Office had no notice of these sums, amounting to nearly $2,000.[1] In October 1898, Joseph H. Shepherd, clerk in the office of Public Accounts, was arrested for deflecting to his own use, three years previously, moneys due Bedford and King William county commissioners of revenue. Shepherd had rubber-stamped three checks of $50 each, with payment to "or bearer." Shepherd was sent to the penitentiary for five years.[2]

In Spring 1891, E. Buford Grymes, clerk in the office of the City Treasurer, went to trial for being responsible for shortage in the amounts of $23.85, paid by Thalhimer Brothers; $6.15 paid by G. E. Schaeffer; $21 paid the Watkins Hardware Company; and $13.20 paid by J. L. Levy. The sums were to pay gas bills. In addition to three embezzlements for the missed gas bills, Grymes was also indicted on forgery counts. In all, the "Grymes deficit" in the treasurer's office amounted to $2,436.79. Found guilty, he went to the penitentiary for a year.[3]

E. A. Randolph, the "colored lawyer," was charged with "unlawfully and feloniously taking, stealing and carrying away, as guardian, the sum of $188.85 belonging to Arthur G. Forrester. Randolph admitted that he failed to invest the money as required by law and that he had spent it."[4]

George E. Crawford, real estate agent and "one of Richmond's first business men and well-known citizens," was charged with misappropriating $3,300 in funds entrusted to his care by Mrs. Catharine Peyronnett. Crawford was the executor of the estate of Mrs. Peyronnett's husband, and had been given the money by Mrs. Peyoronnett to invest. Crawford had lent the $3,300 from the estate to two "negroes," named Banks, on a farm he sold them in Charles City County. The loan was secured by the lien of a second mortgage; the interest was paid regularly until the Banks brothers defaulted on their payments in January 1897. After the case had been postponed three times, a *nolle prosequi* was entered in Hustings Court because of the discovery of a clerical error in the indictment.[5]

Embezzlement contributed to bringing down one of Richmond's most important banks. The Savings Bank of the Grand Fountain United Order of True Believers, the bank arm of the benevolent lodge which had opened in 1888, went under in 1910 amidst emerging revelations of improprieties of the bank's director and cashier. The bank dealt extensively in real estate, and among its many properties were a wholesale grocery establishment, the Hotel Reformer in Richmond, and a convalescent home on a farm just outside the city. Assets in real estate in 1903 amounted to $385,475.52. The bank had gathered capital from insurance, the real estate investments, and individual deposits. The crimes affecting the bank amounted to "criminal negligence and recklessness, fake mortgage transactions, conspiracy between officers and employees of the True Reformers' bank, grand larceny and petty peculations." Most of the depositors who suffered from the wrecking of the bank were "poor and illiterate colored people—laborers, washerwomen, domestics, barbers, waiters, stablemen, farmers and small shopkeepers." The person alleged to be most responsible for the bank's failure, Reuben T. Hill, the cashier, absconded and escaped capture. It was Hill who "got away with all the money that was actually stolen." Largely because of this assumption, the directors were acquitted, but later faced suits in Chancery Court for the unauthorized mortgaging of one specific property.[6]

In another bank swindle, John H. Harding, in 1914, was involved in a $13,000 shortfall that contributed to the folding of the Commonwealth Bank. Specifically, Harding had three grand larceny warrants against him for the theft of $1,400, $410, and $310, on three separate days. At trial, Harding was convicted for embezzlement of $700, and was sentenced to two years at the penitentiary.[7]

A clever scheme involving the search to hire one man wound up recruiting many. Appearing in a newspaper for Wednesday, August 21, 1895, was this notice:

> WANTED, AN HONEST YOUNG MAN of neat appearance (white or colored) between 18 and 24 for steady position of trust; some collecting. All references and $10 security required, and be willing to begin at $9 per week. Address K. P. Dispatch office.

The "shrewd fakir" who placed the advertisement was J. O. Connor. Claiming to be a manager for the Cook Portrait Company, he told the young men who answered his advertisement to report for work at 8:30 a.m., Monday, August 26; each applicant was required to deposit $10 with Connor by 5 p.m. Saturday, August 24. About a dozen white and black men gathered at the photographic gallery as planned on Monday morning, only to discover that Connor had no connection to this firm. Connor fled Richmond, only to return about two weeks later under the pseudonym R. M. Davis, of Baltimore; this time he was seeking a collector, and applicants again were to put up $10. Recognized while out on the street, Davis was identified as Connor, and arrested.[8]

"The man is purely a fraud and fake," so read a telegram sent to a Richmonder in November 1907 from the editorial department of the *New York World*. The reference was to "Diavolo [Jack Diavolo], the robust young man, smooth of face and tongue, who came to Richmond" on November 23, "representing that he had wagered $20,000 with Joseph Pulitzer of the *New York World*, on his (Diavolo's) ability to traverse the length of the United States and return to New York in seven months with $5,000 in his pocket." He carried with him a bogus agreement with Pulitzer that he (Diavolo), as the "champion daredevil bicycle rider of the world," would accumulate the $5,000 "by taking up collections after giving exhibitions on his wheel in the public streets, or by grit." He was prohibited to work or beg. The agreement stated that he had to visit Washington, Baltimore, Richmond, Atlanta, New Orleans, Omaha, Salt Lake City, Cincinnati, Cleveland, Chicago, Denver, and San Francisco. Diavolo "went through Richmond like an electric shock." He collected money from many Broad Street merchants; in one block of Broad he brought in $50. From a jeweler he received a gold ring and some cash; donations were from "a quarter up." In all, Jack Diavolo had 365 names on his donation list.

The *Richmond News-Leader* exposed Diavolo; he was arrested in Richmond and had a date in the Police Court on charges of being a suspicious person and a vagrant. Diavolo refuted the vagrancy charge by stating that he had about $4,500 in a bank; this seemed like a good defense, only no one could find out which bank. Although many retailers came forward saying that the "fakir" had obtained money on false pretenses, Diavolo apparently was only held until some verification from his home city, Columbia, South Carolina, came in. He had a wife there; he had with him a letter from a person supposed to be his wife, which addressed him as "dear Frank," although the name Diavolo was on the envelope.[9] The disposition of the case is not known.

Even clergymen were known to fall to the temptation of embezzlement. In June 1902, the Reverend Nicholas Booker, a black preacher, was charged with embezzling funds to the amount of $8.36 collected by him for the Sunday school of the Pilgrim Baptist Church. Several months previously, warrants had also been taken out on Reverend Booker for theft of approximately $8 of the church's money.[10]

"Perhaps one of the cleverest women who ever visited Richmond" was Mrs. Kate Clayton Howe, noted one reporter in January 1894. Mrs. Howe arrived for the purpose of "getting up an entertainment for the Lee Camp of Confederate veterans." Failing to accomplish this goal, she turned her attention to G.A.R. (Grand Army of the Republic) men. She introduced herself to Colonel John A. Pattee as the wife of Colonel Edward Robbins Howe of the G.A.R. She and the colonel had met on the train from Washington to Richmond, after which she visited him at his office in Richmond. Pattee was the general manager of the Lincoln Building and Loan Association. He helped her move her quarters from the Exchange Hotel to the American Hotel, where Pattee regularly dined. Claiming to have lost her purse, she borrowed $25 from Pattee. Mrs. Howe went off to Newport News, where she wrote a letter to Pattee stating that "she was getting up a large entertainment there for a charitable object," and added that many prominent ladies were connected with her plan. People began to ask questions, and inquiry produced various newspaper stories that revealed the lady's questionable past. She had been born in Amherst, New Hampshire, in 1848. According to her story, in 1862, at age fourteen, she had enlisted in a Massachusetts regiment as a drummer boy. After the war, she made "a pretty good living" on the lecture circuit among G.A.R. posts telling her hair-raising adventures as a drummer boy; she claimed that her true sex was discovered after being wounded at the Battle of Lookout Mountain in 1863. She met her husband at a G.A.R. meeting; once married, they began touring together, with Colonel Howe recounting his "wonderful experiences" as a regimental commander. On the side, Colonel Howe negotiated loans from all the Harvard graduates he could locate. Further investigation forced the phony army duo to "suspend operations on the G.A.R. industry and concentrate on 'touching' Harvard graduates." But even the Harvard game ran its course, and "Ned" was jailed in Chicago. The *Richmond Times* commented, "The next move of his wife, the fair Kate Clayton Howe, is awaited with interest."[11]

Embezzlement also occurred in the commission business. A Virginia law of 1874 made it clear that if any person shall wrongfully and fraudulently use, dispose of, conceal or embezzle any money, bill, note, check, order, draft, bond, bill of lading, or any other property which he shall have received for another or for his employer, principal or bailor, or virtue of his office, trust or employment, or which shall have been instructed or delivered to him by another, &c., &c., shall be deemed guilty of the larceny thereof.

Commission merchants, or their clerks, found it easy to commit financial fraud. Eugene Barnes, twenty-three-year-old bookkeeper to John T. Powers, the "well known commission merchant," disappeared on December 12, 1898, after having overdrawn about $2,000 from his firm's checking account. It seems he then traveled to Baltimore and Atlanta, when he suddenly decided to turn himself in eight days later. Barnes threw himself on the mercy of the court.[12]

A "bogus representative of the well-known tobacco-house of S. Hernsheim & Brothers, of New Orleans" showed up in Richmond in 1877 claiming to be M. Hernsheim himself. The fake tobacconist visited several Richmond tobacco manufacturers. During talk of tobacco business and filling orders, the Impostor borrowed money from his hosts. A telegram to the Hernsheim company in New Orleans revealed that no representative from the company had come to Virginia. The "tobacco sharper" fled Richmond before he could be arrested.[13]

One type of embezzlement was to order goods and then default on payment in full by declaring bankruptcy. Such was the case of Willard F. Trogden, who came to Richmond in February 1878 to purchase goods, representing the firm of W. F. Trogden & Company, merchants, of Greensboro, North Carolina. Including purchases in Baltimore and Philadelphia as well, the North Carolinian ran up a total of $11,000 in debt. Returning to North Carolina, he petitioned for bankruptcy, turning over assets amounting to twenty-five cents on the dollar. A Richmond grand jury indicted Trogden for obtaining goods under false pretenses. Captain James M. Tyler of the Richmond police went to Greensboro, and arresting Trogden, brought him back by train to Richmond. The arrest had "caused a great stir" in Greensboro, but Tyler managed to get away with his prisoner. Among Trogden's largest creditors in Richmond were Milhiser & Company; Gardner, Carlton & Baldwin; Wingo, Ellett & Crump; L. H. Blair & Company; Heller & Fleishman; Putney & Watts; and A. Oppenheimer, Harvey & Blair.

In Hustings Court, Trogden was tried for obtaining goods and then "jumping into bankruptcy." The courtroom was crowded with young men, many of whom "held, or have an ambition to hold, places in business houses." The trial revealed that Trogden had sold the goods he received in North Carolina on court day. The trial ended on June 29, 1878, with Trogden being sentenced to three years at the Virginia State Penitentiary.[14]

Bill collectors converted payments of money to their own use. H. T. Walker, a young man employed as solicitor of city trade and collector of bills for Hall, Powers & Company, wholesale dealers in fancy groceries and confections, faced such a charge.[15] In June 1894, S. S. Cabot similarly was charged with embezzlement of funds of the Live Oak Distillery Company by taking, for his own use, moneys collected from customers. In particular, he was arraigned for collecting $255 from Gonnella Brothers, which he then kept. Cabot was reported to have earned a salary of $250 per month and $170 for traveling expenses.[16]

Tried for embezzlement of $500 from Pettit & Company, with whom he was employed as bookkeeper and collector, was W. L. Francis. Francis claimed that he had been intoxicated at the time of the theft, which moneys had been entrusted to him to deposit in a bank. Francis had been courting a young lady who was working as a stenographer for Pettit & Company. A jury in Hustings Court rejected Francis's plea of temporary insanity, and found him guilty, sentencing him to one year in the penitentiary.[17]

Payroll theft happened. In June 1889, Carmine Gaudiosi, a subcontractor under Harman & Company, general contractors, absconded with money drawn from some thirty Italians who were working on the Belt Line. An Italian named Cancaci, thought to be an accomplice of Gaudiosi, was arrested for embezzlement and also on the charge of carrying a concealed weapon. Harman &Company notified Gaudiosi's bondsmen in New York (Lapenta & Company, Italian National Bank) that unless work was resumed, Gaudiosi would lose his contract.[18]

Richmond proved to be a two-way street for embezzler fugitives. Richmond police had to deal with such out-of-town transgressors who showed up in the city, and, from time to time, they had to go off to retrieve embezzlers in the extradition process.

Among those out-of-state embezzlers apprehended in Richmond, George M. Lindsay, alias G. L. Medicus, who as an agent for the J. L. Stone & Company of Raleigh, North Carolina, "sold a lot of sewing machines, collected the money, and fled from the state." He was tracked down in Richmond at the Exchange Hotel.[19] In December 1900, Jack M. Harris was arrested as a fugitive from justice, being wanted in Wheeling, West Virginia, from his former employer, J. B. McKee, a cigar importer and dealer.[20]

On November 8, 1899, nineteen-year-old Stanley Koeppel walked into a Richmond police station, and confessed he had come from Jersey City, New Jersey, where he had lived with his mother. It was alleged that, while working as a grocery store clerk, he fled with money he was supposed to take to a bank. Richmond authorities were dumbfounded when they heard from the Jersey Police that Koeppel was not wanted. In Police Court a telegram to this effect was read, and Koeppel was "given a half an hour to shake the dust of Richmond from his feet." It was thought that "Koeppel's game was to get transportation to New York and that his story of absconding was a ruse."[21]

Richmond law officers were willing to go great distances to bring wrongdoers back home. That was certainly the case in April 1892, when John T. Davis was charged with embezzling money from Rand & Barbee and Harvey, Blair & Company, both firms at which he had been the bookkeeper. Sergeant Tomlinson, of the Richmond police, traveled all the way to Denver, Colorado, where he picked up Davis. Tomlinson had taken with him a pair of handcuffs with a spring lock; he left the keys in Richmond. For three days and three nights Tomlinson, with his left hand locked to the prisoner's right, traveled back to Richmond. Upon reaching this destination, Tomlinson sent for the key and unlocked the handcuffs.[22] Also arrested in Denver and extradited back to Richmond was Louis L. Gregory, an "absconding cashier" of the Atlantic Coast Line Railroad. Detective-Captain McMahon picked up Gregory in Denver. Two indictments charged Gregory with stealing $3,371.30. Actually, it was believed that Gregory got away with $15,000. Before he was caught, people wondered how he could "keep two automobiles, sport around and live high on a salary of $92 a month." A reward of $1,000 was paid by the American Surety Company of New York, which had bonded Gregory for $30,000, to each of the arresting detectives in Denver and Richmond.[23]

Another long-distance quest to bring back an embezzler involved Sergeant J. M. Duffy going to Mobile, Alabama, to take into custody Milton K. Hirshberg, charged with stealing $1,100 from the safe at the Richmond Inn while a manager there. Walter Krish, Hirshberg's employer, noted that a few nights before the theft, his wife dreamed of rattlesnakes, which she interpreted that a friend was going to rob her husband, a warning obviously not heeded.[24] One who got away was Frank H. Fitzgerald, a "stamp clerk" for the Southern Railroad, who made off with $3,000. Before disappearing, Fitzgerald went to the clerk's office of the Hustings Court, and filed a deed, conveying all his property to his wife. The embezzler remained at large.[25]

One embezzling episode had a happy ending for the accused. Theron

H. Brown, after being placed under arrest, confessed that he had embezzled $13,000 from the Life Insurance Company of Virginia. He had fled. Hunted down by persistent and skilled Pinkerton detectives, he was apprehended in Chicago. At peace with himself, on the train back to Richmond, he remarked, "I am the happiest man on this train." Before he left his cell in Chicago, he knelt down with his wife, who with his children, had joined him in Chicago, and offered silent prayers; "from that time Brown was, it is said, a changed man." There was a "touching scene" when he left Chicago:

> "Please, Mr. Morrison, let Papa wear his own clothes," said his little girl, with great big tears in her eyes, and visions of the convicts in Capitol Square, in their striped suits before her.
> "Take care of Papa," said the little boy, trying in a manly way to be brave, but with water in his eyes.
> The wife broke down completely. She almost collapsed.

Back in Richmond, Brown was sentenced to a year in prison. Fortunately for him (and his family) he won a pardon from the governor. Petitions for clemency were signed by 105 citizens and business houses and nine of the jurors for Brown's trial. Furthermore, accompanying papers asking for pardon came from the president of the Life Insurance Company, the Virginia Trust Company, and pastor of Grace Church, Dr. C. S. Gardner. Brown himself, in a statement, said that he desired pardon not to avoid punishment but to be able to support his family. The citizens petition declared "the ends of justice have been satisfied by his conviction," and further punishment would be a "useless sacrifice" for "one who has truly repented" and who "is needed, sadly needed, by his young children and sorrowing wife."[26]

20

Impostors

A variety of persons showed up in Richmond reflecting a change of identity. One type of impostor was someone who falsely claimed governmental affiliation.

Richmond detectives, on the night of June 30, 1913, arrested Frank H. Woodward at his plush office in the Park building. Woodward, whose real name was Howard F. Porter, posed as an agent for the American Prison Association. In this capacity he had advertised in the newspapers for applicants for jobs in Washington, D.C. as stenographers, clerks, and bookkeepers. Each applicant who came to his office was required to put up a bond of $5–10. Woodford promised to send the applications to Washington and give notification when those chosen should report to work. He also took applications for positions in the federal prison department. An investigation, stirred up by frustrated applicants, soon revealed that Woodward and Porter were one and the same person. Under the latter name he was wanted in New England (chiefly in Lynn, Lawrence, and Salem) for having operated a dubious employment agency there, along with bank robbery. In Richmond, Woodward faced charges of impersonating a government official, operating a confidence game, and attempted jail break (he was caught cutting through the bars of his jail cell with a saw he had concealed by strapping it to his leg under a bandage). The case bogged down in Richmond for difficulty in finding hard evidence of Woodward's actual swindling, but there were alternatives of federal (and other state) prosecution.[1]

A most unusual case of false identity was that of a Richmonder, W. H. Montague, who, while attending a murder trial in Boston, passed himself off as the attorney general of Virginia. Montague called upon Massachusetts's attorney general, Hosea M. Knowlton, and induced him to "cash a draft." Knowlton obliged. Not surprisingly, the note proved worthless. The last that was heard of Montague in Boston was that he was invited by Judge John A. Aiken, who was presiding over the trial, to sit with him on the bench. Montague did so for a short while and then disappeared.[2]

Impostors were also known to pose as government inspectors. Moy Jung, a "well-dressed and be-spectacled young Chinaman," was arrested by Richmond police and turned over to the federal marshal service on a charge of "falsely representing himself to be a government Chinese inspector and obtaining money from local Celestials of linen-cleansing propensities." Two Richmond Chinese men, Leong Long and Ah Chung, filed a complaint against Moy Jung, alleging that he had passed himself off as a government official and had examined their naturalization papers. Pretending to find fault with the documents, Jung demanded money not to report the supposed infractions.[3]

Another kind of bogus inspector were those who purported to represent a firm doing business with the public. For example, a number of clever thieves gained entrance into private homes in the guise of gas line or telephone inspectors.[4] Two such pseudo-inspectors were Charles Taylor and William Beale, who passed themselves off as government collectors of taxes on organs. Confronting Lizzie Jackson at her store, the question was put: "Do you have an organ in your house?" With the answer "yes," Lizzie was threatened with confiscation of the instrument if she did not pay up. Instead of cash, the two phony collectors settled for cans of corn and sardines and one "lot" of crackers.[5]

Richmond detectives arrested George A. Creekmore, using the alias of George Aye, on suspicion of a series of robberies at the Lexington Hotel. Although items found in Creekmore's luggage at his room in the hotel did not match those recently stolen from the hotel's guests, Creekmore was identified by two cards in his possession as "George Aye, Second Lieutenant, United States Secret Service, Washington, D.C.," and "George A. Creekmore, United States Secret Service, Washington, D.C." A check with the Secret Service in Washington revealed his pretense. Creekmore declared that his impersonation was meant as a joke, and, apparently, no crime could be proved against him.[6]

In the spring of 1910 authorities were looking for a fifty-year-old man who passed himself off as an agent of the Pension Bureau. The "smooth-tongued mulatto" spent about a week in Richmond duping African American Civil War veterans out of their alleged pensions. He approached these veterans, telling each one that they were entitled to a large amount of back payments; typically, $700 was given as the amount. The back pension was delivered to a veteran in the form of a bogus check, in return for a $5 fee.

With the impostor able to make many transactions, the fee money rose to a substantial amount.[7]

"Since the breaking out of the Hispano-American war," noted the *Times* in August 1899, "a great many instances have come to light in which unauthorized persons have assumed the uniform of United States Army officers." Falsely wearing the uniform was not illegal as long as there were no attempts at fraud; it was merely considered "strutting around in borrowed plumage." Then there were those military impersonators who sought material gain, such as food, lodging, horse feed, or money. One such case was that of infantry "Captain F. C. Ward, who turned out to be civilian Howard L. Owens of Warrenton, Virginia. He left in the spring of 1899, supposedly to attend the University of Virginia, where he instead borrowed money and moved on to Culpepper, Manassas, Washington, D.C., and Baltimore, giving out worthless checks for loans. He then came to Richmond, where in his army uniform, he hoodwinked Colonel Wilson T. Hartz, the local recruiting officer, for thirty dollars. "Captain Ward" introduced himself as a graduate of West Point and a son of Colonel Thomas Ward, who served in the War Department in Washington. Later, when Wilson tried to cash the impostor's check, he discovered he had been duped. "Ward" was arrested in Richmond and jailed, eventually getting out on bail. For a while, "Ward" was assigned to an insane asylum but soon let go. "Ward" was scheduled to stand trial in the U.S. Circuit Court, but he did not appear; for some reason his bail was not forfeited, "in view of all the circumstances of the case," and the eventual disposition of his case is unknown.[8]

Bogus Confederate War veterans turned up, especially those who claimed to be "one of Pickett's men." It was general knowledge that at meetings of members of Pickett's Camp Confederate Veterans there were "deserters, fakirs and other bogus members of the organization, who couldn't detect gun powder when they smelt [it] on the roster of the camp."[9]

Of course, the public had to be on its guard for those quacks who illegally practiced medicine for monetary gain. The law was quite clear that all physicians obtain a license from the State Board of Medical Examiners. Any person not meeting this requirement would be fined $50–$500 and be "debarred from receiving any compensations for services rendered as such physician or surgeon." The whole Richmond medical community seemed to have taken sides in a controversy in 1892 involving a Boston physician, Dr. R. C. Fowler, who was charged with beginning a practice in Richmond without taking out the license. One of the city's best lawyers,

Judge George L. Christian, served as counsel to Fowler in the Hustings Court. The issue came down to a constitutional one: could a non-resident physician be required to be licensed by Virginia. It was argued that the law applied only to persons living within ten miles of the border of the state.[10]

On a lower level were instances of individuals posing as a physician, of sorts, to be in a position to secure unlawful financial gain. In July 1890, John Jackson (white) and George Taylor, described as "a half-grown negro boy," met Richard Johnson, an "old negro man," near the fair grounds. Upon being informed that Johnson suffered from rheumatism, Jackson said he was a doctor and could cure him for the sum of one dollar. Johnson consented and brought his new acquaintances to his home. There Johnson had his wife bring the money-box. He took out a $5 bill, which Jackson said he could not change. Jackson sent the boy out to change the bill, and then had the old man step out of the room for a few minutes; he sent the man's wife out to get some salt for use on her husband's knees. While alone, Jackson opened the money-box and pulled out the contents—all $20 worth. Then Jackson disappeared. Johnson notified the police. Captured, the phony physician and the boy went to trial; Jackson drew a four-month sentence; the boy, sixty days.[11]

Feigning ties to religion provided yet another opportunity for fraud. Edward Hopkins, a "respectable-looking colored man," came under arrest for soliciting unauthorized contributions to the Colored Free Baptist Church on Navy Hill. By this time he had already collected a considerable sum, which he appropriated for his own use.[12]

Passing himself off as a regularly ordained minister, the Reverend D. D. Rowland, alias Darling R. Philip, talked his way into filling the vacant pulpit at the Second Baptist Church in Richmond. "Such was the vigor and eloquence of his sermons [that] he attracted immense congregations, and soon attained a high reputation for oratory and Christian zeal." Eventually it was discovered that his sermons were plagiarized. Forced to resign, Philip then appeared at the First Baptist Church of Hackensack, New Jersey, where he was installed as the minister of the church. A publication of an article about Philip in the *New York Sun* caught the attention of J.T. Ellyson, a deacon at Richmond's Second Baptist Church. Ellyson tried to get Philip to return to Richmond and prove he was not the same person as Reverend Rowland. Philip refused, and he was dismissed from the New Jersey church until such time as he could prove a single identity as Philip, which of course, could not be done.[13]

Impostors posed as relatives of important or wealthy persons. Consider the case of J. H. Chiles, a deaf mute, who obtained $33.04 from the proprietors of a warehouse, using the false claim that he was the son of John Beasley, a tobacco supplier.[14]

Protesting against a "blarsted outrage," Jack King, thirty years old, who had come from London, England, was remanded to jail in November 1912 for sixty days in default of $100 security. King allegedly defrauded C. M. Carlton out of $7.44 to pay for a cablegram to King's mother in London. But more seriously, King was also wanted for posing as the son of Postmaster Edgar Allan, Jr. In Boston, Montreal, and other places King had obtained money from local postmasters to pay for telegrams to his father, whom he assured the lenders would reimburse them. Of course, none of the postmasters ever heard from Postmaster Allan, and therefore wrote Allan for an explanation. Allan simply replied: "If my son is gallivanting around the country borrowing money, it certainly is news to me, because you see, the only son I have is just 3 years old." In Police Court, Jackson said, "Really, it's all a jolly bit of a mistake." He claimed he had come to Richmond looking for a person who had known his father in England. "I got short of funds—blommin' inconvenient, as you'll agree—and cabled my mother. Some balmy person or other reported that the message wasn't delivered. Queer, eh, what?"[15]

Another Englishman latched onto an even bigger fish. "Every now and then Richmond has a strange visitor," noted the *Times* in January 1894, "but none so strange as Gordon Bryce, poet, magnificent prevaricator, and fakir of the highest order," who "has struck the city for many days." Nobody "knows how he reached the city, and nobody seems to know how he got away." When Bryce first arrived in Richmond, he "casually sauntered into the editorial sanctum of the Times," and introduced himself as the son of the famous James Bryce, member of Parliament and Gladstone's Cabinet, and author of the *American Commonwealth*. The intruder said that his views were the same as his father's, and asked the editor to give him names of "any literary gentlemen whom he might contact. He was given the names of the more prominent Richmond literati. He went to Rosewall Page, who sent him to Frederick L. Davidson, a young English lawyer living in Richmond. Bryce [re]counted his life on a Texas ranch and the loss of over $20,000 due to rascality of his partner"; he displayed the bullet wounds on his body as "illustration of his hair-breadth escapes in his wild life on his ranch." Bryce did not ask for money, but his poverty was apparent. Davidson kindly provided bed and board for Bryce, and then took him to visit the Reverend Hartley Carmichael of St. Paul's Church. It turned out that Reverend Carmichael was an "intimate friend" of James Bryce. Gordon Bryce soon departed the scene. Meanwhile, Carmichael contacted James Bryce in England, and a reply came back that the elder Bryce had no son in America. Gordon Bryce soon departed from Richmond. Davidson said he was not fooled for a minute by the intruder's story, but did believe he was "well connected"; he talked like a gentleman and seemed to be of English lineage. "I think he is probably the son of some prominent man who had been cast off, and is now making his living by imposing on his countrymen." Reports subsequently came in that a person meeting Gordon Bryce's description had pulled off confidence schemes in New York City and Petersburg, Virginia, whereby he obtained funds from certain individuals.[16]

Still other strange foreigners perplexed Richmonders. "Not since the Count of Monte Cristo's day has such strange splendor dazzled and confounded" as that which occurred on New Year's Day 1877. About 1 p.m. in the midst of a snowstorm, a "hansom closed carriage with liveried driver and footman and drawn by aristocratic bays" stopped in front of a house on Franklin Street. The footman, with the aid of a coachman, spread a Turkish carpet from the carriage to the door of the house. A stranger alighted from the carriage, went into the house, where he stayed but a few minutes, departing with the carpet again being stretched out. This proved to be the wrong address. At 1:30 p.m. the stranger made a similar appearance opposite Monroe Park, where he was greeted by a lady of great beauty. The stranger talked to the lady in French and English, with the listener in a state of complete perplexity. He stated that he was on his way to Florida on business and was staying at the Exchange Hotel. The stranger visited several other houses, and generously gave out gratuities to servants in gold and silver coin of France, England, Germany, America, and Turkey. At one residence he visited a French gentleman, and performed on the piano, violin, and guitar "with wonderful skill," and sang in "a rich, highly cultivated tenor voice." Before leaving he gave "Madame" a "lovely enameled locket," with a diamond on its face. At a house on Main and Fourth streets he met a young lady whom he induced to go with him to the rear parlor. He presented her with a sapphire ring, and told her that, if she looked closely, she could read his name inscribed within. As she bent forward to do so, he put his arm around her and drew her to him. The lady screamed, drawing the attention of her companion, an older man, and the "gentleman of the house, who entering the parlor saw the stranger planting kisses on the forehead of the girl. The father rushed upon the stranger but was felled by him." The stranger leaped over his body, and, "springing into his carriage, was off in a trice." No one else reported having seen him in the city, save a barkeep at the Fredericksburg depot, who saw the stranger's "conveyance" pass over a bridge across the river. The assaulted girl claimed that the stranger was in no way a relative or a friend. The mystery was abetted somewhat the following day, January 2, when Richmond authorities received a telegram from Petersburg:

> The mysterious stranger, as to whom telegrams were received here late last evening, was arrested last night at the City Hotel, where he arrived in a blinding snow storm and took an elegant suite of rooms. He refuses to give an account of himself, and his servants, who are Russians, apparently, from their appetite for candies, can give no intelligent answers to questions. It is certain they came from Washington, but who they are is unknown. Doubts of the gentleman's sanity are expressed by those who have conversed with him. He has telegraphed for Hon. R. T. Merrick, signing himself Louis d'Andrasse, and request him to inform Effendi Balthazz, the Turco-Voginian Embassador, as to his whereabouts. He has with him [a] sporting outfit, complete and very handsome.[17]

Women took their turns at various impersonations, including those who passed themselves off as needy. In November 1878, Richmond's police chief, Major Poe, received a telegram from Fredericksburg:

> Dear Sir—Look out for the female impostors. They were made to disgorge here. They have a paper signed "Parkson." They pretend to be in distress. One tall, the other rather low; dressed in black.
>
> J. E. Stone, C. P.

Sure enough, the women in question were picked up on Cary Street near Fourteenth, and taken into custody. Jane Spenser and Annie Kahl were charged with attempting to obtain money "under false pretenses." Jane carried a note on her from the county clerk at Fredericksburg, identifying her as a widow with three children, who had lost everything in a house fire. The justice of the Police Court did not know what to believe, so he dismissed the case but ordered the two women to leave Richmond at once, warning them of a jail sentence if they returned.[18]

Crossdressers, too, got into the act. In June 1893, Charles Smith "was sent to the jig for thirty days in default of security on the charge of being a suspicious character." When Smith was about to be assigned a cell in the men's section of the jail, he informed guards that he was really a woman—Nina Collins, by name—dressed in men's clothes. From the time her husband left her ten years before, she had been "tramping in male attire." A "female outfit" was ordered for Nina, who was said to be about twenty-five years of age.[19] When, in mid-February 1904, police responded to a call that a gang of boys were making a disturbance in a Manchester neighborhood, they arrested what they thought was a masculine quartet, only to discover at lockup that the arrestees were four young ladies, the "daughters of well-known families who had dressed themselves in male attire." The Manchester chief of police kindly lectured the young women and offered to escort them home. The girls then "burst out crying and confessed that their parents didn't know they were out." They were afraid of getting into trouble at home. The policeman then followed them home from a safe distance, ensuring their safety. The girls said they were "just having a valentine lark" and merely visiting some of their friends. The police records did not reveal the girls' names.[20]

"A rather seedy-looking individual, who appeared to be lame and used a crutch" showed up at Sänger Hall, the meeting place of the city's German organization, the Gesangverein Virginia. He introduced himself as Sigmund Friedman, an old comedian, who twenty years ago played at Sänger Hall with a German troupe. Now he was down on his luck and wanted to hire the hall to give a benefit performance for himself. Much wrangling occurred over the rental fee. Friedman finally received guarantee for payment from a local businessman. The old comedian then proceeded to sell tickets to members of the German community (he identified himself as German-Jewish). Needless to say, when it came time for a performance at Sänger Hall, no Friedman could be found. As a local newspaper reported: "It is understood that he left for parts unknown after collecting the cash for some two hundred and fifty or three hundred tickets."[21]

Few bunco-men could match the exploits of "Monster Marvin." His real name was Arthur Merritt, but he went by a variety of aliases, including General Budlong A. Morton, A.B. Morton, David Lindsay, J.B. Lindsay, J.B. Mattieson, Thomas A. Marvin, and A.T. Marvin. For over sixteen years he had a remarkable career, interrupted by a three-year stint in the Auburn, New York, Penitentiary, for committing forgeries and bigamy (with at least eleven women, probably more) ranging from Joplin and St. Louis, Missouri, to Pennsylvania, New York, Connecticut, and Massachusetts. His final downfall came shortly after his marriage to a New Jersey girl in Richmond, Virginia, on July 9, 1881. Leaving almost immediately after the wedding, he wound up in Lynne, Massachusetts, where he was arrested. Richmond authorities were able to secure his extradition back to Richmond. The fifty-one-year-old swindler was presented for examination in the Police Court. After a series of continuances due to difficulty in securing witnesses, the case was finally tried in the Hustings Court, with Judge George L. Christian presiding. Marvin (Merritt) was charged with forgery, obtaining money under false pretenses (involving the First

National Bank in Richmond), and bigamy. The case was regarded as a sensation in Richmond, New England, and New York City, where it had ample newspaper coverage. The defendant decided to plead guilty to both forgery and bigamy. He received a ten-year sentence, five years each for forgery and bigamy.

At the Virginia State Penitentiary Marvin (Merritt) penned verses that found their way into print for private circulation:

> I.
> Listen to our pleading voices,
>   As they fall upon thine ear.
> Borne to you from out our prison:
> Pleadings wrung from pain and fear.
>   From our hearts the cry is sounding—
>   Hearts oppressed by grief and pain.
>   Open wide your hearts in pity
>   Hear our pleading voice again.
>
> II.
> In the dungeons we are pining:
>   Helpless hands we stretch above-
> Give oh give boon of freedom:
>   Give us *Faith* and *Hope* and *Love*.
>   Try the plan of kindly trusting:
>   Mercy brings the giver gain.
>   Oft a cloud seems dark and threatening.
>   Pouring forth refreshing rain.
>
> III.
> From our *faults* the veil lifted.
>   Over years it still may be:
> Do not, then, be cruel-hearted—
>   Grant the boon we ask of thee.
>   You may feel the need of pity.
>   When you know the grief we bear.
>   Will you do a Christian duty
>   And another's burden share?
>
> IV.
> To forgive, the Master taught you:
>   Will you now His teaching heed.
> Shall our deep and heartfelt sorrow
>   Bring the sympathy we need?
>   Then from bondage dark and cruel
>   Let us pass light of yore—
>   Open wide the iron portals:
>   Bid us "Go, and sin no more."[22]

Having entered the state penitentiary on October 5, 1881, Marvin, now sixty-five years old and feeble, was released from his ten-year sentence on June 16, 1890, after serving eight years, eight months, and eleven days, being credited four days each month for good behavior. According to law, he had four days deducted because he had created a disturbance in the prison shoe shop where he had worked. Actually, Marvin had not been an ideal convict. According to the prison warden, Marvin "was one of the most troublesome convicts that ever came under his charge." Marvin's "meanness was done by underhand methods, which defied detection and the attendant punishment." He was "very crafty, would write anonymous notes to the foreman of the shoe-shop, put other prisoners up to mischief, and stirred up strife generally." Marvin refused to be interviewed by the *Dispatch*, saying that "Hogarth was a great caricaturist; Junius a beautiful word painter, but the word painters around this city would put the two combined to shame." At 6:45 p.m. on the day of his release, Marvin boarded a train for Washington, D.C.[23]

21

Drummers

Drummers, sometimes called sample merchants, were traveling salesmen. They had the unenviable task of convincing strangers, on initial acquaintance, to sign up to purchase products. Most drummers represented a wholesale supplier. Then there were those who operated independently, hawking wares on their own.

Selling goods by sample without a license was a violation of city and state ordinances.[1] Any resident merchant could "sell goods by sample, card, or otherwise" by paying a license tax of $10.[2] Out-of-state drummers were excluded from doing business in Virginia. By the mid–1880s, this sample-merchant license tax had risen to $50, and this revenue fee did not "extend to the sale of goods other" than one's own.[3] In 1887, however, the U.S. Supreme Court held that, under the commerce clause of the Constitution, traders from out of state were free to operate under the same conditions as the state's residents.[4]

Soon drummers were claiming that if they were headquartered outside a state in which they were doing business, they did not have to pay for a license. The Supreme Court upheld this claim, but outsiders in Richmond and Virginia were still being arrested for selling without a license.[5]

One Philadelphia sample-merchant, H. N. Hirsch, endured the full impact of Richmond's hostility toward out-of-state unlicensed drummers. On a Saturday morning, October 25, 1873, while walking in Capitol Square, he claimed that he was met by a private detective

> and dragged along to police headquarters, under suspicion of being a sample-merchant. The fellow possessed no proof against me whatever, not having seen any carrying of sample boxes or packages on my part, or my getting the same forwarded to stores. The charge brought up against me was that some gentlemen had called on me at the hotel where I was stopping and probably examined a line of goods.

Tried in Police Court for violating city and state laws in regard to selling goods, Hirsch insisted that he had made no attempt to sell, but merely received calls at his hotel from former customers and talked about old times. Hirsch said that he was a "peaceable citizen, paying a large price for poor accommodations at a so-called first-class hotel," where he joined with friends "in his temporary home." Hirsch, nevertheless, was found guilty of "having a sample-trunk" in his possession. Hirsch refused to pay the $50 fine, and was hurried off to jail to await trial in the Hustings Court for violation of state laws.

His jail treatment was the worst that any felon could expect:

> The twenty-four hours I spent in the lock-up will not soon be effaced from my memory. Kept in a common felon's cell with two inveterate drunkards, surrounded by an army of mice and other animals, perfume de cesspool, locked in from fresh air at 5:30 p.m., I had to go through a night of horror in the above-stated condition, enveloped in a rotten blanket and swarming with vermin, reposing sweetly on the bare and very far from cleanly floor, listening to the rattle of gnawing mice, fighting a regiment of rats in their attempt to feast on my comparatively well-fed body.

The food was so bad, he continued, that he had to reject it. Finally released on bail, Hirsch's case was heard on October 28 before the United States Circuit Court. The hearing went in his favor; the presiding judge declared the state law in reference to sample merchants to be unconstitutional. Subsequently, in Hustings Court, the case was dismissed, with the defendant obliged to pay the city fine only. After revealing his ordeal to the press, Hirsch noted:

> Let all honored fellow-drummers know that, through the martyrdom of the subscriber, to invade the "Old Dominion" is no crime hereafter, but that to come "On to Richmond" ... still costs $10 for a monthly license. Be forewarned by my sad example, dear friends, and do not attempt to perambulate the precinct of this highly *conservative village* without previously interviewing his Honor, Justice J. J. White and forking over the two V's.[6]

Drummers found themselves in trouble in many different ways. A favorite course was for a traveling salesman to announce that he had temporarily run out of funds and needed a little cash to hold him over in room and board. One slick operator who succeeded in "doing the hotels" in 1897 was O. W. Robinson, alias E. V. Lewis, alias George West.[7]

Persons fraudulently passing themselves off as drummers sometimes convinced retailers to advance them money. One such stranger in Richmond, supposedly representing "a commercial house" in Canada, persuaded a local druggist to cash an unsecured check for $35.[8]

Another scheme involved granting more than one "exclusive" franchise for manufacturing and selling a certain commodity. Dr. F. B. Morse was accused of doing this in reference to the Radium Spray Company,

Incorporated, located at 100 N. Seventh Street in Richmond. Morse was arrested in Baltimore on complaint of a man in Washington, D.C., who had paid several hundred dollars for the exclusive right to manufacture the cleaning fluid while Dr. Morse had given the same rights to another dealer. The position of the Richmond company, however, was that it was simply a matter of subletting.[9]

One clever scheme that occurred from time to time was that of someone posing to be the representative of a firm, and then proceeding to place an order for goods to be shipped to that firm. In the meantime, the perpetrator of this fraud would request and generally receive an advance of money made out in a draft upon the receipt of the goods and which purportedly would be included in the amount of the bill. The sharper would then disappear with his money, and no one would ever learn more about the transaction. Usually the person committing the fraud would be operating out of a Northern city, preying upon victims in the South.[10]

Shyster drummers were up to other tricks. So-called "profit-sharing companies" would advertise the availability of a certain product but use various means to substitute inferior items upon delivery. In 1917, for example, the Sprinkle Profit Sharing Piano Company, operating out of Baltimore, advertised that standard-made pianos would be sold in Richmond "at a price far below the cost of manufacture." When a potential customer arrived at a store, he was told that the piano was sold and a salesman would endeavor to sell him a "stencil" piano in its place. A "stencil piano is an inferiorly made instrument" on which "the manufacturer refuses to stamp his name."[11]

There was also chicanery in the sale of tobacco products. One cigar drummer came to Richmond toting "a unique contrivance for cutting and lighting cigars." In purchasing a large quantity of the company's product, a retailer was promised the inclusion of a free cigar cutter-lighter. The drummer would take out one of the high-quality cigars he carried in his pocket for a demonstration. When a retailer received his order for cigars, he found that they were very inferior, some not worth even two cents each.[12]

A phony whiskey drummer operated much the same way. V.S. Wolff, to cite one such con man, would arrive in a city claiming to be a Mason and, within a few days' time, introduce himself to a Mason. Upon giving the name of the company he supposedly represented, he would ask his "fellow" Mason to endorse a check, usually for the amount of $100. Of course, the check was no good. When Wolff was arrested in Richmond, he was already wanted in seven states for this kind of fraud.[13] One young man, R.M. Cary, from Plymouth, Indiana, was sentenced to prison for sixteen months, for cashing four bogus checks on a bicycle company he represented.[14]

No area presented itself for drummer fraud more than in the selling of sewing machines. These devices, especially those made by the Singer Company, enjoyed great popularity in Richmond.[15] As was noted as early as 1876,

> The invention of the sewing machine has not been an unmixed blessing to those who live by the needle.... The machine sews at a rate that fingers cannot compete with.... It has made the possession of a sewing machine a necessity to all seamstresses. The tools that could be had three for a cent have been raised into an article costing sixty-five to seventy dollars, or representing the entire wages of from eight to eighteen weeks. The struggles necessary on the part of a poor girl or woman to pay this extortionate sum for an article not costing the manufacturers more than one-fourth the amount can only be faintly depicted in words.... So easy, indeed, are the terms that if she, by sickness or loss of work, fails in a payment.... The glozing agent ... will have the company's men, armed with a *replevin*, come and carry off the machine and refuse to return her a cent of what she has paid.[16]

Any licensed merchant in Virginia who paid $200 for a license from the state could sell sewing machines in Virginia.[17] In 1886, sewing machines were made to run on an electric dynamo motor, operated by a foot pedal.[18]

Other than harvesting outrageously high prices for sewing machines, some agents involved themselves in further duping customers. Agents had customers sign notes for double the value of the sewing machines, under the pretense that they were merely signing receipts for the item. Great was the surprise for the unsuspecting buyer when receiving notice that payment for the machines was overdue, thus making the likelihood for reclamation by the company for default of payment.[19] Another type of hoodwinking was for a pseudo agent to pick up a sewing machine from a residence on the pretense that the machine needed repairing. Most likely, the machine was taken to an auction house to sell.[20]

Drummers often met up with their kind while on sales excursions. The *Daily Dispatch*, in November 1887, ran an observation on the subject, originally carried in an Omaha, Nebraska, newspaper. A reporter was told by "an old white-haired 'knight of the grip'" that "there is an unwritten code of ethics among commercial travelers that is considered as binding upon each and every one as though each was made to obey it in every particular. The law is known as 'professional courtesy.'" This meant that "no traveler shall take, or seek to take, any unfair advantage of a brother salesman in the same line." A great discourtesy "that one commercial man can show to another is to interrupt him while talking with a customer." One such violation was recalled by the interviewee when he was in St. Louis showing samples to the dress-goods buyer.

> I was booking a nice sale, and had my customer just in the proper frame of mind to place a large order, when who should come in but a young "dude tenderfoot," and, walking up to my man, presented his card and commenced talking up the fine line of laces his house was handling. I was hot enough to consign him to a place where no ice-salesman will ever be found. He was finally informed that the lace-buyer would not be in until the following day, and after leaving his card the youth took his departure. Now nothing is so disastrous to a salesman, especially when he is selling a line of specialties, as an interruption, and it proved so in this case. My customer had had his mind taken away from the subject I had got him interested in, and instead of a very large order, I received a very small one, and had hard work to get that.

The old drummer had his revenge that night. He and several other drummers hatched a scheme that worked to perfection. They informed the young tenderfoot that the lace-buyer would be at the hotel where the drummers were staying that night. But it was pointed out that the prospect enjoyed good food and drink, along with conviviality. In all, there were eight guests and they all marched to the young interloper's hotel room. There, over negotiations for the purchase of a large order of Valenciennes lace, the host ordered up supper, plenty of wine, and fancy cigars for all; the bill came to about $100. A huge order for the lace was made out, and the deal was to be consummated in the morning. Meanwhile, a note was sent to the young tenderfoot, informing him of the trickery. No one signed for the order the next day. A year later, when the perpetrator and victim again met, the young man admitted that the trickery had been the best lesson he ever received. His sponsor company got wind of the event, and the only response he had from them was, "Served you right."[21]

On a different level, peddlers had much of the same problems as did the drummers. State law required $250 for peddling on foot and $500 peddling from a vehicle, except for farmers and truckers hawking their own produce. The city also required a license fee of $100. The state law all but put an end to street peddling. Efforts to have the courts declare the state license law unconstitutional, as being prohibitive of commerce, failed.[22]

Before licensing, peddlers could be held in check by enforcement of the city's nuisance laws. Thus, in 1887, Julius Agrei, a peddler of Hokey-Pokey (a brand of ice cream sold by vendors), was hauled into Police Court on complaint of a citizen for the noise of ringing of bells on his push cart. Agrei was discharged with an "admonition" of the court to the police to report all vendors of Hokey-Pokey who might be caught ringing bells on the street.[23]

Adolphus Byrd, who was "colored, charged with being disorderly in the street while peddling," was fined $5 in Police Court in July 1908. Byrd had a peddler's license. He noisily hawked his fish early in the mornings, disturbing a large portion of the sleeping citizenry. Justice Crutchfield, in the Byrd case, also stipulated that, even when a man had a peddler's license, if he had several men working for him they should remain on the same block as the push cart. If caught beyond the block in which the cart stood, the assistants would be fined for peddling without a license.[24]

When the city cracked down in the summer of 1908 on Hokey-Pokey men who did not have licenses, it was soon learned that nearly all of the thirty-five "push cart peddlers of candy and ice-cream" had "vamped" for Philadelphia. The fleeing vendors simply strapped blankets to their push carts and hired cars to take them northward. Two Greek vendors stayed behind to face the restrictive measures in court.[25]

Changing times forced some vendors out of business. The charcoal vender, who was "once a picturesque if not beautiful figure in Richmond life," disappeared because anthracite coal "supplanted his wares." Also doomed was the slop-man. He "would come into our back-yard every day and there find awaiting him an accumulation of melon-rinds, cabbage leaves, chicken feathers, bones, and other 'slops' from the dining room and the kitchen." He came more frequently than the city's garbage-cart man and

> hadn't as many "rules and regulations" as the municipal representatives have. Almost invariably he was a colored man and a friend of the cook's. Sometimes he possessed a bony horse and a tottering cart with which to haul off the slop. Sometimes he had a wheelbarrow, or push-cart, and we have even seen goat-carts in his service.

Impeding the presence of slop-men was, in part, owing to the city requiring permits for refuse collection. Also, Henrico County prohibiting hog-pens in the city's suburbs "destroyed the chief markets for the slops."[26]

The city did not have much trouble with unlicensed peddlers. Enforcement with heavy fines effectively subdued the traffic. Yet there were occasionally cases involving selling on the street without a license. In December 1913, Louis Berkowitz came before Police Court, upon complaint of Miss Alice Carlisle and Miss Agnes French, who identified articles they had purchased from Berkowitz. The items were "dainty pieces of lingerie which caused the judge to blush" as they were taken out of a wrapper and held up for his inspection.

"My, my," said the court; "take these things away. This is shocking."

A MEMBER OF A GRINDING COMBINATION.

The above was allegedly a "Member of a Grinding Combination," according to the Richmond *Daily Times*, August 13, 1899.

The justice then asked one of the lawyers to whisper the name of each garment and its price. The goods submitted in evidence were worth $100. Berkowitz was fined.[27]

Cases involving peddling without a license could, at times, be difficult to prove. One such example: D. B. Hudson, agent for W. A. Broidy & Son, who was "charged with peddling in the Southside without a license," was dismissed. None of the many witnesses could swear whether Hudson "had agreed to deliver the goods from his sample case or to take their orders for future deliveries." Broidy & Son did an installment business, delivering goods when down payments were made, and then collecting the balance on a weekly or monthly basis.[28]

Two Russians, having previously been arrested for peddling furs without a license, with one item being fined, were back in court in December 1907 for having assaulted each other over the ownership of $1,000 in ladies' furs. Brought into court because of the fight, one of the men, Israel Morgan, was fined $10 and costs, and the other, S. E. Ross, alias Rosinheim, had charges against him dismissed. But after the two defendants left court they again engaged in a physical fight, which was renewed at times after that.[29]

Under the headline "Drummers Flock to Richmond for Great Blowout," a reporter commented, on June 9, 1913, on the great national

HIS AUTOGRAPH.

Policeman—This won't do! The city ordinance says that every peddler must have his name on the side of his wagon!
Peddler—Why, there's my name!
Policeman—That's only a cross!
Peddler—But that's the way I always sign it!—Fliegende Blaetter.

"His Autograph" read the caption of the above image from the Richmond *Daily Times*, May 26, 1901.

"NO!"

"No!" So read the pithy caption of the cartoon from the *Richmond Times-Dispatch*, April 13, 1915.

convention of drummers being held in the city. All day long on June 8, special trains rolled into Richmond bringing delegates from all the states. All these traveling salesmen were immediately taken to the convention headquarters at the Automobile Club rooms at the Jefferson Hotel, where they were registered and supplied with badges. A "big parade" of drummers marched from the Jefferson Hotel at 9:15 a.m. on the 9th. Delegates were issued instructions for the event:

Look for the banner of your State; get in place, and stay there.

Pennants and sample cases will early be given to those who are in place at the marching time.

March four men in a row, two paces behind men and four paces between rows.

Point your nose at the man in front of you, and follow your nose throughout the parade.

March with both feet, and keep time with the drum.

The traveling salesmen looked forward to the political phase of the convention, when there would be "considered friendly rivalry and some lobbying" in the selection of officers. The convention, representing the Travelers' Protective Association of America, boasted one thousand delegates in attendance.[30]

22

Postal Robbers

The Federal Postal Service, with its multiple system of post offices, substations, and branches in retail outlets, attracted a plethora of small-time thieves. They were quite content to clean out a cash drawer, steal stamps, or filch a letter or two for money orders and cash in mail boxes or pouches. Rarely came the big-time postal robbery. When it did, however, it was said to be of "gigantic proportions."

This occurred at the city's central post office, which was being temporarily housed in a building on Franklin Street while renovations were being made, sometime between Saturday night and Monday morning of March 26–28, 1910. Stolen were ninety parcel packages, weighing seven and one-half pounds each, totaling 675 pounds and cash in gold and note, amounting to $1,235.64. Altogether the loss in stamps and the cash totaled $86,295.54. The loot was contained in five trunks, which the thieves placed on a wagon, parked about a block down the street. The trunks were identifiable, as were the stamps, as property of the postal service in Richmond. When the crooks, Eddie Fay, alias Fred Cunningham, and Richard Harris, alias Frank Chester (also known as "little Dick Harris"), arrived in New York City to pick up the loot, which had been shipped by railroad, they were apprehended. Since they were in the custody of federal agents, the two robbers were returned to Richmond without the need of any extradition process. A full handprint on the wall in a hotel room where the robbers had stayed in Richmond, and confessions, were sufficient proof of guilt. A "mysterious third man" involved with the robbery, Herbert Deihm, was not arrested until two years later, in Sandusky, Ohio; Deihm was supposed to pick up one of the trunks with the loot in New York City, but got drunk and met up with a woman while on board a train, and, therefore, did not keep the appointment—thus, the reason he had not been arrested in New York City along with the two other crooks.

Fay and Harris were each sentenced to ten years at the federal penitentiary at Atlanta. In prison "Little Dick" Harris was assigned as head bookkeeper to the shoemaker's department, and Eddie Fay wound up as a clerk to the prison blacksmith. Harris was released in January 1917.[1]

In January 1896, Richmond detectives assisted in the arrest of two black tramps who were suspects in the robbery of a store in Chesterfield County that contained a post office. The burglars entered the building by prying open a back window with a crowbar. Besides taking clothing, tobacco, and cigars, they broke open the till in the post office department, obtaining all the money it contained.[2] Normally thieves would get only stamps, but sometimes they were denied these items because the postal clerk would take them home at night.[3]

Thieves regularly targeted mailboxes.[4] Thomas W. Lacy, in October 1898, was sentenced to two years in a federal penitentiary for robbing a mailbox of a letter containing money addressed to the Reverend Father Donovan.[5]

Occasionally, inside jobs accounted for postal theft.[6] In early 1908, Frank P. Burke, superintendent of Station B of the Richmond Post Office, went on trial in U.S. District Court for mail theft. Burke, along with the postmaster, supervised about eighty persons who had mail-delivery routes. Burke was accused of taking money from letters passing through his postal station; marked money from a decoy letter was found in his possession. At trial he was depicted as having been temporarily mentally unbalanced because of excessive imbibing of "Burke rickys," a concoction of whiskey mixed with carbonated water and lime juice. He customarily had five drinks before breakfast. Miraculously acquitted, Burke resigned from the postal system, and took a job in Philadelphia with the Denniston Manufacturing Company.[7]

W. L. Jordan, a clerk at the Manchester Post Office, caught with $9 in marked money from a letter addressed to William T. Pitt, secretary of a lodge of the Knights of Honor, faced a one–five-year sentence at the state penitentiary.[8] Rena B. Askey appeared to have fared better for a similar crime. A cashier at a postal substation in a drugstore, the twenty-two-year old "very highly connected" woman had a $2,000 shortage in her accounts. The owner of the drugstore, Roy Childrey, promised to make good to the U.S. government the deficient amount, a sum which the young woman's relatives pledged to supply. It is not known whether the case ever came to trial.[9]

Snatching up U.S. mail bags could lead to a big haul. In September 1920, federal agents apprehended three men for stealing $300,000 in cash and Liberty Bonds and twelve karats of uncut diamonds, worth $9,000, from a registered mail pouch on a train en route from Atlanta to Charlotte, North Carolina. Ivy W. West, alias Ben Welburn Franklin, age twenty-four (formerly a street car conductor in Richmond), was picked up at his residence in Richmond. The other two men, Claude Monroe, a railway mail clerk, and Rufus Kight, a plumber's helper, were apprehended in Atlanta. To carry off the theft, West and Kight boarded the train as passengers; Monroe saw to it that the mail storage car was unlocked. Kight made his way into the mail car, slit open the bag of registered mail, pocketed the securities and diamonds, and then left the train. The three met up in Atlanta, where they split the loot. A fair amount of the securities and jewelry were recovered in Richmond pawnshops. The robbers were initially caught as a result of Kight visiting his uncle, a state legislator, in Homerville, Georgia. The uncle, "surmising that something was wrong," reported Kight to the sheriff, who managed to connect the suspect with the robbery.[10]

Going after persons who filched letters from the mail was a rather complicated process. Complaints of missing letters in Richmond amounted to about five per week.

> When an unregistered letter is reported missing at the post-office where the letter was mailed the first duty of the postmaster or his assistant is to ascertain on blank forms provided for the purpose all the facts relating to the letter necessary to a preliminary investigation. Having done this, he proceeds to ascertain by official inquiry whether the letter has reached its destination and been delivered. When a negative reply is received all the correspondence and other papers are transmitted to the Chief Inspector of the Post-Office Department in Washington, D.C., by whom (and not by the postmaster, as many suppose) any further investigation is made. The jurisdiction of a postmaster does not extend beyond the limits of his office. He has no authority in the case of a missing letter to do more than make up and transmit to Washington a full report of the case. His connection with it then ceases unless he is called upon by a post-office inspector for additional information.[11]

In 1878, a post-office transfer agent in Richmond became the source for widespread theft in the delivery of packages of mail to railroads. Three of the railroads servicing Richmond had reported missing mail. Sending out decoy letters had no effect. A special agent, W. T. Henderson, therefore, went into a mailing car, concealing himself in a cabinet. He observed Alonzo W. Wilcox, a local postal agent, enter the car after the regular clerks had left for breakfast. The special agent witnessed Wilcox take a package of letters from a pouch and put it into an overcoat pocket. Wilcox was also seen tearing up and burning a letter in the stove. Wilcox was arrested. He was indicted for unlawfully detaining two letters, and for embezzlement for taking a postal money order from a letter, stealing seventy-five cents in "fractional currency" from another letter, and taking a three-cent postage stamp on a letter. Wilcox came to trial in the U.S. District in Richmond.[12] Similar to this was the case in 1881 of a young man, William Closby, who served as a mail rider in collecting mail pouches and delivering them to train depots. Closby succeeded in "abstracting" letters out of pouches. Finding no money in letters, he threw them out alongside a road, which episode was observed by a witness, thus leading to Closby's arrest. He was lodged in the city jail awaiting trial in federal court.[13]

Mail carriers were also caught, usually by decoy letters, in pilfering postal items. William F. Bowie was such a culprit. Ordered to report regarding "some irregularity of conduct," on September 11, 1873, as he left the post office, "He was observed to take up something from a table and place it under his coat." An assistant postmaster induced him to show what he had concealed. The package proved to be a bundle of letters belonging to his route. Upon further search, twenty-four letters were found in his pockets, most not belonging to his route. A month later four packets of letters assigned to his route were discovered on the top of a furnace in the basement of the post office. At trial, it was shown that Bowie's route, although the smallest in the city, had the highest in volume of letters. On the day in question the number of letters was unusually large. The defense claimed that Bowie, unable to deliver all the letters on his route, fearing that he would be fired if the discrepancy was discovered, simply put them out of sight until, at a later time, he could deliver them. The jury, after twenty minutes of deliberation, came back with a verdict of unlawful detention of letters, but recommended Bowie to the clemency of the court.[14]

Other carriers were arrested for siphoning off letters. It was very difficult, however, to gain convictions by proving intent.[15] One letter carrier was suspended for ten days for entering a saloon while in uniform and drinking a glass of beer.[16]

Some persons used the mails in attempts to conduct swindles. In 1877, W. B. Keater, a locomotive-engineer by trade, hatched a scheme. In an advertisement placed in newspapers, he declared that, as the officer of a new railroad, he wanted to employ 1,000 laborers, 100 locomotive-engineers, 100 conductors, 100 firemen, and 200 brakemen; free transportation to work-sites was promised. All that an interested person had to do was to apply and submit fifty cents. Keater professed to be acting for "A.B. Dixon, Superintendent S. and A.R.R., Chicago." To get hold of the money, Keater sent a postcard to the postmaster of Chicago to forward mail to him as A. B. Dixon, at Richmond. The postcard was turned over to a special agent by the Chicago postmaster; it then wound up in the fraud department of the Post Office Department in Washington, D.C. Keater was arrested in Richmond as he appeared at general delivery when he came for his Chicago mail.[17]

Another postal swindle involved one Robert C. Murray, who tried to sell interest in certain patents which never existed. He was tripped up in an attempt to peddle an electrical writing machine.[18]

One gang victimized wholesale merchants in Montgomery, Chattanooga, Richmond, Charleston, Baltimore, Cincinnati, and elsewhere. The conspirators, using the mails, did a two-fold business: sending orders to wholesale merchants for beer and other liquor, which they would then dispense to "Blind Tigers" (speakeasies) and also using the names and addresses of small rural merchants to dispose of all sorts of goods, including pianos, organs, reapers, and cases of wine. For the liquors, the criminals operated mainly in prohibition counties. Eleven members of the gang pled guilty in federal court in Savannah, Georgia.[19]

John Claflin, six-foot-six and weighing 250 pounds, and "one of the nicest gentlemen" one could meet, operated a swindle in the form of the American Freight Revising Bureau. This "bureau" did a "rushing business" handling thousands of freight bills for revision and correction sent in by complaining shippers. The problem was that the firm produced no results. Indicted by using the United States mails, Claflin managed to vanish, making "good use of the abnormally long legs with which nature endowed him."[20]

A fraud order, in November 1907, was issued to postal authorities in Richmond that prohibited delivery of all mail to the Consolidated Order of Friendships, an African American organization, with headquarters on North Fifth Street. The company, it was later discovered, was a complete fraud. It had issued life insurance policies over four years to "ignorant negroes in nearly every town of size in the State"; earnings had reached into the thousands of dollars. The alleged company had agents in branch offices in Hampton, Roanoke, and Manchester, and had reached into every section of the state. A premium of $10, paid upon the delivery of the insurance, would supposedly bring payment of $200 at death and also carried a benefit of $5 a week in case of sickness. No money was ever paid to a beneficiary.[21]

A novel postal fraud, said to eclipse "in enormity any that were ever perpetrated through the local post office," came to an end in early 1909.

22. Postal Robbers

A gang, F. W. Siebert and his father Christopher, along with two other men, had received as much as $20 per day through their scheme. They had put advertisements in newspapers throughout the North and West. Typical of the advertisements was: "Wanted—A young lady to act as companion to aged infirm old lady in trip abroad. Expenses paid to New York City. Enclose two-cent stamp for reply." A post office box in Richmond was the destination for the response. Some of the letters enclosed as much as ten cents in stamps and one dollar to join the "club." In several months' time, the crooks had received some five thousand replies. Inexplicably, at trial in federal court, F. W. Siebert was only fined $250 and the case against his father was *nolle prosequied*.[22]

There were other instances of misusing the mails. Not the least among them were putting stolen railway tickets on the market,[23] distributing illegal medicines,[24] and sending "obscene postals" to individual persons.[25]

23

Railway Disrupters

Freight and baggage cars stationary at railway yards were susceptible to break-in thefts, and trains, in general, faced the risk of someone interfering with rails, signals, or switches so as to cause wrecks. Railroad officials had to guard against criminals and thrill-seekers alike. The city at the turn of the century was serviced by nine railroads: Richmond and Petersburg; Richmond and Danville; Chesapeake and Ohio; Richmond, Fredericksburg and Potomac; York River; Richmond and York River; Southern Railway; Seaboard Air Line; and Atlantic Coast Line. There were various passenger stations and freight yards. The stations received some consolidation with the establishment of the Main Street Station in 1901 and the Broad Street Station in 1919.[1]

Stealing baggage caused much trouble for the railroads. Usually the method of operation was for a member of a gang to acquire a stack of baggage checks from the baggage room and then substitute the names of wealthy persons on trunks with their own, re-ticketing the trunks.[2]

One gang of baggage thieves that operated for years along the East Coast and Richmond making off with baggage trunks finally met arrest in 1907. The three principal members of the group—Charles Miller, Harry Allen, and Louis Rodgers—each were tried in a Virginia state court and sentenced to five years in the state penitentiary. Miller had been apprehended in London, extradited back to New York and then to Virginia. Having completed their Virginia sentences, they had to stand trial in New York and Pennsylvania.[3]

Special agents rooted out other trunk robbers. More often than not the crooks were looking for liquor. On one occasion, detectives caught their quarry by placing hot-water bags in a trunk, and then poured whiskey over them as well as on top of the trunk. The thieves were arrested as they opened the trunk.[4] Of course, there were always the snatchers of suitcases.[5]

"Thefts on freight cars have long been a great annoyance to railroadmen, and it is often almost impossible to discover where the leak occurs"; so ran a newspaper item in May 1876. One rather effective measure, however, was the freight-car hasp, invented by S. J. Tucker of Richmond. When a car was loaded, a seal covered by a glass was put in the hasp, which could not be opened (even if the lock was broken) without breaking the glass. When a freight train stopped at a station, the location of a theft could be immediately determined.[6]

Thefts, nevertheless, continued, and culprits regularly wound up in Police Court.[7] All members of a gang of five were indicted by a grand jury, in November 1888, for felony. Their crime, if not especially rewarding in terms of loot, covered a wide expanse. The charges against them were

> breaking and entering in the night-time a box-car of the Richmond and Petersburg Railroad Company and stealing ten sacks of flour and four Bibles, all of the value of $19.50; breaking into a car of the Richmond and Alleghany Company and stealing three sacks of flour worth $3.50; and breaking into cars of the Alleghany Company and stealing six pair of boots, six pair of shoes, seven pair of boots, and three sacks of flour of the aggregate value of $37.38.[8]

When possible, entrapment was the best way to catch a freight-car thief. Another sure way was to trace stolen goods to a pawnshop or in the possession of the thief.[9]

Armed guards patrolled freight yards. A thief caught breaking and entering a boxcar could be shot on sight. Guards were kept very busy during wintertime in ferreting out coal thieves. In February 1904, John Newby, a twenty-year-old black man, was accosted by watchman William G. Overby just as Newby had completed filling a large sack of coal. Newby ran, and, refusing to stop when so ordered, Overby shot and killed him.[10]

Some freight-car thieves preferred to operate on moving trains, throwing off goods they stole.[11] One "dare-devil negro," Tom Cooper, kept detectives in a pother for quite a while before being apprehended. He could "mount a freight train when running at almost full speed, rob a car, throw off what he wants, while the train is in rapid motion, and then jump off unhurt."[12]

For persons gaining entry into boxcars, not necessarily for the purpose of robbery, the experience could be fatal. In November 1889, the corpse of a man, about twenty years old, was discovered in a car that had been sealed for ten days. A worker, unloading bales of wood at a freight yard in Richmond, had spotted a foot sticking out from among the bales. The deceased had simply climbed into the car without breaking into it. A post mortem showed only that the man had not died from violence, but from natural causes.[13]

Many of the freight-car robberies could be attributed to boys. In 1883, three "small colored boys," ranging in age from twelve to eighteen years old, proved troublesome over a period of time by raiding cars of the Richmond and Alleghany and the Richmond and Petersburg Railroad companies. The loot consisted mainly of bags of flour, boots, brass, and oddly enough, family Bibles. Several representatives of Wren's Detective Agency shadowed the boys for several days and made the arrest. Of the three culprits, William Morris, the youngest, became a witness for prosecution, while the other two, Phillip Ellis and George Minor, were indicted by a grand jury for felony. Some of the stolen flour was found at the store of John McGrath, who was arrested for receiving stolen property; eventually, however, he was let go.[14]

In February 1904, it was reported that "eight little darkies" were "languishing behind bars," waiting to appear in Police Court. Their ages ranged from thirteen to seventeen years old. They had been apprehended for breaking into a Chesapeake and Ohio freight-car and stealing three boxes of oranges.[15] Another boy, Charles Holzapfel, who had already done two years at the state reformatory, was charged with breaking into railroad cars and stealing various items. Fortunately for Holzapfel, the goods, although amounting to the value of $100, individually were not of the amount constituting a felony; if the breaking-and-entering charge were pursued, however, he could have faced the graver allegation.[16]

A railway larceny of a different type involved a passenger train. A Pullman car was detached from a New York-to-Jacksonville train and detained at Richmond's Byrd Street Station. The cause was the reported robbery of jewelry belonging to Dr. and Madame Edouard Fribourg, residents of Paris, who were on their way to Wilmington, North Carolina, where Dr. Fribourg was engaged to make chemical tests. Before boarding the train in New York City, the Fribourgs dined at the Savoy Hotel.

> Madame Fribourg, who is chic, petite, and all those other French descriptives indicating pretty, vivacious, clever and well dressed, went to dinner smartly gowned for the evening and wearing some stunning jewels—pearl earrings, a beautiful Algerian gold filigree bracelet set with oriental jewels, and two or three diamond rings of brilliant setting, besides a necklace of pearls of most tempting value. Her husband wore three pearl studs in his shirt that seem to have been the pride of his heart.

The Fribourgs went to bed shortly after the train left Jersey City and arose the next morning as the train passed Fredericksburg, Virginia. It was then

23. Railway Disrupters

that Dr. Fribourg noticed missing from a bag three pearl studs, two sets of pearl earrings in golden settings, five diamond-and-turquoise rings, and the Algerian bracelet. The stolen valuables were worth an estimated $10,000. A host of detectives in Richmond and the major cities of the East Coast northward soon were investigating the case. Pullman employees—porters, waiters, and other servants—were rigidly examined. The mystery deepened. Could someone have boarded the train, made the robbery, and then handed the stolen goods to a person on a railroad platform? Or had the Fribourgs been mistaken? During the several-day detention of the train in Richmond, Dr. Fribourg could be seen

> smoking innumerable little Hungarian cigarettes with paper tips and a pungent, dead grass aroma, and plucking occasionally at his crisp, curling beard, while Madame Fribourg turns her dry and anguished eyes appealingly to the police and utters forlorn ejaculations with a perfect Parisian accent which none of them can understand.

Apparently, the case was never solved.[17]

A constant fear of persons seeking to cause train wrecks had the railroads sending out "track viewers," or "train masters," to keep check on the vast expanse of track whether there were any impediments on rails and to spot any potential wrecker. One diabolical plan, fortunately, misfired. Three young tramps—Hamilton Duncan, age seventeen, a white boy, and two black boys, Theodore Hawkins, age nineteen, and William Wallace, age fifteen—decided to wreck a train in order to snatch pocketbooks of passengers. On rails just south of Richmond at a sharp curve on an embankment, the boys put down some fish-bar plates and other pieces of iron. The boys concealed themselves nearby to await the outcome. The engineer did not discover the obstruction until it was too late. The train was heavily jarred, but managed to stay on track. The would-be train wreckers were soon apprehended.[18] In March 1895, two African American boys placed oak logs on the track of an oncoming C & O freight train. As the train was going upgrade, it managed to avoid a wreck. One of the perpetrators, a small fifteen-year-old black boy, was immediately apprehended.[19] Other instances of putting obstruction on the tracks occurred without much harm being done. One time, a train simply cut in two a rail that had been laid crosswise.[20] In February 1913, a five-year-old boy was taken into custody for attempting to place a block of wood on a track.[21]

Besides track obstructing, there was the problem of persons tampering with railroad switches. In June 1884, Robert H. Hopkins and Robert Whitlock were arrested for allegedly moving a switch on a C & O railway, just outside Richmond. The crime had the effect of throwing an express and passenger train from the main track and into a section of empty freight-cars, causing the death of Alexander Hall, engineer of the passenger train. Hopkins was acquitted, and the case against Whitlock was *nolle prosequi*.[22] In August 1915, sixteen-year-old Richard Alexander was arrested for derailment of a C & O baggage car and engine by breaking the switch lock, just north of Richmond.[23]

A most tragic event occurred in September 1919, just south of Petersburg, thirty miles from Richmond. A switch of the Seaboard Air Line was tampered with, causing the wreck of a passenger train. Engineer C. R. Smith and Fireman Harry M. Ferguson were scalded to death, and a "negro" unlawfully trespassing on the train was crushed to death. Although a police bloodhound was employed at the scene of the wreck and the dog managed to follow the trail of the supposed train wreckers, the trail went cold; reportedly, the suspects were seen boarding a train.[24]

In March 1900, Henry Warren, a black yard hand, was charged with uncoupling a C & O train on the track at an incline in Richmond; the rear half, therefore, was in danger of running into another train. Fortunately, no accident ensued.[25]

The city, without any wrongdoing involved, had its share of horrific mishaps comparable to those experienced elsewhere in the country.[26] In November 1912, a charred body was discovered from a boxcar fire of the Southern Railroad.[27] A few months later, at the Byrd Street yards, a shifting engine of the Atlantic Coast Line moved in the same direction as a car inspector, J.E. Baugh, was working on the tracks. Struck by the engine, Baugh's head was completely severed from his body, and the rest of him was badly mangled.[28]

24

On Board Troublemakers

From the 1880s to about 1910, train robberies flared up across the country.[1] Besides the train robbery that aroused much anxiety among Virginia citizens at Aquia Creek in 1894 (see chapter 25), there were scattered holdups and violence on passenger and excursion trains that were routed through Richmond.

In December 1892, an east-bound C & O passenger train heading toward Richmond was held up just outside Huntington, West Virginia. Two men boarded the train at midnight. One wore a broad sombrero and looked like a cowboy; the other was a red-headed boy, about eighteen years old, described as being "coarsely and commonly dressed." They both wore belts "heavily burdened with weapons." They put on masks, pulled out large Colt revolvers, and entered a car next to the Pullman car. The robbers ordered all hands up and searched the passengers. They shot and killed one passenger, and wounded another in the foot. "A panic ensued, during which trainmen reached the scene, and a general fight ensued." The cowboy pulled the cord, and the train stopped. The two robbers jumped off and disappeared into some woods; they remained at large.[2]

"As woolly and as wild a Western bit of train robbery" as had happened in "many a decade," occurred near Richmond on June 27, 1904. Two black men held up "an entire car-load of colored excursionists" on the C & O Railroad returning from Buckroe Beach. The conductor in charge of the train received a heavy blow to the head. The robbers, identified as John Brown and Jeffry Shelton, took $140 from the treasurer for the excursion party and then "touched" ten passengers. "When the cry of robbery was raised, the conductor locked the doors of the coach and stood guard with a loaded revolver." The thieves, however, managed to knock down the conductor and seize his weapon. They then bolted through a window and fled down a country road. The two thieves were captured by

Richmond detectives. The prisoners were "young and tough-looking customers." It was expected that they would also face charges in a dozen other cases. Three other blacks were also arrested for the excursion train robbery. Of the five-member gang, two went to the penitentiary for five years, one was fined $10 and costs, one had to give security for twelve months, and one was acquitted.[3]

On another excursion train, returning to Richmond from Winston-Salem, North Carolina, a fight occurred in the "refreshment car," resulting in a shooting." Too much whiskey was attributed as cause for the attack. Nathaniel Benson was charged.

A robbery in a Pullman car on the Seaboard Air Line, Florida Limited, southbound from Richmond on December 31, 1906, occurred at 2:30 a.m. as the train reached La Crosse, Mecklenburg County, North Carolina. One man singlehandedly held up the passengers. Percy Martin was apprehended in Huntington, West Virginia, and brought back to Richmond by detectives. Martin confessed to the crime.[4]

The actions of two men on Halloween night, October 31, 1917, resembled mischief rather than outright train robbery. D.C. Clark, a black man employed as a railroad watchman who went by the ironic alias "Snowball," and James Foley, an ironworker, took off in a switch engine of the C & O Railroad. They got as far as one mile before they were caught. A freight train was flagged just in time to avert a collision.[5]

Often, violence on a train involved a conductor. On Saturday night, December 3, 1881, Thomas Curtley boarded a southbound R, F & P train at Milford in Caroline County, headed for Richmond. Curtley claimed free passage by being a lineman for the Western Union Telegraph Company. Captain Thomas H. Stratton, the conductor, demanded payment for a ticket or that the passenger show his pass. After some contention, Curtley paid for a ticket and took a seat. Just before coming to Richmond, Curtley went up to Stratton and cursed him. Stratton responded by punching Curtley in the face. After other blows were exchanged, two passengers separated them. Stratton was bleeding profusely from a cut. Curtley was arrested and sent to Caroline County for prosecution since the offence happened while the train traversed that county.[6]

A similar episode happened in September 1885 when Captain Woolfolk, conductor of an R, F & P train, attempted to eject an African American man occupying a seat in the ladies' car. The passenger refused to leave, prompting Woolfolk to have the porter lock up the man in the smoking car. The detained passenger then became violent and broke the glass pane on the door of the car. Woolfolk then unlocked the door and immediately received a "furious attack" from the passenger. In an attempt to ward off blows, the conductor was severely cut on both arms. The assailant then came at him again with a knife, but, thankfully, Woolfolk was able to restrain him. The "lunatic" passenger wound up lodged in a cell at the Second Police Station.[7]

Violence with weaponry involving trains was reported from time to time. In February 1891, fifteen-year-old John Higgins was shot and seriously wounded by George Branzell, a brakeman of the C & O Railroad. A fracas started when the brakeman threw a lump of coal at Higgins, who was playing at the bottom of Libby Hill. One of the boys stooped to pick up a rock, but before he could throw it, the brakeman shot at the group, a ball striking Higgins in the back. The boy recovered. Branzell, himself only nineteen years old, was arrested. In his defense, Branzell said that the boys had been rocking the train.[8]

On June 13, 1892, Major J. B. Johnson, commander of a "colored" battalion riding aboard an excursion train on its way from Newport News to Richmond, shot at W. H. T. Massey, who had been beating a woman. Massey had questioned Johnson's right to interfere and advanced toward Johnson. The bullet had passed through Massey's chin and caused the loss of an eye. Johnson, brought into Police Court on a charge of "intent to maim," was discharged on grounds of self-defense.[9]

On the Fourth of July, 1895, a full-scale riot took place aboard an excursion train on its return trip to Richmond from West Point, Virginia. Hundreds of men, women, and children were "compelled to witness the disgraceful brawls in all their disgusting details." The train was crowded, and many persons could not get seats. The fight began at the front of the train, and soon more than a dozen men were engaged in conflict. Several fights went on at the same time. "Fortunately, the fight was done with Nature's weapons and no one was badly hurt." In one of the fights, a "drunken crowd" started a battle in a coach near the rear of the train. "Two ladies in this coach and another in the car adjoining fainted or went into spasms through fright during the excitement." Another woman "swooned away and did not recover consciousness for two hours." One participant in the fights had a fit of "delitrium [sic] tremens," yelling and "fighting imaginary snakes." The cause of the riotous behavior was assigned to the fact that much beer was sold on board. Several bartenders dispensed the beer in the refreshment car "under the pseudonym of ginger ale." In addition, some "negro assistants" went through the train with baskets of bottled beer, selling to all who would buy. A reporter commented that "probably no saloon in this city sold as much beer" as "did the men in the refreshment car." Drunken men "staggered through the coaches singing, swearing and annoying ladies and gentlemen everywhere." The "trainmen" did not intervene and could not be seen near any of the fighting parties. To add to the disorder, the train broke in two (a draw bar having broken off), causing an hour's delay.[10] A year later, on an excursion train returning to Richmond from Buckroe Beach, a railway porter was stabbed. The assailant disappeared from the train.[11]

"Interest in the foul murder on a Pullman car" of D. F. Connell, a business man of Portsmouth, Ohio, while on his way to Richmond in August 1891, carried on for many years. A man had entered Connell's berth with the intention of robbing him. During the ensuing struggle, the assailant shot and killed Connell. Several black men were arrested for the crime, including "Jack" Prince, but no one was convicted. A year after the killing of Connell, Prince, along with an associate, was arrested for wounding a train conductor who had accosted them for not paying fare. Prince received a sentence of nine years in the penitentiary, but taken sick with dropsy, died after having served two years of his sentence. Prince's pal was turned over to West Virginia authorities and hanged for the murder of a railroad man. But Prince, while in prison, confided to a cellmate that another man had been involved with him in the Connell murder and had done the actual shooting. Though the alleged murderer had spent time in the penitentiary, he seems never to have been caught to answer for the Connell murder; a revived investigation five years after the murder appears not to have led to an arrest.[12]

Passengers aboard the Seaboard Air Line train, a fast train out of New York City, heading toward southern cities, panicked over the pandemonium that broke out in Richmond one Saturday night in May 1911. A policeman, F. M. Bosquett, while walking down the length of the coaches, spotted two figures huddled between the tender and the baggage car. Upon the order to come forward, one of the stowaways yanked out a revolver and fired at Bosquett before the policeman could get hold of his own pistol. Bosquett returned fire, and "a lightning-like exchange of shots" ensued. The two men clambered down from the "blind baggage" and started running around the train. The policeman gave chase as the runaways exited the train. The punctuation of the "staccato-like sound of pistol shots" frightened the passengers alighting from the train. The men were swift runners and made good their escape. Panic reigned in the station for several minutes, and many who had awakened aboard the train thought the excitement was the result of the train being held up.[13]

25

The "Big Train Robbery"

"The fast mail train, No. 78, on the Richmond, Fredericksburg and Potomac railroad, was held up by train robbers near the drawbridge over Aquia creek last evening about 9:30 o'clock" and "it is supposed that a large amount of money and valuables were secured," read the headline news of October 13, 1894.[1] Another newspaper's account referred to the event as "the most daring train robbery ever committed in Virginia, if not in the entire country."[2] The train consisted of mail, express, baggage and smoker cars, a first-class passenger coach, and "three sleepers."

At 7 p.m. on the night of October 12, the train left Byrd Street Station, for the scheduled run to Washington. The train paused at Fredericksburg to take on water. As the train started up slowly, at the drawbridge over Aquia creek, just beyond Fredericksburg, sixty miles from Richmond, two masked men climbed aboard, on to the top of the train. From there they jumped on to the tender and then into the locomotive, compelling Engineer Frank T. Gallagher, at cocked pistols, to halt the train. To give the impression of a large gang, the robbers ran up and down the train firing their pistols in the air. The holdup men demanded admittance to the express car, but the agents inside, B.F. Crutchfield and Henry Murray, bolted the express door. The robbers placed a dynamite cartridge on the sill of the door, and the ensuing explosion shattered it. In the express car, the agents were forced to open the safe. All valuables therein were taken.

While the thieves rifled the express car, five other masked men, each holding a large revolver, stood guard outside the express car. After securing the plunder, the two robbers inside compelled the fireman, Henry Washington, to cut the locomotive loose. The train headed for Quantico, eight miles away, while the five men that were on the outside disappeared on foot. About a mile from the scene of the robbery, the two holdup men left the engine, leaving open the throttle; "the big machine was turned loose to do destruction to whatever might be in its path." Fortunately, one of the agents telegraphed ahead that the locomotive was coming, and a switchman was able to divert it to a side track; the engine hurled itself into four empty coal cars with both the engine and the cars becoming total wrecks.

The conductor of the train, M. A. Birdsong, managed immediately to send a telegram to Major E.T.D. Myers, president of the R, F & P, in Richmond. The R, F & P offered a reward of $1,000 for the arrest of those involved in the robbery, and the governor of Virginia, Charles T. O'Ferrall, added another $1,000. It was estimated that the robbers had stolen a total of $180,000—$150,000 from the safe, and $30,000 from express packages.[3]

The morning following the robbery, many detectives from New York, Philadelphia, and Washington, accompanied by officers of the Adams Express Company, came to investigate the crime.[4] At every railroad town there was an intense lookout for suspicious persons. At Front Royal, Virginia, about fifty miles from the scene of the robbery, two strangers carrying heavy satchels were observed; they "spent money freely, and had plenty of gold and silver." Witnesses received a good impression of what the men looked like and what they were wearing. Before the local sheriff could get to them, the two suspicious characters boarded a Norfolk and Western train. The next day, Tuesday, October 16, one of the suspects was arrested in Cumberland, Maryland, as he was about to board a train for Pittsburgh. The captive was Charles J. Searcy, who claimed to be from Kansas (but actually was from Texas). He admitted he had been in Front Royal the day before. Found on his person were $1,050, two watches, two pawn tickets from Washington, D.C., a large navy revolver, fifty shells, a pair of gold spectacles, and New Honduras lottery tickets. Put under charge of detectives and immediately sent to Washington, all the while Searcy was interrogated ceaselessly through day and night; "the screws were kept turned on him, questions of all kinds were put to him."[5] Finally, after nonstop interrogation for nearly two days, Searcy broke down and confessed; he revealed all aspects of the plot, what was done with the booty, and where his companions had fled. Among the evidence against Searcy was a wax express seal found on his person.[6]

Searcy fingered as his companion in the robbery Charles August Morganfield, alias Charles Morgan, whom Searcy noted was the instigator. Morganfield was located in Cincinnati, where he was in a hospital after having broken his leg from jumping off a train. Morganfield and Searcy had been acquaintances over a long period of time and had met in Washington, D.C., just prior to committing the crime.[7] Virginia authorities sought the extradition of Morganfield for trial in the state but had to wait three months before Morganfield could walk again, with crutches, plus time for the legal maneuvering. Meanwhile, on November 21, 1894, a grand jury in the Stafford County Court, just outside of Fredericksburg, returned five indictments each for Morganfield and Searcy, involving assault with intent to kill, breaking and entering a railway car, and robbery.[8]

Morganfield, under the charge of detectives, arrived on January 19, 1895, at Fredericksburg, there to be tried for the train robbery. Charles Searcy would be tried separately at a later time.

Early in the morning of February 20, 1895, both Morganfield and Searcy were taken from the Fredericksburg jail and placed on a train for the ride to the Stafford County Courthouse. Morganfield was arraigned and his trial began; Searcy had to wait his turn. The Stafford County Courthouse, according to one observer, was "more like a place where a train might be successfully held up than where the perpetrators of one of the most daring train robberies on record" were to be tried. "The courthouse, the jail, the clerk's house, two stores and other houses constitute the village." It was "four miles from the railroad, in the most thinly settled part of the county." The prisoners were secured by two superintendents of the Pinkerton detective agency and three other guards armed with Winchester repeating shotguns, there being a fear that gang members might attempt a rescue. A throng of country people mixed with state and Adams Express dignitaries. Morganfield pled not guilty.[9]

W.S. Thomas, a prominent attorney from Baltimore, led the prosecution; State Senator William A. Little and Colonel Shay argued for the defense. Little went to work, impugning the testimony of the prosecution's witnesses, saying that corporate wealth, namely that of the Adams Express Company, was trying to gain a quick conviction at any cost. Little exclaimed that "money is all powerful; men sell their honor and women their virtue for money; but thank God, the women of Stafford are with us." The defense attorney was alluding to the fact that a Stafford female citizen had written a letter protesting the awarding of $1,000 for the capture of the train robbers but only $150 for the arrest of the murderer of "one of Stafford's oldest and best citizens." Little also emphasized a partner in crime, Charles Searcy, being an infamous criminal, should not be allowed to incriminate Morganfield with uncorroborated testimony.[10]

Morganfield's trial lasted exactly one week, ending February 28. The jury found him guilty of train robbery generally, but deferred from deciding on specific counts, for which it was expected that the defendant would face another trial. Morganfield was sentenced to eighteen years in the penitentiary. In protesting his sentence, Morganfield declared that he had not been ready for trial and was not in fit physical condition to be tried. The prosecuting attorney then announced it was ready to try Searcy, and also Morganfield again, on the three remaining indictments against him. A continuance on these cases was granted. Both Morganfield and Searcy were conveyed back to the Fredericksburg jail.[11]

Morganfield was fortunate not to face trial on the remaining indictments. Searcy stood trial at the Stafford County Courthouse on May 16, 1895. He pled guilty. Before the case went to the jury, Searcy was allowed to speak, pointing out that he was guilty only as an accessory to the robbery and that he was not involved in the breaking and entering; attention was also called to the fact that, if he confessed and pled guilty, he was promised that he would be liable to a maximum prison term of five years. Prosecutor White stated that he reluctantly agreed to a five-year term because "it brought to justice two noted criminals" and contributed to breaking up gangs. White, however, noted that both Searcy and Morganfield should be hanged. The jury, after deliberating one hour and fifty-three minutes, returned with a verdict of guilty, going beyond the recommended punishment, assessing a sentence of eight years in the penitentiary. The judge commented that Searcy was as guilty, or perhaps guiltier, than Morganfield and should at least have received a sentence of eighteen years, as did his partner in crime.[12]

While in prison, Searcy several times applied for a pardon to Virginia governors Charles T. O'Ferrall, J. Hoge Tyler, and Andrew J. Montague; his appeals were all denied.[13] Charles J. Searcy, at age forty-four, walked out of the state penitentiary at 8 a.m., May 2, 1902, having completed his term, serving nearly seven years of his eight-year term, gaining forty-eight days a year for good behavior.[14] He had enough money to hold him over, having worked in a shoe factory at the penitentiary. But his stopping at the Stafford Courthouse area raised suspicion, as his visit there allegedly to visit friends seemed to set Searcy with plenty of money, supposedly recovered from the train robbery. The newly freed man, however, had to move on quickly as word was out that law enforcement agents from Arkansas had come to Virginia to arrest him for a crime committed in that state ten years before. He bought a ticket for Washington, D.C., and disappeared.[15]

Charles Morganfield, the "famous train robber," as he was called though he persisted in claiming his innocence, now age fifty-two, was released from the state penitentiary, Saturday morning, December 31, 1910, with only $2, a pair of crutches, and the clothes on his back, after having served fifteen years, seven months, and fifteen days of an eighteen-year sentence. Morganfield had lived in prison in constant dread of the brutal guards. He served six years of his sentence in the prison hospital as a means of self-protection. A motto of the guards had been: "Any damned thing is good enough for a convict."[16]

Upon his release, Morganfield announced he was going on a speaking circuit on behalf of the 1,200 men who remained in the prison, to expose the extreme brutality of the penitentiary guards and especially how the shoe company, allowed to use prisoners in the making of shoes for forty-two cents a day, exploited the prison employees. He appeared at the Academy of Music in Richmond on January 10, 1911, for an hour-and-a-half address, and subsequently was also signed on to give a presentation at the Wells Theater. In the meantime, Morganfield gave interviews to newspapers, declaring his allegations against the prison system. He claimed he had been innocent of participating in the Aquia train robbery.

A prison surgeon, Dr. Charles V. Carrington, attested to the credibility of Morganfield's statements. The clothing of prisoners, said Carrington, was "sometimes stiff with blood, their backs sometimes horribly lacerated and mangled, and sometimes their health completely ruined by the beatings they received." Morganfield, himself a "maimed helpless creature" because his broken leg did not mend, endured three such beatings in one week. In his address, billed as "Fifteen Years in Hell," he told of the savagery of the guards towards prisoners. He noted that in the basement of the penitentiary were bodies of black prisoners, which "had been given burial within the walls of the penitentiary for the reason that their mutilated carcasses were deemed not fit even for the dissecting tables in medical colleges." He told of how men were "stretched upon the cross in the dungeon until rats nibbled their finger tips and ears."

The prisoner shoe factory, operated by a New England company, had a vested interest in keeping prisoners from acquiring time off for good behavior. The workers became skilled, and the company could only replace them with a financial loss. Morganfield favored unionizing prison workers. He did not hesitate to attack Virginia's "political machine," and asserted that pardons were often based on political patronage. Morganfield promised, through an ensuing lecture series, to rectify the inhumanity at the penitentiary. He would take his case to the governor, the legislature, and the people. "I am going after the Big Top on the hill. I intend to fight to the finish."[17] Thus Charles Morganfield exchanged the notoriety of being an alleged train robber for the mission of reform in the treatment of convicts.

26

Gold Brick Caper

"One of the boldest pieces of swindling every perpetrated in Richmond" was nipped in the bud during the first days of January 1895. The victim was Alfred W. Withers, a wealthy thirty-year-old of Gloucester County. The perpetrators were two men, claiming to be John Williams, a miner from Arizona, and Thomas H. Parker, an assayer of the United States mint in Philadelphia. Another person in the case was described as "an Indian, who turned out to be a white man, very probably Parker himself, who wore a red mask and black wig."

Williams and Parker had come to Richmond and were staying at the Ford Hotel. According to the narrative that developed in the case, Williams visited Withers at his home in Gloucester County. Williams claimed that he had come to Virginia in search of an uncle named Alfred Withers, who had taken him out west when he was seven years old and "cared for him until he grew to manhood." The uncle, several years ago, had returned to Virginia, and Williams lost touch with him. Williams told Withers that, back in Arizona, he had been out hunting and found lying in the woods two Indians—one dead, and one badly injured. "The living Indian was taken up and nursed back to health by Williams, and to show his gratitude for the kindness he had received at the hands of the paleface, the redskin took Williams to a very rare and rich gold vein." There, twelve bars of gold were found. Williams took eight of the gold bricks, and the Indian kept four. Realizing that the bricks in his possession were very valuable, Williams decided to visit his uncle in Virginia and divide his wealth with him. In Norfolk, Williams was informed that an Alfred Withers lived nearby, in Gloucester County.

Williams told Withers that he had brought with him to Virginia the Indian, who had the four gold bricks he wished to sell. Withers came to Richmond with Williams. Informed that the Indian was very disappointed at not being able to sell his gold, Withers consented to go with Williams a few miles out of the city, into Henrico County, where the Indian was encamped in a strip of woods. Reaching the spot in a cab, Williams told Withers to wait for him while he went to converse with the Indian. Withers could see the Indian at a distance and observed an "animated conversation" after Williams reached him. When he returned, Williams said that the Indian was on a twenty-one-day furlough from his reservation, and the time was about to expire. Williams said that if the "redface" could get money in order to return home, he would put up as collateral two gold bars, worth about $23,000. Williams got one of the gold bars and bored through it with an auger. Williams exclaimed, "You see, it is the same all the way through." Williams and Withers went back to the city with the shavings. Williams allegedly took the shavings to three jewelers, all of whom proclaimed that the shavings were of fine-quality gold, twenty-four-carat, worth $20.70 an ounce. The two men then took the gold bricks to Thomas Parker, allegedly an assayer from Philadelphia, then staying at the Ford Hotel.

Parker, a "tall, neatly-dressed man, with iron gray Vandyke whiskers, sharp, dark eyes, of exceedingly suave manner" looked at one of the gold bars "through his gold-rimmed eye-glasses with a dignity that would have been becoming to an admiral in the French navy, and with due reticence and modesty" agreed to make the test. Going to Parker's room, the supposed assayer took out utensils from a valise, applying acid to the gold bars, and went to work. Parker declared the gold to be of the highest quality and said he wished to buy it and take it back to the mint in Philadelphia. Williams then said that the Indian did not want to sell the brick at a sacrifice, but would put up two of the bars with Withers to secure a loan of $5,000. The next day Withers paid the money.[1]

Meanwhile, Withers was called upon at the hotel by Simon Capps, who requested payment toward a debt Withers owed him. Not wanting to go back to the bank for more funds, Withers visited Joseph Bryan and asked for a loan of $1,500. Bryan replied that he usually required good security for lending money. Withers, of course, had the bricks of gold which he had just deposited in a vault at the Virginia Trust Company. The bricks were taken out, and Bryan, not exactly accepting Withers's account of how the bricks were acquired, decided to have the bricks tested again. At the Nowlan (jewelry) Company on Main Street, it required only a "cursory examination" to establish that "the two bricks of yellow metal" were made of brass and copper "with a coating of the poorest sort of bronze, which appeared to have been put on with a brush."[2]

Getting wind immediately that their gold bunco scam had been exposed, Parker and Williams hightailed it out of Richmond. Parker hired a horse and buggy from Bennett Brothers' Stable and made it to Petersburg; there he boarded a Norfolk and Western train for Lynchburg, followed by Williams. Authorities immediately put out an all-points bulletin for urban areas to be on the lookout for the two men. Both were caught quickly and brought back to Richmond. Parker was taken from a Pullman sleeper on a train just beginning to head westward. Williams was grabbed in Lynchburg.[3]

The mystery of an Indian being involved in the gold bunco scam was put to rest. At the Second Police Station, officers decided to create a little burlesque of the situation. They obtained a dummy from a clothing store and outfitted him as Lo, a poor Pamunkey Indian. He was decked out with a mask, wig, blanket, peace pipe, "and other properties" to resemble the figure Alfred Withers had spotted in the woods at an encampment in Henrico County. The only thing missing was evincing of a guttural "Olla gamolo," given upon the salutation of John Williams that night of the bunco gold-brick transaction with Withers. An "unbroken stream of grinning visitors" called at the station to view the handmade Indian. Richmond detectives made a visit to the "Indian camp," where they found two more bars of "brazen coated metal" and a derby hat. There was no doubt, in the eyes of Richmond's lawmen, that Lo, the Indian, was one and the same as Thomas Parker.[4]

The gold-brick case became even more confused as new actors entered the stage. John T. Norris, who claimed to be a detective from Springfield, Ohio, turned up and declared he was on the trail of gold brickers, and, if given a commission, he would recover the money Withers had paid. Contact with the Pinkerton agency in New York City revealed that Norris was well known "as a deep and shrewd a scoundrel as ever operated in league with notorious crooks" and that he had served a term in prison in Illinois for blackmail. Norris, while staying at the Ford Hotel, tried unsuccessfully to bribe the Commonwealth's attorney, H.M. Smith, to turn Parker over to him to take back to Ohio. Norris was arrested for attempting to bribe Smith. Ironically, Norris had on his person out-of-state papers for the arrest of Parker, known also as Francis Lockwood Smith, wanted for many crimes, mostly related to gold-brick and tin-box scams. Norris had been shadowing Parker and John Williams, alias Cameron Bostetter, for a long time, giving rise to the suspicion that Norris was part of the gold-brick gang. Norris, however, had fallen out with Williams, who had informed a New Jersey district attorney that Norris was "operating hand in glove with the gold-brick syndicate." Also entering the picture was

Samuel Emery, a turfman (bookmaker) who had come from New York City, hopeful of securing Parker's release. Emery, too, was thrown into jail as a suspicious person, but soon released on $1,000 bail. Norris could not meet his bail for $1,000 and remained in jail until the Parker case was heard in Police Court. On January 17, 1895, the Police Court remanded Parker's case to the grand jury for felony indictment and decided to discharge Norris from custody.[5]

Meanwhile, a half-dozen persons from out of state arrived in Richmond and claimed to have been victimized by Parker in gold-brick and other schemes. One of the victims who came to Richmond was Mrs. E.O. Dwelly of Sandusky, Ohio; she had purchased two of the phony gold bricks for $4,000 from an "Indian" out in the countryside, just like the Richmond case.[6]

Parker, who insisted on his innocence in the Richmond gold brick case, came to trial in the Henrico County Court on April 16, 1895. Defense Attorney L.O. Wendenberg pressed hard the leading prosecution witness, Alfred Withers, in cross-examination. It was shown that Withers, now twenty-nine years of age, had run away from home at age fourteen and wound up "running around the country, gambling, and looking after skin-games." Several of Parker's victims from out of state testified to their being conned by Parker. The defendant called no witnesses. Yet the case was considered as one that could be decided either way. Guilt depended upon whether the defendant attempted intentionally to defraud Alfred Withers. Judge Wickham instructed the jury that to prove fraud four things had to concur: intent to defraud; an actual fraud committed; false pretense used in perpetrating the fraud; and fraud must be accomplished by means of false pretense. If any one of these elements were not proved beyond a reasonable doubt, the jury must find the accused not guilty. The jury, which deliberated from April 18th through the 24th, declared it could not reach a decision; after being sent back to reconsider, it returned the next day with the verdict. Despite this, the judge had no option but to declare a mistrial. It was alleged (but not proven) that one of the jurors had been bribed.[7]

Parker continued in the Henrico jail, unable to meet bail of $50,000. A second trial in the Henrico County Court was scheduled to begin May 27, and then postponed until June 20. Two factors, however, worked to preclude this event. Parker's attorney, L.O. Wendenburg, went to Emporia, Virginia, and sued for a writ of habeas corpus, which was granted by the Greensville County Court, and Parker was brought to that county. A warrant for obtaining the custody of Parker by federal authorities for trial in a U.S. Circuit Court was issued on the charge of impersonating a federal assayer. With the writ for habeas corpus being issued by the Greensville Court, Judge Wickham had little choice but to lower bail to the point that Parker could be freed. This was done, with Parker meeting $7,000 bail. But upon return to Richmond, Parker settled down in the city jail, this time as a federal prisoner. Before he could be released, he had to appear before Judge Hughes of the federal court. Since Parker had already met bail in Henrico County, Judge Hughes, on June 16, released Parker from federal custody with only $100 bail. Parker was still expected to appear before the Henrico Court on June 20.[8]

Parker wasted no time in getting out of Richmond; he did so just in the nick of time. At his departure, the governor was meeting with attorneys to arrange warrants for his re-arrest. Being let go, Parker met his friend Emery at Rueger's saloon, where they had sandwiches. The two men left the city in a "double-drag" for Ashland, ten miles away, where they boarded a northbound R, F & P train.[9] Predictably, Parker was a no-show for his scheduled trial in the Henrico Court. Sheriff Simon Solomon stood on the courthouse steps and called out several times, "Thomas H. Parker!" With no response but "the jeering of the jaded upon the railings," Solomon went back into the courtroom and declared that "the prisoner at the bar" was obviously elsewhere. Parker's bail, put up by the Virginia Trust Company, was forfeited.[10] Also not appearing for trial in U.S. Circuit Court in Richmond, Parker's bail at that venue was withdrawn.[11]

It would be quite a while until Richmonders would learn the whereabouts of "the king of bunco"—the gold-brick hoaxer Thomas Parker. As one observer noted, "For a gold-brick man to come down here and swindle one of our citizens out of $5,000 and depart unwhipt of justice is bad enough, but for him to be able to charge the State Treasury as this fellow did, is taxing our patience and pockets overmuch." Parker's case had caused great expense to the state of Virginia: Richmond and Henrico County officers incurred costs to capture Parker; there was the expenditure to bring witnesses from other states to Richmond to testify.[12]

Famed folk musician Polk Miller, leader of the Old South Quartette, had come to Richmond at the time that Parker absconded. He commented that letting Parker go reminded him of a "possum hunt" when he was a boy:

> I went out 'possum hunting one night and had the good luck to catch the biggest one I had ever seen. The next day, Sunday, I was at church and told all the boys that I had the finest 'possum dogs in the world. When they heard of my catch the night before, they became very much interested and wanted to go with me the next

26. Gold Brick Caper

night. Monday morning, I took the varmint out of the barrel in which he was safely imprisoned till I could give the neighbors a regular "'possum roast," and called all the dogs for a chase. I had a half dozen or more dogs, and made the little darkies hold them while I let loose the 'possum in full view. I thought, of course, that the dogs would soon overtake and tree him, and I wanted to make them rank for 'possum by the time the boys got there that night. Imagine my mortification and chagrin when, on turning the dogs loose (bailing him, as it were), not a single dog I had would follow him, but stood around looking at me as if to say, "We caught him after a hard chase, and you turned him loose, and now we ain't going to bother ourselves any more about 'possums"—and they didn't. When the boys came that night, we went out, but the dogs were listless and indifferent, wouldn't hunt for 'possums at all. And to this day, I have felt that I "went back on my dogs" when I turned that 'possum loose.[13]

Parker had been involved with so many gold-brick schemes over the years that he could not resist returning to his old habit. Having wound up in Canada, Parker returned to the States by hooking up with a gold-

The above unfortunate was "a Prosperous Bunco Man" in Alaska, as depicted in the Richmond *Daily Times*, September 19, 1897.

brick gang, consisting of himself and three other men. In August 1900, near Hogansville, New York, his victim was "a guileless farmer" who "invested in a brick which the usual Indian had brought from the West, paying $6,000 for it." Parker, along with his accomplices, were arrested.[14]

Still, at the turn of the century, "the making of gold bricks with which confidence men rob the granger 'come-ons,' and even smart merchants and bankers" became "an established industry." It was not a crime to make a gold brick, only when "the spurious article is sold." One such con man publicly revealed the way to produce a "quality" gold brick. A copper and zinc mixture was used. A half-dollar's worth of real gold was sufficient for a covering.

> Our science is known as water gilding because the last touch we give is to chill it in iced water. We buy our gold in leaves from the beater. These leaves we place in a crucible with mercury, seven parts of mercury to one of gold. The mercury is first heated, and, under the action of a furnace, the mixture is made red hot. Then it is allowed to cool down. We squeeze the amalgam through chamois leather for the purpose of ejecting the superfluous mercury, and the gold, with twice its weight of mercury, remains behind. It is then a yellowish mass of the consistency of butter, and with this the metal is coated with a brush. This is the first step in turning the brick into gold.
>
> After receiving the first coat the brick is subjected to a strong heat for the purpose of evaporating the remaining mercury. It is then in fine form, but far from perfect. There will be little irregularities, and these are removed with a delicate brass brush. After the brushing a lack of true golden tone is apparent, but we have any easy remedy for this. We coat the brick over with gilding wax, which is a preparation of red ocher, verdigris, alum, and borax. Then the brick is again exposed to the action of fire till the wax is entirely burnt away. It's real gold then but we are bound to make it a few carats finer, so our customers can have no possible ground for questioning the quality of their treasure. We do this by covering it with a saline composition and again exposing it to a high temperature. It is finally chilled in cold water, and is beautiful to look on—a perfect gold brick.[15]

When Alfred W. Withers was swindled by the gold-brick men back in January 1895, it "was thought that no other person would ever be caught by this trick," so read a newspaper account of January 1900. But the nephew of the man who was tricked "proved that all is not gold that glitters." D.F. Withers, of Gloucester, while out hunting, met two young men from Baltimore who were hunting quail. Withers and the newcomers immediately became friends and agreed to hunt together. The two outsiders declared to Withers that they owned a mine in California that would soon produce $25 million in gold. They said they were in the East to pick up machinery to produce the gold. Withers happily invested $3,000 in the scheme, and, as security, the two strangers promised to give him a lump of gold they had brought from the mine. All three went to Baltimore, with

Withers taking along the $3,000. In Baltimore, the men went to a popular restaurant, where Withers was filled with oysters and champagne. The two gold-brick men and Withers took a cab to the outskirts of the city. Leaving the cab, they went to a "shabby house," where they accosted "a huge painted Indian." Reluctantly, the Indian pulled from under his bed "a greasy old army blanket," from which he took a piece of yellow metal, giving it to Withers. The $3,000 was handed over to the two other white men, and then Withers left. The following day, Withers realized that he had been swindled. Within two days, detectives ran down the two gold-brick men. One of the perpetrators was the son of a wealthy widow; he made restitution of the $3,000 and paid traveling expenses of Withers and the cost of hiring detectives.[16]

Gold-bricking hoaxes subsequently happened elsewhere. In August 1900, James Blackwell and an accomplice, Frank Smith, were arrested in a gold-brick swindle on a farmer in Springfield, Massachusetts. As in the precedent-setting scheme, Blackwell had disguised himself as an Indian.[17] In spring 1901, three Chicago men duped a citizen of Greensboro, North Carolina, into purchasing a phony gold brick; the men were caught and sentenced to seven years in the state penitentiary; on the recommendation of an Illinois senator and other influential persons, one of the culprits received a pardon in August 1902.[18] A $10,000 gold-brick hoax occurred in 1909 in South Bend, Washington, but was not revealed until three years after the death of the victim. The cheese-shaped brick, weighing 100 pounds, was determined to be made of copper, coated with pure gold.[19]

Precious-metal swindling was not confined to the manufacture of counterfeit gold bricks. The Klondike gold rush in the 1890s had excited Americans everywhere. "Two alleged visitors to the far regions" appeared in Richmond, exhibiting glittering nuggets. The young men, who "had oily tongues and who evidently had been near the chemical works," had their pockets filled with lumps of pyrites, with "the hope of making as though the lumps were gathered in that much sought for place, the Klondike," and thereby being able to sell them. The ruse was discovered when the two bunco men presented one of the nuggets for inspection at a store. The would-be defrauders quickly fled.[20]

Not coincidentally, while Americans learned of the gold-brick hoaxes, they debated the feasibility of diluting the gold monetary standard with making the value of silver at a high-fixed ratio in relation to gold. Gold bugs portrayed the silverites as seeking to lead Americans into a buncoland—accepting an inflated, inferior currency.

Glossary

ballyhoo—entertainment offered in front of a sideshow
barker—a person who stands in front of a sideshow, bidding persons to enter
Big Top—state penitentiary
Black Jane—the city cart for carrying away a corpse
Blackleg—swindler, especially in racing or gambling
bone-shakers—crap shooters
bones—dice or dominoes
boodle—stolen goods
boodle game—to purchase with money something worth much more; the purchase of counterfeit money with real money at lesser amount
boosters—men who stand around fake gambling games and keep on winning to induce persons to gamble and lose
brace—a dishonest faro game
buck the tiger—gamble, especially at faro
bucket shop—a fraudulent brokerage house that speculates on its own account against its customers' interest
bug—a sore on the body that tramps replicate with croton oil
bumper—a person employed to mingle with the crowd in front of a showplace's entrance and jostle potential customers toward a ticket stand
bunco-steering—leading a person to a bunco operation
Cash Corner—Cary and Eighteenth streets, "place of roost for all the outcasts of the city"
cat—a tramp who will do anything but beg
check flasher—forger
cinch—something sure and easy
cookshops—restaurants that served as a cover for dealing in stolen goods
crapster—crap shooter
crib—a house regarded by thieves as a likely place to burglarize
Devil's Headquarters (also known as Hell's Half Acre)—intersection of Broad and Adams streets with Brook Avenue; triangular lot, uptown rival of Cash Corner

Dutch gold—an alloy of copper and zinc in the form of thin sheets that could pass as gold
faker—a street vendor of articles of dubious value
fakir—a confidence man; the name is derived from that used to identify a member of any Islamic religious order
fixer—the man who "squares it" with officials so that you can rob anybody
flimflammer—one who engages in deception, trickery
footpad—one who robs a pedestrian; highwayman
gaff—dealer at faro games
gay cat—a tramp who will take part in a robbery if certain he will not be caught
grifter—swindler, dishonest gambler, or the like; a manager of a sideshow at a circus or fair
healers—men who do the "dirty work" for the gamblers running thieving games
hokeypokey men—street vendors who sold candy, ice cream, and "other joys from push carts"
hoodlum—gangster, racketeer; a rowdy, destructive juvenile
Johnnie squad—groups of youngsters loitering on Broad Street sidewalks between Seventh and Ninth streets
lemon tongue—fist
lizard—an instrument for cheating at cards
Louse Level—building at rear of Sixth Street Market; stores on ground floor, ladder through trap door above leads to den of crime
Major Helm's hostelry—state penitentiary
nippers—handcuffs
peeties—loaded dice made to throw sure numbers
pennyweigher—a sharper who disposes of phony diamond rings
plunger—reckless bettor or speculator; dealer at faro game
policy—a daily lottery betting that certain numbers will be drawn from a lottery wheel
policy shop—place with a policy wheel
pulled—arrested
resort—illegal gambling place, usually along an alleyway
resurrection men—grave robbers who sell corpses to medical schools
rookery—crowded tenement house
shinplaster—paper money of amount less than one dollar; issued during wartime
Shockoe—Richmond City Jail
shoving the queer—passing counterfeit money
skag—a gamecock
skin game—any cheating or fraudulent tricks
snatch thief—pickpocket, shoplifter, purse snatcher, yeggman

spieler—a barker, such as at a circus sideshow
stake and **chain red eye**—bad whiskey
stool pigeon—person as decoy or informer for the police
Valley Inn—Richmond City Jail
wisenheimer—smart aleck; wiseacre
yegg, or **"Johnny Yegg"**—hobo robber
yeggman—itinerant burglar; also safe cracker
Zulu—savage African American

Chapter Notes

KEY TO NEWSPAPERS

Daily Dispatch (*DD*)
Daily Richmond Examiner (*DRE*)
Daily Times (*Times*)
Evening Leader (*EL*)
Richmond Dispatch (*RD*)
Richmond News (*News*)
Richmond News Leader (*NL*)
Richmond Times-Dispatch (*RTD*)
The State (*State*)

Preface

1. *The Random House Dictionary of the English Language* (New York: Random House, 1966), 197.
2. *RD*, October 8, 1895.
3. Elaine Hatfield and Richard L. Rapson, *Flimflam Artists: True Tales of Cults, Crackpots, Cranks, Cretins, Crooks, Creeps, Con Artists, and Charlatans* (Thorofare, NJ: Xlibris, 2011), 55.
4. *News*, June 20, 1900.

Chapter 1

1. *RTD*, July 2, 1904.
2. Christopher Silver, *Twentieth-Century Richmond: Planning, Politics, and Race* (Knoxville: University of Tennessee Press, 1984), 122.
3. *Times*, July 7, 1893, and October 15, 1898; *RD*, January 20 and March 2, 9, 10, 1897; *RTD*, May 5, 1903.
4. *Times*, August 6, 1899.
5. *NL*, July 7, 1911.
6. Jerry Lazarus, "The Good Old Days: Were They Really Better?" *RTD*, February 11, 1979.
7. *DRE*, May 7, 1866.
8. *DD*, July 10 and November 4, 1872; December 6 and 23, 1873; May 2, 1874; January 9, 1875; and June 7, 1879; Lazarus, "Good old Days."
9. *RD*, November 8, 1901.
10. *NL*, December 10, 1908.
11. *EL*, February 11, 1899.
12. *RD*, June 12, 1913.
13. *RD*, July 14, 1873, and April 19, 1896.
14. Lazarus, "Good Old Days"; Gustavus A. Weber, *Report on Housing and Living Conditions in Neglected Sections of Richmond* (Richmond: Whittet & Shepperson, 1913), 15.
15. Weber, *Report on Housing*, 63.
16. *Times*, July 29, 1893, and August 18, 1895.
17. *Time and the River: The Story of Richmond's Drinking Water* (Richmond: Department of Utilities, revised 1956), 3-5.
18. *NL*, October 1, 1908.
19. *NL*, February 16, 1909.
20. *EL*, February 1, 1898.
21. *State*, June 16, 1885.
22. *DD*, February 27, 1878.
23. *Times*, January 1, 1902; *NL*, January 1, 1916.
24. *NL*, January 6 and November 30, 1920.
25. *RTD*, January 11, 1909.
26. *Times*, August 18, 1895.
27. *Times*, September 20, 1894; *RTD*, October 1, 1911.
28. *DD*, January 15, 1877; *Times*, September 20, 1894, and August 14 and December 10, 1897; *EL*, August 22 and September 28, 1898.
29. *State*, September 16, 1897.
30. Paul W. Keve, *The History of Correc-*

tions in Virginia (Charlottesville: University Press of Virginia, 1986), 149; Harry M. Ward, Public Executions in Richmond, Virginia, 1782–1907 (Jefferson, NC: McFarland, 2012), 152.
31. DD, July 1, 1878; State, October 10, 1878; Times, November 13, 1889; NL, March 13, 1919.
32. Times, May 25, 1899.
33. Times, March 26, 1893.

Chapter 2

1. DD, November 16, 1883, and January 22, 1884; Times, October 10, 1901.
2. State, January 8, 1894.
3. Times, September 30, and October 5, 1902.
4. George A. Sala, America Revisited, 2 vols. (London: Vizetelli and Company, 1882), 1: 241.
5. James Breeden, "Body Snatchers and Anatomy Professors: Medical Education in Nineteenth-Century Virginia," Virginia Magazine of History and Biography, 83 (1975): 67; DD, November 18, 1867.
6. RD, January 20, 1892.
7. Times, June 9 and August 6, 1902; T. Tyler Porterfield, Nonesuch Place: A History of the Richmond Landscape (Charleston: The History Press, 2009), 89.
8. DD, January 7, 12, 16, and 26, 1880.
9. Breeden, "Body Snatchers," 322–23.
10. Sala, America Revisited, 241.
11. Times, October 28, 1886.
12. DD, January 21, 1881.
13. NL, October 4, 1904.
14. DD, January 18, 1884.
15. DD, March 3, 1887.
16. NL, December 8, 1915.
17. George E. Barksdale, "The Legend of Chris Baker," published article, Tompkins-McCaw Library archives.
18. Charles R. Robins, "Chris Baker," article, Tompkins-McCaw Library archives.
19. State, March 8, 1897.
20. RD, March 13, 1896.
21. NL, September 14, 1904.
22. State, February 24, 1891; DD, May 1, 1896.
23. State, February 21, 1891.
24. State, May 23, 1892.
25. Times, November 13, 1896.
26. NL, March 29, 1909.
27. Times, June 16, 1895.

Chapter 3

1. Times, July 30 and August 14, 1903.
2. Times, October 1, 1899.
3. Times, January 25, 1894.
4. News, June 8, 1901.
5. RTD, November 29, 1909.
6. DD, October 12, 1877.
7. Times, May 21, 1899, and January 8, 1903.
8. State, September 10, 1897.
9. News, March 5, 1900.
10. Times, February 6, 1902.
11. EL, January 4, 1898; RD, January 4, 1898.
12. RTD, May 1, 1912.
13. NL, December 4, 1914, and August 7, 1915.
14. Times, October 21, 1900.
15. State, September 4, 1895.
16. News, February 20, 1900.
17. News, February 21, 1900.
18. RTD, May 20, 1903.
19. NL, January 7, 1914.
20. NL, July 16, 1915.
21. NL, March 20, and April 21, 1913.
22. NL, March 13, 1876.
23. Times, May 11, 1890.
24. State, February 21, 1896.
25. NL, May 1, 1916.
26. RD, March 5, 1891; William S. Kroger, Clinical and Experimental Hypnosis in Medicine, Dentistry, and Psychology, 2d ed. (Philadelphia: J.B. Lippincott, 1977), 3.
27. Times, January 24, 1896.
28. Times, April 2, 1897.
29. Times, November 30, 1897.
30. NL, January 15 and 17, 1910.
31. State, January 13 and 15, 1896.
32. State, November 7, 1896; Times, November 8, 1896.
33. EL, December 16, 1898.
34. News, June 19, 1900.
35. NL, January 16, 1911.
36. DD, October 22 and 24, 1872, and October 17 and 31, 1874.
37. State, March 25, 1981; DD, September 6, 1883.
38. State, March 19, 1879, and May 19, 1884.

39. *Times*, October 7, 1893.
40. *Times*, September 27 and 30, 1896.
41. *RD*, November 25, 1900; Kenneth Silverman, "Harry Houdini," in John A. Garraty and Marck C. Carnes, eds., *American National Biography* (New York: Oxford University Press, 1999), 11: 247.
42. *Times*, July 3, 1887.
43. *State*, July 24, 1994.
44. *RD*, October 3, 1894.
45. *State*, May 3, 1897.
46. *NL*, June 29, 1911.
47. *Times*, October 27, 1901.
48. *RTD*, June 21, 1908.
49. *State*, May 3, 1897.
50. *NL*, April 3, 1908.
51. *News*, May 10, 1900.
52. *EL*, June 5, 1999.
53. *State*, May 6, 1897.

Chapter 4

1. Isaac Weld, quoted in Harry M. Ward, *Richmond: An Illustrated History* (Northridge, CA: Windsor Publications, 1985), 66.
2. *Times*, January 21, 1896.
3. *RD*, June 26, 1892.
4. *DD*, October 24, 1886; *State*, January 3, 1889; *NL*, December 23, 1911.
5. *State*, November 1, 1896.
6. *NL*, August 19, 1909.
7. *RTD*, January 28, 1903, January 26 and 27, 1904, July 19, 1914, and July 17, 1918.
8. See John Morris, ed., *Wanderings of a Vagabond* (New York: John Norris, 1873), 56-59, and Harry M. Ward, *Children of the Streets of Richmond, 1865-1920* (Jefferson, NC: McFarland, 2015).
9. *Times*, December 21, 1886.
10. *Times*, June 14, 1893, October 18, 1894, July 11, 1999; *RTD*, March 12, 1909; *NL*, Jan. 1, 1909, and September 27, 1915.
11. *RTD*, August 10, 1908.
12. *RD*, October 10, 1897.
13. *RTD*, February 1, 1903.
14. *RTD*, July 3, 1909.
15. *NL*, January 14, 1907.
16. *DD*, September 13, 1870, April 30, 1871, October 22 and November 2, 1874, March 23, 1881, and February 11-13, 1887.
17. *State*, May 1, 1877; *State*, May 9, 1898.
18. *Times*, March 8, 1890, *State*, May 9, 1898; *NL*, December 5, 1910.

19. *State*, March 15, 1888; *RD*, April 4, 1889, and October 4, 1890.
20. *State*, December 12, 1892; *RTD*, September 1, 1909.
21. *RTD*, February 12, 1903.
22. *State*, June 18, 1894, and September 4, 1897; *Times*, October 2 and 12, 1898.
23. *Times*, September 25, 1898.
24. *Times*, September 25, 1898.
25. *NL*, June 29, 1906.
26. *State*, July 11, 1893.
27. Ward, *Richmond: Illustrated History*; Virginia C. Johnson and Barbara Crookshanks, *Virginia Horse Racing: Triumphs of the Turf* (Charleston: History Press, 2008), 100-02; Virginius Dabney, *Richmond: The Story of a City* (Garden City, NY: Doubleday, 1976), 86.
28. *Times*, October 8, 1883, and May 2, 1894.
29. *Times*, January 11 and March 19, 1896.
30. *NL*, April 22, 1904.
31. *Times*, April 3, 1901; *RTD*, January 30-31, 1903; *NL*, February 23, 1910, and May 28, 1912.
32. *Times*, January 1, 1897; *RD*, December 6, 1891.
33. *Times*, January 15, 1891.
34. *Times*, February 4, 1899.
35. *Times*, December 22, 1896; Porterfield, *Nonesuch Place*, 26.
36. *Times*, November 14, 1897.
37. *NL*, January 9, 1909.
38. *State*, December 12, 1877.
39. *State*, December 4, 1879.
40. *NL*, January 9 and February 1, 1909; *Charter and ... Ordinances of the City of Richmond* (1910), 389-99.
41. *NL*, August 2, 1918.
42. *Times*, August 26, 1902; *NL*, June 10, 1907, August 5, 1912, and July 14 and August 12, 1914.
43. *DD*, July 2, 1889; *RTD*, Jan 28, 1903, and June 18, 1906; *NL*, August 18, 1903, August 8 1907, and October 22, 1914.
44. *NL*, June 30, 1913.
45. Morris, *Wanderings of a Vagabond*, 208-14.
46. *Times*, February 15, 1893.
47. "The Gamblers," *The Idea*, vol. 4, no. 78, July 30, 1910, 8-9.
48. *NL*, January 27, 1908; "Fake Club," *The Idea*, vol. 4, no. 31, September 18, 1910, 12-13.

49. *Times*, April 7, 1895, and September 10 and 16, 1902.
50. *State*, September 6, 1886; *DD*, October 20, 1886; *RD*, July 18, 1895; *Times*, April 8, 1902; *NL*, December 3, 1907.
51. *NL*, December 3, 1907.

Chapter 5

1. *DD*, April 29, 1872.
2. *State*, May 8, 1897.
3. *DD*, August 27, 1877.
4. *Times*, November 13, 1900.
5. *NL*, April 1, 1913.
6. *NL*, April 1, 1913.
7. *NL*, October 11, 1910.
8. *Times*, November 23, 1895.
9. *State*, December 13, 1895.
10. *NL*, July 3 and 14, 1917.
11. *State*, November 3, 1877.
12. *DD*, December 31, 1877.
13. *State*, March 2, 1897.
14. *NL*, December 7, 1910.
15. *DD*, February 10, 1888.

Chapter 6

1. *EL*, February 2, 1899.
2. *NL*, December 1, 1916.
3. *NL*, January 7, 1919.
4. *RTD*, March 16, 1919.
5. *Times*, December 20, 1891; *RTD*, March 12, 1909; *NL*, December 8, 1911.
6. *Times*, June 1, 1902.
7. *NL*, March 30-31, 1911.
8. *RD*, November 14, 1894.
9. *NL*, April 6, 1908.
10. *Times*, January 23, 1892; *NL*, October 3, 1912.
11. *RD*, April 29, 1902.
12. *NL*, June 10, 1905.
13. *Times*, September 17, 1901.
14. *Times*, April 20, 1901.
15. *NL*, September 21, 1911.
16. *Times*, May 15, 1889.
17. *NL*, October 6, 1908.
18. "The Loan Sharks," *The Idea*, vol. 4, no. 23, June 4, 1910, 10.
19. *NL*, November 9-10, 13, 26, and 28, and December 1-2, 1914; *RTD*, December 31, 1914.
20. *NL*, December 2, 1914.
21. *NL*, August 27, 1915.
22. *NL*, May 5, 1915.
23. *RTD*, December 1, 1909.
24. *RD*, January 21, 1896.
25. *NL*, September 29, and December 29, 1911.

Chapter 7

1. *DD*, October 24, 1873, and October 29, 1878; *State*, October 17, 1881, and November 1, 1882; *RD*, June 18, 1897; *NL*, October 3, 1910.
2. *State*, October 17, 1881; *DD*, October 3, 1888.
3. *Times*, October 21, 1891.
4. *NL*, October 9, 1911.
5. *RD*, October 29, 1891.
6. *RTD*, October 6 and 9, 1919.
7. *NL*, October 11, 1906.
8. *NL*, October 9, 1908.
9. *NL*, October 12, 1911.
10. *State*, October 26, 1885; *NL*, October 9, 1913.
11. *Times*, October 10, 1894.
12. *State*, October 9, 1894. Management of burlesque shows in the city were fined when their presentations became too risqué (e.g., *NL*, October 20, 1914).
13. *NL*, September 9, 1908.
14. *News*, October 24, 1900.
15. *RD*, October 29, 1891.
16. Ibid.
17. *Times*, October 9, 1894.
18. *State*, October 26, 1880, and October 26, 1885; *RTD*, October 11, 1913.
19. *RTD*, May 18, 1909.
20. *DD*, October 27, 1874, and October 28, 1875.
21. *DD*, November 2, 1876.
22. *Times*, September 30, 1888.
23. *NL*, October 1, 1910.
24. *RTD*, October 6, 1915.
25. *DD*, September 6 and November 2, 1876; *State*, November 3, 1876.
26. *RTD*, September 29, 1914.
27. *NL*, October 3, 1908.
28. *NL*, October 30, 1908.
29. *Times*, October 9, 1894.
30. *DD*, May 19, 1876.
31. *DD*, October 29, 1879.
32. *State*, May 7, 1907.
33. *DD*, April 17 and 21 and September 19, 1877, October 4-5, 1878, and October 7,

1881; *State*, August 26-27, 1880, September 3, 1885, and September 9, 1895; *RD*, May 15, 1900 and November 2, 1902; *RTD*, August 8, 1920; Ernest Albrecht, "Charles Ringling," *American National Biography*, 18: 527-8.
34. *RD*, April 16, 1899, and May 15, 1900; *RTD*, May 15, 1900, October 2, 1906, May 23, 1913, and October 10, 1920.
35. *DD*, October 24, 1877, and October 4, 1878.
36. *DD*, April 17, 1877.
37. *NL*, January 4, 1910.
38. *DD*, September 19, 1876.
39. *NL*, November 14, 1903.
40. *RTD*, June 8, 1911.
41. *DD*, April 19, 1877.
42. *State*, July 9 and 11, 1896.
43. e.g., *State*, April 23, 1883.
44. *RD*, May 15-16, and May 18 and 20, 1900.
45. *RD*, October 6, 8-10, 12-13, and 17, 1901.
46. *NL*, September 27, 1920.

Chapter 8

1. *DD*, January 17, 1886.
2. Ibid.
3. *Times*, September 1, 1893; *RTD*, September 10, 1903; *NL*, November 9, 1904.
4. *NL*, June 7, 1913.
5. *DD*, September 21, 1876; *State*, June 6, 1885; *RD*, March 4, 1900.
6. *State*, June 26, 1885.
7. *NL*, February 20, 1895.
8. *NL*, October 14, 1913.
9. *State*, April 12, 1877.
10. *Times*, February 9, 1896.
11. *RD*, July 14, 1894.
12. *Times*, January 3, 1897.
13. *Times*, November 13, 1897.
14. *State*, March 8, 1897; *Times*, November 23, 1898 and September 26, 1900.
15. *NL*, March 5, 1907.
16. *DD*, June 7, 1870.
17. *State*, February 18, 1878.
18. *NL*, May 12, 1916.
19. *State*, June 11, 1878.
20. *Times*, May 7, 1899.
21. *NL*, October 14, 1913.
22. *NL*, November 25, 1912.
23. *EL*, May 6 and June 10, 1899.
24. *NL*, April 15-16 and 10, 1909.

25. *DD*, April 17, 1887.
26. *Times*, April 10, 1895; *RD*, April 10, 1899.
27. *RTD*, May 4, 1920.
28. *State*, September 20, 1888.
29. *RD*, March 10, 1892.
30. *NL*, January 6, 1906.

Chapter 9

1. *RTD*, December 3, 1903; Claire Mee, "Inside the Criminal Mind," *New York Times*, Sunday Review section, May 31, 2015, 9
2. *DD*, January 31, 1886; *RD*, January 13, 1891; *NL*, June 9, 1904, June 6, 1914, December 6, 1915, and January 5, 1918; *Times*, December 9, 1887, January 3, 1889, April 10, 1898, and February 24, 1900.
3. *State*, November 9, 1885.
4. *NL*, December 6, 1915.
5. *NL*, May 9 and October 16, 1919.
6. *State*, May 20, 1884; *DD*, January 17, 1886.
7. *DD*, March 10, 1881; *State*, May 20, 1884; *RD*, October 14, 1891; *Times*, May 25, 1892.
8. *State*, September 2, 1878.
9. *State*, August 9, 1886.
10. *State*, May 25 and 26, 1877.
11. *State*, December 13, 1877.
12. *RTD*, October 31, 1910.
13. *NL*, May 12-13 and 18, 1918.
14. *State*, September 3, 1896.
15. *Times*, September 23, 1899.
16. *Times*, August 18, 1901.
17. *DD*, December 20, 1891; *State*, January 1, 1894; *NL*, June 22, 1906, July 8, 1907, and April 2, 1912.
18. *Times*, January 22, 1889; *State*, July 9, 1890. *RD*, August 22, 1901; *NL*, September 21, 1903.
19. *DD*, July 27, 1870; *State*, August 31, 1878, and September 7, 1896; *Times*, November 23, 1888, and April 20, 1901; *EL*, October 17, 1900; *NL*, September 21, 1903, July 30, 1910, and February 12, 1920.
20. *NL*, August 5, 1903.
21. *State*, September 7, 1896.
22. *Times*, June 2, 1889.
23. *NL*, August 10, 1907.
24. *DD*, January 20, 1868, July 7, 1877, and January 24, 1883; *State*, July 3, 1883, and

January 14, 1888; *Times*, December 11, 1886, April 1, 1896, August 14 and December 26, 1899, and July 17, 1901; *EL*, March 22, 1898, and January 5, 1900; *NL*, September 2, 1903, and August 27, 1907.
25. *DD*, December 11 and 18, 1872, January 12, 1877; *State*, September 20, 1889; *NL*, November 2, 11, and 14, December 30, 1914.
26. *DD*, January 3, 1886.
27. *NL*, December 16, 1916.
28. *RD*, April 27, 1897.
29. *RD*, November 15, 1899.
30. *NL*, June 17, 1910.
31. *RTD*, October 8, 1915.
32. *Times*, June 26-27, 1900, April 4, 1901, and January 14, 1902; NL, November 30, 1908, July 29, 1911, and July 5, 1916.
33. *Times*, January 27, 1900.
34. *Times*, October 17, 1895; *RTD*, January 11, 1909.
35. *NL*, July 28, 1910.
36. *NL*, July 1, 1916.
37. *NL*, August 15, 1910.
38. *NL*, March 10, 1914.
39. *NL*, February 17, 1908.
40. *NL*, October 2, 1908.
41. *DD*, December 12, 1876; *State*, March 18, 1881, and August 6, 1885.
42. *State*, May 11, 1886; *DD*, January 8, 1885; *NL*, April 19, 1907.
43. *Times*, January 19, 1896; *RTD*, September 18, 1908.
44. *NL*, September 22, 1906.
45. *NL*, July 3, 1907.
46. *State*, January 13, 1891.
47. *RTD*, April 15, 1913.

Chapter 10

1. *Times*, October 28, 1894, and December 22, 1896; *RD*, February 26, 1897; *NL*, Feb 29, 1904, September 8, 1906, December 8, 1909, and April 6, 1910; *RTD*, November 16, 1908.
2. *RD*, October 28 and 30, 1894; *Times*, October 28, 1894.
3. *NL*, September 29, 1903.
4. *RD*, February 26, 1897.
5. *Times*, January 5, 1897.
6. *NL*, July 3, 1906.
7. *NL*, October 5, 1916.
8. *RD*, July 11, 1890.

9. *Times*, June 3, 1894, and March 11, April 8 and 12, and October 12, 1902; *NL*, September 30, 1903, April 10, 1905, July 13 and September 24, 1906, January 5, 1912, December 8, 1915, March 31, 1916, and April 15, 1920; *RTD*, November 16, 1909.
10. *NL*, October 26, 1914.
11. *NL*, March 31, 1916.
12. *NL*, January 13, 1911.
13. *State*, June 16, 1879.
14. *NL*, July 8, 1907.
15. *Times*, September 12, 1893.
16. *NL*, January 5 and 27, 1916.
17. *NL*, December 2, 1919.
18. *NL*, September 24, 1906; *State*, August 20, 1880.
19. *NL*, August 21, 1919.
20. *NL*, November 1, 1912.
21. *NL*, February 29, 1904.
22. *RTD*, October 11, 1913.
23. *NL*, July 9, 1913.
24. *RTD*, September 10, 1915.
25. *News*, October 29, 1900; *NL*, December 29, 1903, April 20, 1904, October 9, 1908, and August 12, 1910.

Chapter 11

1. *Times*, October 24, 1888.
2. Ibid.
3. *State*, July 9, 1894; *NL*, November 19, 1903.
4. *NL*, October 14, 1904.
5. *Times*, October 24, 1888.
6. *NL*, March 6, 1905.
7. *DD*, February 26, 1887; *EL*, November 25, 1898; *Times*, November 26, 1898 and February 17, and June 9 and 19, 1900; *NL*, January 2, 1904, November 29, 1907, and January 4, 1910.
8. *State*, March 17-18 and 22-25 and May 11, 14, and 18-20, 1886.
9. *NL*, November 6, 1903.
10. *News*, August 9, 1900. (For Topeka Joe, see chapter 17.)
11. *Times*, July 18, 1900.
12. *NL*, September 21, 1908.
13. *NL*, December 17, 1912.

Chapter 12

1. *State*, July 7, 1896.
2. *RTD*, November 25, 1910.

3. *NL*, December 29, 1910, and March 8, 1911.
4. *State*, September 21, 1896.
5. *NL*, October 7, 1907.
6. *RD*, October 31, 1873; *RTD*, January 12, 1912; *NL*, December 1, 1916.
7. *NL*, January 1, 1914.
8. *State*, May 13, 1878; *NL*, December 24, 1919.
9. *Times*, November 2, 1891, and November 2, 1901; *NL*, December 20, 1913, October 16, 1919, and October 4, 1920.
10. *State*, October 30, 1877; *NL*, October 11, 1906.
11. *DD*, January 3, 1872, November 3, 1874, November 3, 1877, and October 31, 1878; *State*, November 6, 1877; *NL*, July 7, 1906, September 28, 1910, September 26, October 12, 1911, and January 4, 1916.
12. *NL*, October 15, 1906.
13. *DD*, October 29, 1886.
14. *Times*, September 28, 1893, and March 29, 1900.
15. *RTD*, November 20, 1903.
16. *NL*, October 13, 1906.
17. *State*, May 6, 1878.
18. *State*, March 28, 1881.
19. *Times*, May 20, 1899.
20. *NL*, July 17, 1911.
21. *Times*, July 22, 1898.
22. *State*, February 8 and August 21, 1877, March 12 and July 9, 1879, and October 2, 1895; *DD*, August 22, 177; *Times*, August 15, 1899; *NL*, June 30 and December 19, 1910, December 3, 1915, August 21, 1919; *RTD*, November 24, 1903.
23. *NL*, June 10, 1910.
24. *State*, July 10, 1893.
25. *NL*, December 11, 1906.
26. From St. Louis, *Times*, April 4, 1901.
27. *State*, July 7, 1896.
28. *State*, November 5, 1877.
29. *DD*, November 14, 1877.
30. *State*, May 3, 1878.
31. *DD*, November 14, 1877.
32. *NL*, February 25, 1904.

Chapter 13

1. *Times*, April 10, 1898.
2. *EL*, August 16, 1898; *Times*, August 31, 1898; *NL*, November 30, 1899.
3. *EL*, January 7, 1899; *News*, January 5, 1900.
4. *NL*, January 15, 1907.
5. *State*, February 27, 1897.
6. *NL*, February 27, 1918.
7. *State*, January 1, 1897.
8. *Times*, May 13, 1897.
9. *EL*, December 22, 1899.
10. *EL*, December 19, 1899.
11. *News*, May 22, 1900.
12. *Charter and ... Ordinances of the City of Richmond* (1867), 216-17.
13. *Ordinances of the Council of the City of Richmond* (Richmond: O.H. Flanhart, 1898), September 17, 1898, 119; *Certain Resolutions of the Council of the City of Richmond* (Richmond: Ware and Duke, 1900).
14. *Times*, August 9, 1898, and October 2, 1900.
15. *Times*, October 27, 1891.
16. *RTD*, November 14, 1908.
17. *EL*, April 17, 1899.
18. *NL*, November 20, 1906.
19. See chapter 14.
20. *DD*, July 24, 1874.
21. *DD*, August 21, 1874.
22. *Times*, December 5, 1900.
23. *Times*, October 31, 1894, and February 2, 1895.
24. *NL*, April 11, 1912.
25. *Times*, March 4, 1902.
26. *NL*, January 1, 1907.
27. *Times*, September 21, 1897.
28. *EL*, February 3, 1898.
29. *NL*, January 2, 1909.
30. *State*, February 9, 1893.
31. *Times*, November 5, 1902.
32. *NL*, December 7, 1914.
33. *RD*, January 1, 1890; *Times*, June 4, 1891, and February 15, 1899; *EL*, July 9, 1898.
34. *NL*, January 26, 1905.
35. Most prominent being the William Byrd Community House, *NL*, January 27, 1905, and November 9, 1915; *Eighth Annual Report of the State Board of Charities and Corrections ... Year Ending 1916* (Richmond: 1917), 106-10.
36. *Times*, April 20, 1893.
37. *NL*, February 16, 1906.
38. *RTD*, May 24, 1903, and July 31, 1938.
39. *Times*, August 24, 1890; *RTD*, November 2, 1937, and December 1, 1941.
40. *State*, July 14, 1876.

Chapter 14

1. *State*, November 1, 1893.
2. *State*, December 21, 1901.
3. *DD*, April 21, 1869; *RD*, October 3, 1892; *Times*, March 4, 1897, and June 15, 1900; *State*, May 10, 1897; *EL*, February 18, March 9, and April 5, 1898.
4. *Times*, March 4, 1897.
5. *Times*, September 29, 1901.
6. *State*, December 21, 1896.
7. *EL*, March 19, 1898.
8. *RD*, April 6, 1900.
9. *RD*, April 6, 1900.
10. *EL*, July 27–28, 1897; January 29, 1898, and November 17, 1800; *Times*, July 27–28, 1897, January 28, 1900, and July 21 and November 6, 1901; *State*, November 17, 1897; *RD*, November 6, 1898; *NL*, July 21, 1901, and May 4, 1906.
11. *Times*, November 6, 1901.
12. *RTD*, May 18, 1910.
13. *State*, August 31, 1882.
14. *RD*, October 11, 1902.
15. *Times*, September 1, 1893.
16. *EL*, July 27–28, 1897.
17. *Times*, October 6, 1894.
18. *Times*, April 1 and December 27, 1900.
19. *DD*, January 4, 1881.
20. *State*, September 25, 1894.
21. *RD*, November 19–20, 1889.
22. *DD*, January 18, 1877, and November 23, 1887.
23. *DD*, May 18, 1886; *Times*, October 4, and November 12, 1898, and June 12, 1902.
24. *State*, March 3 and 9, 1897.
25. *State*, June 5, 1897.
26. *RTD*, December 21, 1914.
27. *State*, January 2, 1894.
28. *State*, August 30, 1898.
29. *RTD*, December 31, 1909.
30. *NL*, August 12, 1912.
31. *EL*, March 11, 1899.
32. *RD*, December 29, 1895.
33. *State*, October 31, 1893, and Jan 2, 1897.
34. *RD*, November 1, 1899; *Times*, April 4, 1899, and January 28, 1900.
35. *State*, February 25, 1899; *EL*, December 14, 1898; *RD*, March 16, 1901.
36. *DD*, June 26, 1877.
37. *State*, January 2, 1897.
38. *News*, May 30, 1900.
39. *EL*, November 16, 1898.
40. *News*, January 6, 1900.
41. *Times*, January 28, 1900.
42. *NL*, January 15, 1907.
43. *State*, January 11, 1877 and August 8, 1893; *DD*, November 7, 1880.
44. *State*, December 23, 1876.
45. *State*, January 5, 1897.
46. *State*, August 25, 1897.

Chapter 15

1. *State*, December 8–9, 1892; *Times*, August 19, 1894, October 20, 1901, and June 1, 1902; *NL*, November 5, 1903, October 6, 1904, November 26, and December 20, 1907.
2. *NL*, September 13, 1918.
3. *NL*, December 14 and 29, 1914.
4. *Times*, September 1, 1895; *NL*, April 13, 1907, and March 23 and 30, April 8, October 2, 1908.
5. *NL*, February 9 and April 1909.
6. *NL*, November 18, 1908.
7. *NL*, December 30, 1914.
8. *NL*, November 21, 1913.
9. *NL*, July 21, 1915, and September 27, 1920; Louis Filler, *A Dictionary of American Social Reform* (New York: Philosophical Society, 1963), 590; Alfred H. Kelley and Winfred A. Harbison, *The American Constitution: Its Origins and Development* (New York: W.W. Norton and Company, 1955), 590.
10. *Times*, January 8, 1889.
11. *RTD*, May 3, and 19, 1903; *NL*, April 20 and 24, 1918.
12. Page Smith, *Rise of Industrial America*, vol. 6 (New York: McGraw-Hill, 1984), 93.
13. *DD*, May 26, 1883.
14. *State*, September 7, 1895.
15. *NL*, July 19, 1906, December 23, 1907, and April 7, 1908; *RTD*, March 7 and June 7, 1909, and February 20, 1917.
16. *NL*, November 29, 1907.
17. *NL*, January 11, 1909.
18. *Times*. April 24, 1894.
19. *NL*, October 16, 1908.
20. *NL*, October 7, 1910.
21. *NL*, April 2, 1904.
22. *NL*, April 4, 1906.
23. Ibid.

24. *NL*, June 30, 1917; J. C. Furnas, *Great Times: An Informal Social History of the United States, 1914-1929* (New York: G.P. Putnam's Sons, 1974), 275.
25. *NL*, September 21, 1917.
26. *NL*, December 12, 1916.
27. *NL*, March 26, 1904.
28. *NL*, March 28, 1904.
29. *RTD*, April 1, 1906.
30. *RD*, March 21, 1901.
31. *NL*, May 4, 1906.
32. *NL*, January 9, 1906.
33. *RTD*, December 29, 1914; *NL*, January 6, 1915.
34. *NL*, December 21, 1914.
35. *NL*, October 18, 1915.

Chapter 16

1. e.g., *RD*, July 27, 1874; *Times*, December 9, 1900; *NL*, August 12 and 18, 1911, January 2 and July 19, 1912, and June 6, 1913.
2. *Times*, May 4, 1888.
3. *NL*, September 11, 1912.
4. *NL*, January 7, 1911.
5. *NL*, April 3, 1903.
6. *NL*, July 7, 1909.
7. *DD*, March 1 and 4, 1875.
8. *NL*, May 10, 1916.
9. *NL*, July 7, 1911.
10. *RTD*, February 19, 1910.
11. *NL*, March 28, 1907.
12. *NL*, November 9, 1907.
13. *RTD*, October 31, 1910; Ernest A. Bell, *Fighting the Traffic in Young Girls: War on the White Slave Trade* (Chicago: G.S. Ball, 1910), 388.
14. "Another Sacrifice to Richmond's White Slave Trade, Fostered by the Police Board," *The Idea*, vol. 5, no. 8, July 22, 1911, 8-9.
15. Anna Maquire, "The Richmond White Slave Trade," *The Idea*, vol. 4, no. 18, April 30, 1910, 14-15.
16. *DD*, April 3, 1881.
17. *NL*, June 3, 1905.
18. "Another Sacrifice...," *The Idea*, vol. 5, no. 8, 8-9.
19. *NL*, April 7, 10, and 12, 1905; April 13, 1913; February 27 and March 6, 1907.
20. *DD*, August 17, 1869, June 3 and 22 and August 19, 1871; July 1-2, 1872, November 21, 1874, January 17, 1875, June 30 and August 13, 1878; July 22, 1879, September 9 and October 29, 1882; July 8, 1883; January 21, 1887; *EL*, October 22, 1898; "Justice John Issues Bench Warrant ...," *The Idea*, vol. 5, no. 5, March 1910, 11.
21. *DD*, June 15, 1876.
22. *NL*, January 8 and February 9-11, 1915; Arthur W. James, *Virginia's Social Awakening* (Richmond: Garrett and Massie, 1939), 114-15.
23. See Harry M. Ward, *Children of the Streets of Richmond*, 58-68.
24. *DD*, July 3, 1883; *State*, August 24, 1888; *Times*, July 12, 1898; *EL*, October 21, 1898, and September 27, 1899.
25. *State*, August 24, 1888.
26. *DD*, July 31, 1883.
27. *NL*, January 29, 1913.
28. *State*, October 30, 1895; *RD*, July 1, 1902; *NL*, July 17 and October 18, 1902; *Times*, January 1, 1903; *EL*, January 20, 1903.
29. *Times*, May 23, 1894.
30. *NL*, July 2 and 7-8, 1910.
31. *State*, January 11, 1887.
32. *NL*, October 31, 1910.
33. *NL*, December 6, 1910, and October 30, 1915.
34. *DD*, June 18, 1879.
35. *NL*, September 10, 1907.
36. *NL*, March 9, 1916.
37. *NL*, January 7, 1907.
38. *RTD*, December 19, 1907.

Chapter 17

1. *State*, November 18, 1876.
2. *DD*, March 14, 1882.
3. *State*, July 13, 1885.
4. *Times*, April 13 and May 4, 1889, September 15, 1893, and April 3, 1894; *RTD*, July 7, 1904.
5. *NL*, March 28, 1916.
6. *State*, November 29-30, 1878.
7. *State*, June 14, 1879. Similar attempts of escape: *State*, March 22, 1886, and *RD*, December 4, 1900.
8. *State*, September 14-16, 1885.
9. *State*, March 1, 1886.
10. *State*, November 24, 1888.
11. *Times*, April 24, 1889.
12. *Times*, August 13, 1899.
13. *NL*, December 11, 1916; *RTD*, December 11, 1916.

14. *RTD*, January 4, 1917.
15. *State*, August 12, 1878.
16. *DD*, July 20, 1874.
17. *Times*, December 25, 1900, and April 20, 1901.
18. *NL*, January 1, 1908.
19. *DD*, February 16 and June 10, 1876; *State*, September 23, 1878, October 30, 1888, and September 26-28, 1897; *Times*, July 12, 1888, and December 4, 1900; *RD*, February 25, 1899.
20. *Times*, October 25, 1894.
21. *Times*, September 23 and 25-26, 1900, March 24, May 28, July 31, and September 29, 1901, and August 7 and 10, 1904.
22. *RTD*, June 30, 1903.

Chapter 18

1. *DD*, October 8, 1876; *State*, September 5, 1885; *Times*, April 22, 1891; *NL*, January 13, 1909, and August 18-19, 1914.
2. *Times*, September 13, 1891.
3. *DD*, January 5, 1872, January 29, 1879, March 25, 1881, June 14, 1883, July 14, and December 27, 1888; *State*, August 26 and December 15, 1876, August 26, 1878, September 6, 1879, April 8, 1880, June 10 and September 5, 1885, March 31, 1890, April 13, July 21, and August 28, 1893, July 16, 1894, and June 12, 1897; *Times*, May 25, 1879, and September 13, 1891; *RTD*, June 27, 1913; *NL*, July 3 and August 19, 1914, and January 2, 1919.
4. *State*, March 8, 1897; *RTD*, October 31, 1912.
5. *State*, March 25, 1881, May 23, 1890, and February 10-12 and April 7, 1893; *RD*, June 15, 1897; *RTD*, June 27, 1903; *NL*, January 5, 1916.
6. *State*, June 11, 1895; *RD*, June 13, 1897; *NL*, April 23, 1904 and February 14, 1914; *RTD*, November 26, 1910.
7. *State*, May 23, 1890.
8. *RD*, June 15, 1891.
9. *NL*, March 30, 1914.
10. *State*, April 13, 1893.
11. *NL*, July 3, 1911.
12. *NL*, December 2, 1915.
13. *Times*, December 18, 1892.
14. *NL*, February 24, 1913.
15. *DD*, January 5, 1872.
16. *RD*, July 13, 1914.

17. *State*, March 15, 1880.
18. *Times*, March 8-9, 1895.
19. *NL*, July 1, 1918.
20. *DD*, March 27 and May 3-7 and 7, 1877.
21. *RD*, August 25-26, 28, 1891, September 3 and 22, October 21-25 and 27, November 10, and December 5, 1891; *Times*, September 3 and October 20-25 and 27, 1891.
22. *NL*, August 22, 1908; *NL*, January 3-6 and 8, 1917, April 4 and 18, 1918, and April 5, 1920.
23. *RTD*, January 2-8, 1917.
24. *RTD*, September 18, 1904.
25. *RTD*, May 30, 1916.
26. *EL*, February 4, 1899.
27. *State*, January 5, 1887.
28. *DD*, January 6, 1877.
29. *State*, January 5, 1887.
30. *NL*, July 11, 1904.

Chapter 19

1. *DD*, December 4, 1884.
2. *Times*, April 24-25, 1901; *RD*, July 16, 1901.
3. *Times*, January 1, April 7-8, 14, 16 and May 12-16, 1891; *State*, March 4, 1891; *RD*, March 5, 7-8, 10-11, April 11, 21-22, and May 15, 1891, May 13, 1892, December 31, 1895, and January 1, 1896.
4. *Times*, September 24, 1894.
5. *Times*, May 5, 1897; *RD*, May 5-6 and July 1, 1897.
6. *NL*, August 1, December 5, and December 12, 1911; *RTD*, May 29-30 and June 1, 1912; Steven J. Hoffman, *Race, Class and Power in the Building of Richmond, 1870-1920* (Jefferson, NC: McFarland, 2004), 151-56.
7. *NL*, January 1 and April 24, 1914.
8. *State*, August 26 and September 7, 1895.
9. *NL*, November 25-27 and December 3, 1907.
10. *Times*, June 10, 1902.
11. *Times*, January 9, 1894.
12. *RD*, December 13, 18, 21, 1898.
13. *DD*, April 9, 1877.
14. *State*, June 7-8 and 27-28 and July 12, 16, 1878.
15. *DD*, November 15, 1887.

16. *Times*, June 20, 1894.
17. *NL*, January 15, 1907.
18. *RD*, June 22, 1889.
19. *State*, August 21, 1980.
20. *RD*, December 12, 1900.
21. *Times*, November 9-10, 12, 1899.
22. *State*, April 20, 1892.
23. *RTD*, June 23, 1911.
24. *NL*, January 26, 1920.
25. *Times*, January 14, 1902.
26. *RTD*, February 29, March 4-5, and April 5, 1904.

Chapter 20

1. *NL*, July 1-2, 6-10, 1914.
2. *RD*, May 11, 1901.
3. *NL*, February 21 and April 12, 1904.
4. *NL*, June 20, 1913, February 27, 1914, and December 16, 1916.
5. *EL*, March 10, 1898.
6. *NL*, April 12, 1907.
7. *NL*, March 23, 1910.
8. *Times*, August 12-13, 15, 1899.
9. *Times*, February 22, 1898.
10. *RD*, March 29, 1892, and June 21, 1901.
11. *State*, July 14, 1890.
12. *State*, December 14, 1876.
13. *DD*, October 1, 1877.
14. *State*, February 15, 1878.
15. *NL*, November 12, 1912.
16. *Times*, January 6 and 12, 1894.
17. *State*, January 2, 1877.
18. *State*, November 21, 1878.
19. *Times*, June 14, 1893.
20. *NL*, February 16, 1904.
21. *Times*, November 6, 1896.
22. *DD*, August 20, 23-24, 30-31, September 1-2, 7-8, 11, 13, 18, 20-25, October 5-6, 1881, and May 16, 1883.
23. *RD*, June 17, 1890.

Chapter 21

1. *DD*, March 25, 1872, October 28, 1873, January 29, 1875, and March 18 and September 25, 1876.
2. *State*, April 10, 1877.
3. *DD*, March 14, 1884.
4. *DD*, March 8, 1897.
5. *Times*, January 26, 1880; *State*, March 26 and September 8, 1886; *DD*, September 26, 1886, and February 9, 1887; *NL*, March 5, 1912.
6. *RD*, November 7, 1873.
7. *State*, June 12, 1897.
8. *State*, October 31, 1893.
9. *NL*, May 13, 1911.
10. *State*, April 21, 1881; *DD*, April 23, 1881.
11. *NL*, January 12, 1917.
12. *Times*, May 4, 1900.
13. *Times*, January 7, 1900.
14. *EL*, March 21, 1898.
15. *State*, April 15, 1890.
16. *DD*, July 6, 1876.
17. *State*, May 15, 1882.
18. *State*, February 25, 1886.
19. *RD*, September 5, 1901.
20. *Times*, January 15, 1896; *RD*, May 27, 1897.
21. *DD*, November 25, 1887.
22. *RD*, December 8, 1888; *Times*, February 22 and May 28, 1901.
23. *State*, May 26, 1887.
24. *NL*, July 30, 1908.
25. *NL*, June 10, 1908.
26. *RD*, September 1, 1901.
27. *NL*, December 18, 1913.
28. *NL*, March 20, 1911.
29. *NL*, December 4, 1907.
30. *RTD*, June 9, 1913; *NL*, June 9 and 18, 1913.

Chapter 22

1. *NL*, March 29-30, and April 15, 18, 20-21, 25, 1910, August 12, 1912, and July 5, 1913.
2. *Times*, January 7, 1896.
3. *Times*, January 7, 1896; *NL*, August 18, 1911.
4. *State*, July 28, 1894; *RD*, October 7, 1898; *Times*, July 10, 1902.
5. *Times*, October 8 and 15, 1898.
6. *News*, May 14, 1900.
7. *RTD*, January 31, February 1-2, 4, 1908; *NL*, April 12-13 and June 30, 1909.
8. *Times*, October 19, 1889.
9. *NL*, September 20, 1910.
10. *NL*, September 28-29, 1920.
11. *DD*, November 15, 1882.
12. *State*, December 21, 1878.
13. *State*, March 19, 1881.
14. *RD*, October 22, 1873.

15. *State*, June 19, 1877; *Times*, May 2, 1890.
16. *Times*, March 6, 1895.
17. *DD*, August 2, 1877.
18. *Times*, August 17, 1899.
19. *Times*, March 22, 1900.
20. *NL*, June 7, 1907.
21. *NL*, November 30, 1907.
22. *NL*, April 11, 14, 16, 1909.
23. *NL*, March 24, 1906.
24. *RD*, October 15, 1902.
25. *NL*, September 27, 1910.

Chapter 23

1. Ward, *Richmond*, 200 and 202; Hoffman, *Race, Class and Power*, 7; William E. Griffin, Jr., *One Hundred Fifty Years of History along the Richmond, Fredericksburg and Potomac Railroad* (Richmond: Whittet and Shepperson, 1984), 44-45, 52, 58-59; John S. and Emily Salmon, *Historic Photos of Richmond* (Nashville: Turner Publishing Company, 2007), 98, 130.
2. *DD*, February 7, 1876; *NL*, January 11, June 29, and July 1, 1907.
3. *NL*, June 11 and 29, July 1, and October 18, 1907, April 1-2, 4, 1908.
4. *NL*, June 18, 1910, and September 29, 1919.
5. *NL*, July 15, 1914.
6. *DD*, May 16, 1876; *Times*, April 16, 1899.
7. *DD*, December 9, 1872; *RTD*, November 21, 1910.
8. *DD*, November 21, 1888.
9. *Times*, October 29, 1899.
10. *NL*, February 29, 1904.
11. *NL*, February 18, 1909.
12. *Times*, July 21, 1900.
13. *Times*, November 20, 1889.
14. *RD*, November 16 and December 1, 1888.
15. *NL*, February 25, 1904.
16. *NL*, March 2, 1907.
17. *NL*, December 3, 1907.
18. *RD*, July 18, 1891.
19. *Times*, March 15, 1895.
20. *DD*, September 2, 1872, and March 5, 1874; *State*, September 17, 1881.
21. *NL*, February 5, 1913.
22. *DD*, February 11-14, 1885.
23. *NL*, August 5, 1915.
24. *NL*, September 30, 1919.
25. *Times*, March 13, 1900.
26. *DD*, June 25, 1881; *NL*, Mary 15, 1905.
27. *NL*, November 27, 1912.
28. *NL*, April 2, 1913.

Chapter 24

1. *State*, January 2, 1879, July 22 and September 5, 1885, September 15, 1892, November 1, 1894, March 27 and July 5, 1895, and April 1, 1896; *DD*, February 2, 1883, and February 4, 1886; *RD*, September 2 and December 2, 1891, March 15, 1892, January 3, 1896, January 3 and October 2, 1897, July 14, 1900, July 5 and October 24, 1901; *Times*, April 24-25, 1901, and July 5, 1902; *NL*, April 22 and June 8, 1904, January 12, 1907, and September 17, 1912.
2. *Times*, December 14, 1892.
3. *NL*, June 29 and July 5, 9, 15, 1904.
4. *NL*, January 3-5, 7-8, and 10, 1907, and August 13, 1909.
5. *NL*, January 15, 1877.
6. *State*, December 5, 1881.
7. *State*, September 14, 1885.
8. *RD*, February 27 and March 15, 1891.
9. *State*, September 15, 1892.
10. *State*, July 5, 1895.
11. *State*, August 21, 1900.
12. *State*, April 17-18, 1896.
13. *NL*, May 15, 1911.

Chapter 25

1. *Times*, October 13, 1894.
2. *State*, October 13, 1894.
3. *Times*, October 13, 1894.
4. *State*, October 15, 1894; *Times*, October 14, 1894.
5. *State*, October 15 and 17, 1894; *Times*, October 23, 1894.
6. *Times*, October 19-20, 1894.
7. *Times*, October 21, 24-27, and 31, and December 23, 25, 1894; *RD*, October 31, 1894; *State*, January 18, 1895.
8. *RD*, January 12, 1895.
9. *State*, January 12 and February 20, February 1, 1895; *RD*, January 19 and 22, 1895.
10. *RD*, February 27-28, 1895; *Times*, February 28, 1895.
11. *RD*, March 1, 1895; *Times*, March 1-2, 21, 1895.

12. *RD*, March 22 and May 16, 1895; *Times*, May 16, 1895.
13. *Times*, November 12-13, 1898, July 9 and 26, 1901, and April 9, 1902; *RD*, November 12, 1898, July 9, 1901, and May 1, 1902.
14. *Times*, May 2, 1902; *RD*, May 3, 1902.
15. *Times*, May 4, 1902; *RD*, May 10, 1902.
16. *NL*, January 3, 1911.
17. *NL*, January 6-7, 11, 1911.

Chapter 26

1. *RD*, January 5, 1895.
2. *RD*, January 5-6, 1895.
3. *Times*, January 5-6, 1895; *State*, January 5, 7, 1895; *RD*, January 8, 1895.
4. *Times*, January 8, 1895.
5. *State*, January 8-10, 12, 14, 17, 1895; *Times*, January 9-10, 12, 15, 1895; *RD*, January 10, 12-13, 1895.
6. *State*, January 11, 18, 1895; *RD*, January 11, 1895; *Times*, January 12, 18, 20, 1895.
7. *RD*, March 2, April 18-19, 21, 23, 25, 30 and May 16, 19, 1895; *State*, April 19-20, 29 and May 17, 1895; *Times*, April 20, 26, 30, 1895.
8. *RD*, May 11, 18, 21 and June 9, 11-12, 1895; *Times*, May 1, 11, 28, 1895.
9. *State*, June 11, 1895; *RD*, June 12, 1895.
10. *RD*, June 21, 1895; *Times*, June 21, 1895.
11. *Times*, October 13, 1895; Dabney, *Richmond*, 261.
12. *RD*, June 21, 1895.
13. *State*, July 2, 1895.
14. *News*, August 11, 1900; *RD*, August 12, 1900.
15. *Times*, March 24, 1899.
16. *Times*, January 7, 1900.
17. *EL*, August 13, 1900.
18. *Times*, August 5, 1902.
19. *NL*, September 13, 1912.
20. *State*, September 26, 1897.

Bibliography

Acts of City Council of Richmond. Richmond: O.E. Flanhart Printing Company, 1898.

Albrecht, Ernest. "Charles Ringling." In American National Biography (24 vol.) John A. Garraty and Mark C. Carnes, eds. New York: Oxford University Press, 1999.

"Andy Griffith: Policy King." The Idea, vol. 3, no. 8, July 25, 1909, 13–15.

"Anna Maquire: The Richmond White Slave Trade." The Idea, vol. 4, no. 18, April 30, 1910, 14–15.

"Another Sacrifice to Richmond's White Slave Trade, Fostered by the Police Board." The Idea, vol. 5, no. 8, July 22, 1911, 8–9.

Barksdale, George E., et al. "The Legend of Chris Baker." Unsourced article, Tompkins-McCaw Library Archives, 3–5.

Bell, Ernest A. Fighting the Traffic in Young Girls, or War on the White Slave Trade. Chicago: G.S. Bell, 1910.

Blanton, Wyndham B. Medicine in Virginia in the Nineteenth Century. Richmond: Garrett and Massie, 1933.

Breeden, James. "Body Snatchers and Anatomy Professors: Medical Education in Nineteenth-Century Virginia." Virginia Magazine of History and Biography, 83 (1975): 321–45.

Burton, Peter J. Police Court Pictures. Richmond: C.N. Williams, Printers, 1892.

Cei, Louis B. "Law Enforcement in Richmond: A History of Police-Community Relations, 1737–1970." PhD diss., Florida State University, 1975.

Certain Resolutions and Ordinances of the Council of the City of Richmond. Richmond, 1900.

Charter and ... Ordinances of the City of Richmond. Richmond, 1869, 1885, and 1910.

Chesson, Michael B. Richmond after the War, 1865–1890. Richmond: Virginia State Library, 1981.

Christian, W. Asbury. Richmond: Her Past and Present. Richmond: L.H. Jenkins, 1912.

Courtwright, David T. "The Cycles of American Drug Policy." The American Historian (August 2015): 24–29.

"Crime Protected." The Idea, vol. 3 no. 25, 5.

Dabney, Virginius. Richmond: The Story of a City. Garden City, NY: Doubleday, 1976.

"Death Hovering over Mysterious 'Chris.'" Newspaper article, Tompkins-McCaw Library archives.

"Did They Want to Convict the Gamblers?" The Idea, vol. 3, no. 12, August 28, 1909, 11–13.

Ezekiel, Herbert T. Recollections of a Virginia Newspaper Man. Richmond: Herbert T. Ezekiel, 1920.

"Fake Club." The Idea, vol. 4, no. 31, Sept. 18, 1910.

Filler, Louis. A Dictionary of American Social Reform. New York: Philosophical Society, 1963.

Furnas, J. C. Great Times: An Informal Social History of the United States, 1914–1929. New York: G.P. Putnam's Sons, 1974.

"The Gamblers." The Idea, vol. 4, no. 28, July 30, 1910, 8–10.

Griffin, William E. One Hundred Years of History along the Richmond, Fredericksburg and Potomac Railroad. Richmond: Whittet and Shepperson, 1984.

Griset, Rich. "Black Market." *Style Weekly,* August 17, 2010.
Hatfield, Elaine, and Richard L. Rapson. *Flimflam Artists: True Tales of Cults, Crackpots, Cranks, Cretins, Crooks, Creeps, Con Artists, and Charlatans.* Thorofare, NJ: Xlibris, 2011.
Hoffman, Steven J. *Race, Class and Power in the Building of Richmond, 1870-1920.* Jefferson, NC: McFarland, 2003.
"Huche Kuche at the Fair." *The Idea,* vol. 4, no. 34, October 1, 1910, 5.
James, Arthur W. *Virginia's Social Awakening.* Richmond: Garrett and Massie, 1939.
James, Watson, Jr. "Chris Baker: Faithful Servant of Medical Science in Virginia." *Virginia Record,* October 1957, 22-23; 50-54.
Johnson, Virginia C., and Barbara Crookshanks. *Virginia Horseracing.* Charleston: The History Press, 2008.
Kelly, Alfred H., and Winfred A. Harbison. *The American Constitution: Its Origins and Development.* New York: W.W. Norton and Company, 1955.
Keve, Paul W. *The History of Corrections in Virginia.* Charlottesville: University Press of Virginia, 1986.
Kollatz, Harry, Jr. *Richmond in Ragtime.* Charleston: The History Press, 2005.
Kovistra, Paul G. "Cole Younger." In *American National Biography* 24: 193-94.
Kroger, William S. *Clinical and Experimental Hypnosis in Medicine, Dentistry, and Psychology.* 2d ed. Philadelphia: J.B. Lippincott, 1977.
Lambert, William. *Show Life in America.* East Point, GA.: Will Delavoye, 1921.
Lazarus, Jerry. "The Good Old Days: Were They Really Better?" *RTD,* February 11, 1979.
"Loan Sharks." *The Idea,* vol. 4, nos. 23-24, June 4 and 11, 1910, 1-2 and 10, resp.
Lowry, Thomas P. *The Story the Soldiers Wouldn't Tell: Sex in the Civil War.* Mechanicsburg, PA: Stackpole Books, 1994.
Mee, Claire. "Inside the Criminal Mind." *New York Times,* Sunday Review, May 31, 2015, 9.
Meier, August, and Elliot Rudwick. "Negro Boycotts of Segregated Streetcars in Virginia, 1904-7." *Virginia Magazine of History and Biography,* 81 (1973): 479-87.
Moore, James R. "P.T. Barnum." In *American National Biography* 2: 211-14.
Morris, John, ed. *Wanderings of a Vagabond.* New York: John Norris, 1873.
Mustian, Thomas E. *Facts and Legends of Richmond Area Streets.* Richmond: Carroll Publishing Company, 1936.
"Old Chris—The Anatomical Purveyor." Typescript, n. d. Tompkins-McCaw Library Archives.
Ordinances ... of the Council of the City of Richmond. Richmond: O. H. Flanhart, 1898.
"Policy Shops." *The Idea,* vol. 3, no. 12, August 21, 1909, 12-13.
Porterfield, T. Tyler. *Nonesuch Place: A History of the Richmond Landscape.* Charleston: The History Press, 2009.
Random House Dictionary of the English Language. New York: Random House, 1966.
Rathge, Adam. "Pondering Pot: Marijuana's History and the Future of the War on Drugs." *The American Historian,* August 2015, 30-36.
"Rich Gamblers Go Free, Poor Ones Suffer." *The Idea,* vol. 3, no. 2, June 12, 1909, 8-10.
Robins, Charles H. "Chris Baker." Typescript, Tompkins-McCaw Library Archives.
Sala, George A. *America Revisited.* 2 vols. London: Vizetelly and Company, 1882.
Salmon, John S., and Emily J. Salmon. *Historic Photos of Richmond.* Nashville: Turner Publishing Company, 2007.
Silver, Christopher. *Twentieth-Century Richmond: Planning, Politics, and Race.* Knoxville: University of Tennessee Press, 1984.
Silverman, Kenneth. "Harry Houdini." In *American National Biography* 11: 247-49.
Smith, Page. *The Rise of Industrial America,* vol. 6. New York: McGraw-Hill, 1984.
Time and the River: The Story of Richmond's Drinking Water. Richmond: Richmond Department of Public Utilities, revised 1956.
Wallington, J. Rufus. *Get-Rich-Quick Character in Stories by George R. Chester.* N.p., 1908.
Walthall, Ernest T. *Hidden Things Brought to Light.* Richmond: Dietz Printing Company, 1933.
Ward, Harry M. *Children of the Streets of*

Richmond, 1865–1920. Jefferson, NC: McFarland, 2015.
_____. *Public Executions in Richmond, Virginia 1882–1907.* Jefferson, NC: McFarland, 2012.
_____. *Richmond: An Illustrated History.* Northridge, CA: Windsor Publishing, 1985.
Warner, John H., and James M. Edmonson. *Dissection: Forensics of a Rite of Passage in American Medicine, 1880–1930.* New York: Blast Books.
Weber, Gustavus A. *Report on Housing and Living Conditions in the Neglected Sections of Richmond.* Richmond: Whittet and Shepperson, 1913.
"Why Police Don't Bother Big Gamblers." *The Idea.* Vol. 5, no. 9. August 22, 1911, 5.

Index

A. Oppenheimer, Harvey & Blair 160
Academy of Music 27, 203
Adams Express Company 201
Agee, John 70
Agrei, Julius 178
Albemarle Club 44
Alexander, Richard 194
Allen, Harry 190
Allen, R.W. 95
Allen, Thomas 105
Alley, John 121
American Hotel 159
"American nobility" 118
Anderson, Rev. E. 138
Anderson, J.E. 94
Andrews, G.L. 79
Angle, Capt. James B. 100
Aquia Creek 195
Armistead, Frank 132
Armstrong, Lillian 104
Armstrong, Mark 131, 132
Arthur, J.L. 151
Ashland 208
Askey, Rena B. 185
Aso, Eso (Antonio Frederick) 18
Atlantic Coast Line Railroad 162, 190, 194
Aye, George 165

Bachrach, Samuel 54
Baker, Chris 11, 13, 14, 15
Baker, Jacob 149
Baldwin, Kittie 27
Barbour, James 151, 152
Barnes, Eugene 160
Barnum and Bailey circuses 69
Batton, Albert G. 142
Batton, James T. 142
Batton, O.W. 142
Baugh, J.E. 194
Beale, William 165
Beasley, Frances 55
Beasley, John 168
Beatty, Jennie *see* "Irish Jennie"

begging game" 115
Bell, Robert O. 97
Belle Island 118
Benson, Nathaniel 196
Berkowitz, Louis 179
Berriman, George R. 30
Bijou Theater 21
Bird, Billy 103
Birdsong, M.A. 200
Black Hand *see* Italian Mafia
Black Jane" 11
Blair, J. Harvey 149
Blanchard, Henry C. 30
"Blind Tigers" 188
Bonucelli, Angelo 94
Booker, Rev. Nicholas 159
Booth, Robert 73
Bosco, the Magician 31
Bosquett, F.M. 198
Bostock Wild Animal Show 69
Bouldin, C.W. 143
Bowie, William F. 187
Bradley, Joseph 122
Brannan, T.L. 14
Branzell, George 197
Bratke, A.K. 53
Broad Rock race course 42
Broad Street Station 190
Brooker, Dr. Boyce D. 132
"Brooklyn Johnny" *see* Hamilton, John
Brooks, Robert J. 100
Brotherhood of Railroad Tramp Association 119
Brown, Abraham 134
Brown, Betty 133
Brown, J. Randell 27
Brown, Jessie 95
Brown, John 195
Brown, Joseph 134
Brown, Marshall 40
Brown, Theron H. 162
Bryan, Joseph 205
Bryce, Gordon 168, 169

Bryce, James 168, 169
Buffalo Bill's Wild West Show 69
Bundy, Harrison 38
Burke, Frank P. 185
Burruss, Asby 55
Burruss, Joe 140
Burton, John (alias Jimmie Bryant) 103
Butchertown 5
Butler, John (alias "Frisco Slim") 146
Byers, Henry 143
Byrd, Adolphus 179
Byrd Island 118
Byrd Street Station 192, 199

C & O (Chesapeake and Ohio) Railroad 103, 190, 192, 195, 196
Cabot, S.S. 161
Callaway, J.H. 48
Cameron, William E. 14
Campbell, Stephen 107
Cannabelloca 130
Capps, Simon 205
Cardozo, Vincent 80
Carlisle, Miss Alice 179
Carlton, C.M. 168
Carmichael, Rev. Hartley 168, 169
Carney, Edward (alias "Hutch") 146
Carr, John 68
Carrington, Dr. Charles V. 203
Cary, R.M. 177
Chambers, Catherine 48
Chancery Court 157
Charity, Lou 106
Chesapeake and Ohio railroad *see* C & O Railroad
Chester, Frank *see* Harris, Richard (alias "little Dick Harris")
Chesterfield County Court House 119
"Child Jack" 146
Children's Home Society 6
Childrey, Robert H. 132
Childrey, Roy 185
Chiles, J.H. 168
Chinese "opium joints" 128
Ching Lee Foo 21
Christian, Judge George L. 167, 171
Christian Endeavor Societies 149
Chung, Ah 165
Church Hill 21, 84
City Small Pox Hospital 83
Claffin, John 188
Clark, D.C. (alias "Snowball") 196
Clarke, Aleck 85
Closby, William 187
cocaine 127, 128; dens 129
cockfighting 42
"Cockney Tim" *see* Madden, Tim
Cohen, Hermie 110
Coles, Marie 88

Cole's Great New York and New Orleans Menagerie and Circus 69
Collector of the Internal Revenue Service 128
Collins, Columbia 145
Collins, John 47, 48
Collins, Nina 170
Collins, Susanna 145
Collins, Sylvester (alias "Dashing Billy") 146
Colored Free Baptist Church on Navy Hill 167
Community Chest *see* United Way
Connell, D.F. 198
Connor, J.O. 158
Connors, Jimmie *see* O'Connor, Edward
Consolidated Order of Friendships 188
Cooke, Professor H. 20
Cooper, Tom 191
Corbin, Samuel 82
Coup's United Shows 69
Courtland Moon 133
Cousins, Warren 140
Crawford, George E. 156
Creekmore, George A. 165
Crittenden, Col. C.T. 151
Crittenden, William 102
Crutchfield, B.F. 199
Crutchfield, Justice John Jeter 3, 7, 8, 19, 20, 38, 95, 101, 108, 110, 113, 115, 116, 125, 126, 179, 199
Cunningham, Fred *see* Fay, Eddie
Cunningham, Judson 132
Curtley, Thomas 196

Dabney, Samuel 135
Daily Dispatch 51, 177
Dashiell, William S. 152
"Dashing Billy" *see* Collins, Sylvester
Davidson, Frederick L. 168
Davis, Fred 101
Davis, John T. 162
Davis, R.M. 158
Deane, James 30
Deihm, Herbert 184
Delaney, Captain 87
Dempsey, George 115
Dennis, E.R. 113
"Denver Harry" 146
"Denver Ned" 104
Department of Outdoor Poor 6
Deputy, David 125
Diavolo, Jack 158
"Dick Turpin" 95
Dickerson, Robert 17
Dickinson, Dr. Luther R. 150
Dickinson, W. Allen 33
Dillard, H. 47, 48
Dixon, A.B. 188
Dodson, Lizzie 145
Doer, William (alias Dutch; Nobb Myers) 103

Donovan, Rev. Father 185
Dowell, Percy 97
Doyle, C.H. 153
Duffy, Sgt. J.M. 162
Dula, Mrs. Grover C. 97
Dumbarton School 136
Duncan, Hamilton 193
Dungee, Rev. J.W. 154
"Dutch" see Doer, William
Dutch gold 110
Duval, John T. 91
Dwelly, Mrs. E.O. 207

Ebenezer Cemetery 17
Edouard, Madame 192
Edwards, Jones 91
Ellis, Phillip 192
Emery, Samuel 207, 208
Epps, Robert Henry 155
Evans, Joseph R. 101
Evergreen Cemetery 11, 16
Exchange Alley 6
Exchange Hotel 154, 159, 161, 169

Fagan, E.E. 132
Fairfield race course 42
fakirs 59, 65
Fasi, Carlo 80, 81
Fasi, George 80, 81
Fasi, Maddelena Moscari 80, 81
Fast, Emile 80
Fay, Eddie (alias Fred Cunningham) 184
Ferguson, Harry M. 194
Fey, Anna Eva 19
Fick, John 138
Field, Maj. Gen. James G. 151
"Fifteen Years in Hell" 203
First National Bank 172
Fitzgerald, Frank H. 162
Flasher, Annie 121
Florida Limited 196
Foley, James 196
Ford, William (alias Molincant) 103
Ford, W.J. 105
Ford Hotel 204, 205
Forepaugh's Circus 69, 70, 73
Forrester, Arthur G. 156
Foster, Lottie May 132
Fowler, Hester 84
Fowler, Dr. R.C. 166
Fox, Kate 19, 20
Fox, Martha 19, 20
Francis, W.L. 161
Franklin, Ben Welburn see West, Ivy W.
French, Miss Agnes 179
Fribourg, Dr. 192
Friedman, Sigmund 171
"Frisco Slim" see Butler, John
Fulton Bottom 5

Gaddy, Percy 144
Gaines, Henry 68
Gallagher, Frank T. 199
G.A.R. see Grand Army of the Republic
Gardner, Carlton & Baldwin 160
Gates, N.C. 153
Gaudiosi, Carmine 161
Gentry, Harry 95
George, Wesley 149
Gilchrist, John (alias "Providence Slim") 146
Gladstone Club 44
Glen Allen Station 136
Gloucester, County 204
Gonnella Brothers 161
Goochland County 8
Graham, Mrs. Allie 105
Grand Army of the Republic 159
Graves, James 108
Great American Army of Tramps 122
Great John Robinson and Franklin Brothers Show 69
Green, Edward 142
"green goods men" 82
Greenwald, Aaron 93
Gregory, Louis L. 162
Grimes, Joe 50
Grymes, Buford 156
gypsy bands 117

Hall, Alexander 194
Hall, Dr. G. Stanley 28
Hall, Mary 145
Hall, Powers & Company 161
"Hall-Thieves Brigade" 84
Hamilton, John (alias "Brooklyn Johnny") 146
Hamilton, Lillie 88
Hammond, William A. 54
Hancock, C.L. 128
Hanover County 14
Harding, John H. 157
Harman & Company 161
Harris, Jack M. 161
Harris, Richard (alias Frank Chester; "little Dick Harris") 184
Harrison Act 131
Harrison-Hoalder gang 117
Harrison Narcotics Law 128
Hartz, Col. Wilson T. 166
Harvey, Samuel (alias Sam Jackson) 103
Harvey, Blair & Company 162
Hatcher, Cody 131
Hawkins, Theodore 193
Hayden, Dr. Wynne 30
Heckler, Harry G. 144
Heller & Fleishman 160
Henderson, W.T. 186
Henrico County 90, 208
Henrico County Court 207

Index

Henry, Dr. John 28
heroin 127
Higgins, John 197
Hill, Reuben T. 157
Hippodrome and Wild West Show 70
Hirsch, H.N. 174, 175
Hirshberg, Milton K. 162
"Hobo" Leighton 131
Hokey-Pokey 179
Hollywood Cemetery 83
Holzapfel, Charles 192
Hoodooism 21
Hooper, John R. 20
Hopkins, Alfred 154
Hopkins, Edward 167
Hopkins, Robert H. 193
Horwitz, Leon 110
Hotel Jefferson 49
Hotel Reformer in Richmond 157
"Houche Khouche dance" 64
Houdini, Harry 32
Houston, Samuel 50
Howard, B.F. 102
Howard, George 22
Howe, Col. Edward Robbins 159
Howe, Mrs. Kate Layton Howe 159
Howe's London Circus 69
Hudson, D.B. 180
Hughes, Judge 208
Hupp, J.D. 121
"Hutch" see Carney, Edward
Hustings Court 7, 27, 53, 54, 100, 108, 110, 138, 152, 154, 160, 161, 162, 171
Hutchings, Adalaide 135

"Imposing ballyhoos" 63
"Indian Bill" see Jefferson, William
Industrial Home for Colored Girls in Hanover County 88
"Irish Jennie" 145
Italian Mafia 135
Italian National Bank 161

Jackson, Giles B. 93
Jackson, John 167
Jackson, Lizzie 165
Jackson, Sam see Harvey, Samuel
Jackson, Tennessee 87
Jackson Ward 5
James E. Wells 140
Jefferson, William (alias "Indian Bill") 144
Jenkins, R.L. 104, 105
Jeter, Rev. Jeremiah Bell 150
Jewish Club 45
J.L. Stone & Company 161
"Johnnie squads" see "loafing gangs"
Johnson, Charles 144
Johnson, Hannah 105
Johnson, Maj. J.B. 197

Johnson, John 103
Johnson, Richard 167
Jones, Annie 95
Jones, Eddie 105
Jones, Squire "Sugar Bottom" Frank 8
Jordan, W.L. 185
Jung, Moy 165
Juvenile and Domestic Relations Court 8, 154

Kahl, Annie 170
Kahn, W.E. 23
Keater, W.B. 187, 188
Keene, William B. 140
Keller, the Illusionist 31
Kelly, George 130
Kelly, Sarah 135
Kelso, Anna 28
Kelso, Marie 28
Kidd, Leo 136
Kight, Rufus 186
King, Jack 168
King, Scott (alias Tom Walker) 144
King, W.T. 92
King William County 21, 151
Kirby Station 122
Knowles, J.C. see Schwabacher, Albert
Koeppel, Stanley 161, 162
Krish, Walter 162

Lacy, Alberta 38
Lacy, Thomas W. 185
Landstreet, John 154
Lane, Julian T. 90
Lapenta & Company 161
laudanum 129
Lavender, George 140
Layton, Ernest 101
Lee Camp of Confederate Veterans 159
Leopold, Sylvain A. 20
Levy, J.L. 156
Lewis, E.V. see Robinson, O.W.
L.H. Blair & Company 160
Life Insurance Company of Virginia 163
"Light-Fingered Gentry" 103
Lime Kiln 118
Lincoln Building and Loan Association 159
Lindsay, David see Merritt, Arthur
Lindsay, George M. (alias G.L. Medicus) 161
Lindsay, J.B. see Merritt, Arthur
"little Dick Harris" see Harris, Richard
Live Oak Distillery Company 161
"loafing gangs" ("johnnie squads") 112
Long, Leong 165
Lonzo, Wilbur 27
Lucas, F.B. 105, 106
Ludwig, J.L. 152
Ludwig, William C. 152

Index

Mack, Patrick J. 124
Madden, Tim ("Cockney Tim") 101
Main Street Station 103, 190
Mallory, Ruth 139
Manhattan Club 44
Mann Act of 1910 136
Mapp Prohibition Act 131
Martin, Percy 196
Martin, William 47
Marvin, A.T. see Merritt, Arthur
Marvin, Thomas A. see Merritt, Arthur
Massey, N.L. 151
Massey, W.H.T. 197
Mattieson, J.B. see Merritt, Arthur
Maxwell, James 143
May, Moses 32
Mayo Street 136
"Mayor Taylor's Hand" 25
McClintlock, Bob 20
McCormick, D.J. 79
McGiffin, Nick 34
McGrath, John 192
McGruder, Wade 17
McLean, Rev. Charles 30
McMahon, Detective-Captain 162
Meade, Richard H. 94
Mechanics Cemetery 16
Medical School of Virginia's Egyptian Building 10, 15
Medicus, G.L. see Lindsay, George M.
Merritt, Arthur (alias A.B. Morton; A.T. Marvin; David Lindsay; General Budlong A. Morton; J.B. Lindsay; J.B. Mattieson; Thomas A. Marvin) 171
Merritt, Walter 91, 92
"Michigan Red" 146
Milhiser & Company 160
Miller, Charles 190
Minor, George 192
Mr. Fetig 95
Monroe, Claude 186
Monroe Club 44
Monta, George 144
"Monster Marvin" see Merritt, Arthur
Montague, Andrew J. 202
Montague, W.H. 164
Moon, Cortland 133
Moore, Lucile 154
Moore, Thomas L. 97
Moore, William (alias "Black Jew") 103
Morgan, Charles see Morganfield, Charles August
Morgan, Israel 181
Morganfield, Charles August (alias Charles Morgan) 200, 201, 203
morphine 127
Morris, A.J. 23
Morris, George 125
Morris, Lizzie ("Sixth Street Liz") 105

Morris, William 192
Morse, Dr. F.B. 175
Morton, A.B. see Merritt, Arthur
Morton, Gen. Budlong A. see Merritt, Arthur
Moses, Roseberry 133
Mozart Academy 27
Mrs. Masson 26
Murphy, C.J. 115
Murphy's Hotel 19, 30
Murray, Henry 199
Murray, Robert C. 188
Myers, E.T.D. 200
Myers, Nob see Doer, William
Myers, William 103

Napier, Henry 85
National Bank of Virginia 154
Nelson, W.H. 149
Newby, John 191
News Leader 133
Nixon, Hugh 142
Norris, John T. 206
Nowlan (jewelry) Company 205
Nugent, Daniel 103

Oakwood Cemetery 11, 14, 17, 33
O'Connor, Edward (alias Jimmie Connors) 103
O'Ferrall, Charles T. 200, 202
"Old Billy" 11, 14
Old Bob Lock 117
O'Neil, Dennis 139
opium 127
Oregon Hill 5
Orr, Annie 121
Orr, Jane 121
Overby, William G. 191
Owens, Howard L. 166
Owens, Ida 146

Page, Daniel 105
palmistry 24
Paradise Club 44
Parker, Thomas H. see Smith, Francis Lockwood
Parker, Dr. W.H., Sr. 29
Pattee, Col. John A. 159
Patterson, George 122
Pawnee Bill's Circus 70
Peerless Minstrels 139
Peninsular Bank of Williamsburg 146
Penitentiary Bottom 5
Pettit & Company 161
Peyronnet, Mrs. Catharine 156
Philip, Darling R. (alias Rev. D.D. Rowland) 167
Phillip, Louis B. 149
Pilgrim Baptist Church 159

238 Index

Pinkerton National Detective Agency 151, 201
Pitt, William T. 185
Pizzini, Annie 153
Pizzini, William B. 153
Poindexter, J.W. 151
Police Court 7, 17, 19, 37, 38, 40, 85, 95, 101, 112, 113, 115, 119, 120, 125, 126, 128, 135, 137, 144, 158, 170, 171, 174, 178, 179, 191, 192, 197, 207
Poll, George 110
Pollard, Miss Bernice 102
Porter, Howard F. 164
Potter's Field 11
Powers, John T. 160
Priddy, Charles 22
Prince, "Jack" 198
"Professor Jackson" 22
"Professor Lee" 22
"Providence Slim" see Gilchrist, John
"P.T. Barnum New and Greatest Show on Earth" 71
Purcell, John 150
Putney & Watts 160

R.A. Patterson and Company 154
Radium Spray Company Incorporated 175
Rand & Barbee 162
Randolph, E.A. 156
Randolph, Mrs. Norman V. 149
Rapley, Joseph (alias "Topeka Joe") 146
Reed, H.C. 51
Reid, Mary 22
Reinheimer, Mr. Lee 32
Religious Herald 150
Renfrew, Frank 144
"Resurrection Men" 10
Rhoda Royal Circus 70
Richmond Almshouse 117
Richmond and Alleghany railroad 192
Richmond and Danville railroad 190
Richmond and Petersburg railroad 121, 190, 192
Richmond and York River 190
Richmond Billiard Academy 84
Richmond Club 44
Richmond, Fredericksburg and Potomac railroad 190, 199
Richmond Home Social Club 45
Richmond Inn 162
Richmond Jail 8
Richmond News 24, 25
Richmond News-Leader 158
Richmond Theater 27
Richmond Times 159
Riley, "Lone-Hand" 59
Riley, Morton 144
Ringling Brothers' World Greatest Shows 69
Riverview Cemetery 11, 17, 18
Roberts, George 126

Robinson, Charles 128
Robinson, Gladys 88
Robinson, J.H. 143
Robinson, O.W. (alias E.V. Lewis; George West) 175
Rodgers, Louis 190
Ross, S.E. (alias Rosinheim) 181
Rosinheim see Ross, S.E.
Roussell, Amelia 145
Rowland, Rev. D.D. (alias Darling R. Philip) 167
Rueger's saloon 208
Runyon, Elley B. 139

St. Clair, Fannie 103
St. Vitus's Dance 116
Sales, Clarence 89
Sales, John 20
Salvation Army 6
Samuel, T.H. 68
Sanger Hall 171
Sangster, George E. 94
The Savings Bank of the Grand Fountain United Order of True Believers 157
Schaeffer, G.E. 156
Scheisinger, Dr. Louis 19
Schmidt, Hermann 100
Schrader, August 30
Schwabacher, Albert (alias J.C. Knowles) 153
Schwane, Anthony 78
Seaboard Air Line 122, 190, 194, 196, 198
Searcy, Charles J. 200, 201, 202
Second Baptist Church in Richmond 167
Second Police Station 85, 154, 206
Sells Brothers Circus 69
Semon, Zera 31
Seybold, Thomas 81
Shaw, Charles 100
Sheltering Arms Hospital 14
Shelton, Jeffry 195
Shelton, Lizzie 88
"Shenandoah Red" 146
Shepherd, Joseph H. 156
Shield, John 135
Shockoe Creek 6, 126
Shockoe Hill 84
Shockoe Hill Cemetery 11
Siebert, Christopher 189
Siebert, F.W. 189
Sig Alascon's Wild West Show 69
"Sixth Street Liz" see Morris, Lizzie
Smith, Charles 170
Smith, Engineer C.R. 194
Smith, Francis Lockwood (alias Thomas H. Parker) 204, 206, 207, 208, 209
Smith, H.M. 100, 206
Smith, James C. 100
Smith, Myron A. 57
Smith, Patsy 133

Smith, William E. 156
"Snowball" *see* Clark, D.C.
Society of Associated Charities *see* United Way
Solomon, Sheriff Simon 208
Southern Planter and Farm 150
Southern Railway 190, 194
Spears, Asby 136
Spenser, Jane 170
Spiritualist Movement 19
Stafford County Court 201
Stoner, Harry 68
Strang, Frank 140
Strange, Jennie 146
Stratton, Thomas H. 196
Stuart, Henry C. 23
Sullivan, Timothy 80

Taylor, Burnley 150
Taylor, Charles 165
Taylor, Charles E. 150
Taylor, George 167
Taylor, George B. 150
Thalhimer Brothers 156
Thaxton, Olaa 137
Theatre Comique 80
Thompson, R.H. 148
Thurston, Edward F. 139
Thurston, Howard 31
Tisdale, Kid 103
Tomlinson, Alexander M. 100
Tomlinson, Captain 154
Tomlinson, Sergeant 162
"Topeka Joe" *see* Rapley, Joseph
Traine, August 80
Trogden, Willard F. 160, 161
Tucker, Mrs. L.C. 108
Turner, B.F. 95
Turner, Mother Frances 135
"Turpin, Dick" 95
Turpin, Walter 81
Tyler, J. Hoge 202
Tyler, Capt. James M. 160
Tyler, W.N. 95

United Order of True Reformers 149
United States Circuit Court 175
United Way 117

Van Ness, James K. 150
Vaughan, Charles 11
Vaughan, Mollie 11
Virginia-Carolina Wheel Works 118
Virginia Club 44
Virginia Code of 1904
Virginia Maternity Home 135
Virginia State Penitentiary 143
Virginia Trust Company 205, 208

W.A. Broidy & Son 180
Walby, William 113
Walke, John 12
Walker, H.T. 161
Walker, Tom *see* King, Scott
Wallace, William 193
Wankin, Henrietta 105
Ward, Capt. F.C. 166
Ward, Richard 105
Ward, Col. Thomas 166
Warren, Henry 194
Washington, Henry 199
Watkins Hardware Company 156
Weatherford's Row 37
Webster, Mrs. E.F. 149
Wells, Charlie 140
Wendenberg, Attorney L.O. 207
West, George *see* Robinson, O.W.
West, Ivy W. (alias Ben Welburn Franklin) 186
West, Johnston, and Co. 78
Wharton, Mrs. M.E. 24
Whitlock, Robert 193
Wickham, Judge 208
Wilcox, Alonzo W. 186
Williams, Agnes 117
Williams, Charles 144
Williams, Dr. J. 132
Williams, Jack 110, 125
Williams, John 204, 205, 206
Williams, Joseph B. 12, 47
Williams, Stanley 146
Williams, William 132
Willson, Ded 110, 125
Wilson, Willie 124
Wingfield, George A. 50
Wingo, Ellett & Crump 160
Wippermann, Carl 100
Wise, John S. 151
Withers, Alfred W. 204, 205, 206, 207, 210, 211
Withers, D.F. 210
Wolff, J. 103
Wolff, V.S. 176
Wollard, Dr. A.G. 51
Wombwell's British Menagerie 69, 74
Woods, George 103
Woodson, S.P. 154
Woodward, Frank H. 164
Wren, John 54
Wright, Augusta 121
Wyman the Wizard 31

York River railroad 190
Young, James 144, 145
Young, Mary 151

Zimmerman, Samuel 134

www.ingramcontent.com/pod-product-compliance
Ingram Content Group UK Ltd.
Pitfield, Milton Keynes, MK11 3LW, UK
UKHW041942140426
5217IPUK00014B/612